GROUP COUNSELING
Theory and Practice

GROUP COUNSELING
Theory and Practice

Rickey L. George
University of Missouri-St. Louis

Dick Dustin
University of Iowa

PRENTICE HALL Englewood Cliffs, New Jersey 07632

Library of Congress Cataloging-in-Publication Data

George, Rickey L.
  Group counseling.

  Includes bibliographies and index.
  1. Group counseling. I. Dustin, E. Richard,
1936-   . II. Title.
BF637.C6G417 1988   158'.5   87-14405
ISBN 0-13-365156-8

Editorial/production supervision and interior design: Ann L. Mohan
Cover design: Ben Santora
Manufacturing buyer: Carol Bystrom

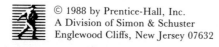 © 1988 by Prentice-Hall, Inc.
A Division of Simon & Schuster
Englewood Cliffs, New Jersey 07632

Printed in the United States of America

10 9 8 7 6 5 4 3 2 1

ISBN 0-13-365156-8   001

Prentice-Hall International (UK) Limited, *London*
Prentice-Hall of Australia Pty. Limited, *Sydney*
Prentice-Hall Canada Inc., *Toronto*
Prentice-Hall Hispanoamericana, S.A., *Mexico*
Prentice-Hall of India Private Limited, *New Dehli*
Prentice-Hall of Japan, Inc., *Tokyo*
Simon & Schuster Asia Pte. Ltd., *Singapore*
Editora Prentice-Hall do Brasil, Ltda., *Rio de Janeiro*

To Our Families

RG: Kathy, Amanda, Laura, and Susan
DD: Pat, Rob, and Sue

CONTENTS

PREFACE

The goal of this text on group counseling and therapy is to present the methods and processes of group approaches in an integrative way that focuses on *how* effectiveness with a group is facilitated as well as *why*. We have attempted to integrate theory and practice in a manner that will provide an analysis of the skills and information needed by the group leader as well as a summary of the major issues related to these practices.

Although the book is written for use as a major textbook in beginning courses in group counseling, it is based on the premise that students already are familiar with the major counseling theories and techniques. Since the emphasis is on the application of theoretical concepts and strategies in a group setting, the material may be a valuable resource for more advanced readers as well. It is designed to address a wide audience including counselors, counseling psychologists, and social workers who work—or are preparing to work—in a variety of settings.

While the book is current and thorough, we have been selective regarding the material and ideas included. The book gives wide enough coverage to explain the *how* and *why* of group counseling without presenting all of the supportive research findings and includes a comprehensive list of references to provide direction for readers seeking greater depth.

We believe that this book differs from other existing textbooks in several fundamental ways. Although we do not attempt to present a comprehensive view of the major theoretical approaches, we believe that the book has a strong theoretical foundation in its analysis and description of the dynamics of various group counseling concepts and techniques. Thus it integrates the thorough, scholarly strengths of some books with the readable, practical applications of others.

We wish to express our gratitude to our spouses—Kathy and Pat—and to our children—Mandy, Laura, Susan, Rob, and Susan—for their support, encouragement, and understanding during the preparation of the manuscript. In addition, we wish to give special thanks to our mentors and colleagues over the years who have contributed to our professional development in so many ways.

Special thanks also to Eileen Lagermann, Reta Litton, and Ginny Travis, who typed the manuscript and who put up with our demands for speed. Finally, we would like to express our appreciation to the Prentice Hall staff—especially Wayne Spohr, Susan Willig, and Shirley Chlopak—for their confidence and assistance.

R.G.
D.D.

CHAPTER 1
INTRODUCTION TO GROUP COUNSELING

INTRODUCTION

During the past two decades, there has been an increasing emphasis on the use of group processes to meet the counseling needs of various individuals. However, the use of groups as a means of meeting individual needs has existed from the very beginning of counseling as a process. In the early days, group approaches consisted primarily of "group guidance" activities, mainly in the areas of vocational, educational, and avocational guidance (Brewer, 1942). With the founding of the American Group Psychotherapy Association in 1942, followed by the results of small group research which generated new insights into group processes, group counseling has become a legitimate approach to dealing with the various objectives and goals of counseling.

HISTORICAL PERSPECTIVE

Although there are earlier records of group approaches to mental health and guidance, the first psychotherapy group is traditionally recognized as one begun by Joseph Hersey Pratt in 1905. Pratt, a Boston internist, treated patients suffering from tuberculosis who could not afford hospital treatment. To save time, Pratt began to gather the patients in groups of about 20 to instruct them in basic hygiene and the need for proper rest, diet, and environment. Journals kept by the patients show progress and the development of a degree of cohesiveness of mutual concern. While the group was formed primarily for economic reasons, Pratt later became convinced that the new rapport created by the patients was therapeutic and began to emphasize the beneficial influence that patients could have upon each other.

Pratt's work, however, was pushed into the background by the increasing interest in the ideas coming from the beginning psychoanalytic movement of Freud. Although Freud himself was interested in groups primarily as a means of learning about mass psychology and the influence of strong, powerful leaders, one of his colleagues, Alfred Adler, made some progress in adapting the methods of psychoanalysis to small groups. Other individuals from within the psychoanalytic school who focused on group activities included Samuel Slavson, Alexander Woll, and Emanual Schwartz. These three believed that a group setting evoked psychoanalytic concepts more powerfully than did individual therapy. They were particularly impressed by the interactions and dynamics of the group.

In the mid 1940s, a training group in Bethel, Maine, devised a method to analyze its own behavior. The leaders of this group had worked with Kurt Lewin, a psychologist at the Massachusetts Institute of Technology who had developed the idea that training in human relations skills was an important, but overlooked, type of education in modern society. Forming shortly after Lewin's death, the group focused on experience-based learning, that is, analyzing, discussing, and trying to improve their own behavior in the group situation. Observing the nature of their interactions with others and the group process, participants believed, gave them a better understanding of their own way of functioning in a group, making them more competent in dealing with interpersonal relations. The warm, caring relationships that developed among the participants led to very deep personal change in individuals.

As a result of these group experiences and the learning that resulted, those individuals organized the National Training Laboratories, which quickly became a model for training leaders in industry and education. The major impact of NTL was a new emphasis on the *process* by which a group operates, rather than on content. Group leaders placed far more importance on *how* something was said and the effects this had on other individuals than on the words themselves. Thus, participants in the group experience were not interested in learning content, but were focusing on *how* to learn, especially within the area of interpersonal relationships.

Although experience-based learning has undergone enormous changes in the last few decades, its impact is still powerful. Thousands of individuals have received training to become leaders and millions have been involved in such a group experience. As a result, group approaches have seen a considerable expansion in practice, research, and writing. These philosophical concepts became the basis for various encounter, growth, and development groups.

DEFINITION OF GROUP COUNSELING

While the term *group counseling* has become very popular and practices under this name have been introduced in a variety of settings, there is still variation in what it means to different individuals. Professionals working in counseling and related fields have been asked to reach a consensus as to what a group is beyond the definition that a group consists of three or more members who influence each other and are influenced by others. Such a group of individuals who meet and interact with one another in a face-to-face setting tend to believe that they belong to a particular group for the purpose of achieving some objective or goal. Most professionals would agree that individuals meet to satisfy personal needs and to develop an interdependence upon one another. As will be shown in later chapters, these individuals establish roles and norms as a result of sharing common attitudes, feelings, and times. In addition, these groups go through stages that can be observed and described by those who study such group behavior.

Before looking at some specific definitions of group counseling, it may be valuable to look at distinctions between three major types of group activities. Gazda (1978) says that *group guidance* is "organized to prevent the development of problems" (p. 6). In such activities, the content includes information about social-personal-vocational-educational issues that are not ordinarily taught in regular courses. Such activities usually occur in the classroom, involving the entire class.

The primary purpose is to provide accurate information for use in improved understanding of self, others, or a particular area of interest.

On the other hand, *group counseling* is seen as more than prevention oriented; it is "growth engendering and prevention and remediation oriented" (Gazda, 1978, p. 7). Attitude change, behavior change, and changes in cognitive processing are examples of potential goals of group counseling. Gazda (1978) suggests three major differences between group guidance and group counseling, while acknowledging that they share a great deal of similarity. First, he points out that group guidance is recommended for all individuals on a regular basis, while group counseling is generally recommended only for those who are experiencing some coping difficulties in their lives. Second, he points out that group guidance makes an indirect attempt to change attitudes and behaviors, while group counseling makes a direct attempt to modify attitudes and behaviors. Third, Gazda says that group guidance can be done with large, classroom-size groups; whereas group counseling is most effective in small, intimate groups.

A third type of group activity is that of *group psychotherapy*. Used primarily as part of in-patient treatment for individuals who are suffering from severe emotional distress, group psychotherapy is most often seen to be remediative-adjustive-therapeutic, while counseling is thought of as developmental-educative-preventive (Blocher, 1966). While most professionals in the field believe that there is a difference between group counseling and group psychotherapy, most also agree that there is a great deal of overlap between them.

It is important to note that the distinctions between group counseling and group therapy are difficult to define, although it is generally accepted that such differences exist. George and Cristiani (1986) suggest that a clear distinction between the two can best be made by giving counseling and psychotherapy as points on a continuum in regard to various elements: goals, clients, settings, practitioners, and methods. Overall, differences may be best understood in terms of the kind of goals that are seen for each. Whereas counseling is most often described as being educational, supportive, vocational, problem-solving, conscious awareness, and short-term in nature; psychotherapy is most often perceived as being reconstructive, analytical, and long term, with an emphasis on severe emotional problems.

The confusion resulting from a lack of agreement concerning a definition of group counseling can be seen by looking at various definitions that have already been offered. In 1962, Glanz offered his definition of group counseling:

> The establishment of a group of persons for the purposes of individual growth and development in the area of personal and emotional problem solving. (p. 326)

Muro and Freeman (1968) proposed that group counseling be used to refer to:

A form of small group activity in which the participants are psychologically healthy and engaging in mutually supportive and stimulating inquiry into the values and meanings which are becoming attached to their lives in the larger world outside the group. (p. 9)

Ten years later, Gazda (1978) offered a further developed definition of a group:

Group work refers to the dynamic interaction between collections of individuals for prevention or remediation of difficulties or for the enhancement of patient growth/enrichment through the interaction of those who meet together for a commonly agreed on purpose and at prearranged times. (p. 260)

Finally, the definition of Weiner (1984) is offered as a simple, but important definition for us. Weiner suggests that while any group interaction can have a positive influence on the lives of individuals who are involved in that interaction and that therefore any group can be therapeutic, he defines group therapy as "a deliberate effort to alter the thinking, feelings, and behaviors of the group members" (p. 2). For the purpose of this book, we wish to define group counseling as the *use of group interaction to facilitate self-understanding as well as individual behavior change* (Dustin & George, 1973).

NEED FOR GROUP COUNSELING

From the moment most individuals wake up in the morning until the time they go to bed at night, they interact first in one group and then in another. Most individuals work as a part of a group, most individuals interact with social acquaintances as part of a group, and most individuals spend much of their leisure time as part of a group. Since the realities of community existence require community interaction, people are highly concerned with the nature of their relationships with family, friends, and colleagues. These relationships produce and/or reduce stress, feelings of loneliness, low self-esteem, a sense of failure, or a desire to improve their lives. In a sense, the counseling group provides an opportunity for the individual to participate in a small microcosm of society the individual experiences daily. As such, the group process reflects the world beyond and adds an ingredient of realism to a setting and interaction which can often be seen as artificial. Group counseling can make factors such as peer group pressure, social influence, and conformity come into play as part of the therapeutic process, just as they influence and affect the individual's attitude and behavior change outside the group. Corey (1985) points out that "the group process provides a sample of reality. The struggles and conflicts that people experience in the group situation are no different from those they experience outside of it" (p. 9).

In such a setting, participants have the opportunity to explore their styles of relating with others and to learn more effective behaviors in those relationships. As a result, the group setting becomes an opportunity to receive feedback and support from others concerning their perceptions of one another of how each is experienced in the group. As such, the individuals often learn to take risks regarding new attitudes such as trusting, caring, and helping, as well as new behaviors. Group members have the opportunity to get to know others at a relatively intimate level, if they wish, as a result of experiencing one another in a highly safe environment.

Thus, a group setting provides a good setting for the individual to learn and practice new skills. The risk of making an error is minimized and success is reinforced by other members of the group. As a result, new social skills can be learned in a positive environment by practicing until the skills are sufficiently well learned to be used in ordinary social relationships. In addition, in a group setting the peer pressure that is involved often brings about a greater push to action both within the group and outside the group. Thus, members of the group are urged toward activity involved in facing and acting on the real issues and concerns in their lives. Likewise, the possibility of learning new behaviors is increased by the opportunity to observe other members of the group who may be seen as role models in terms of the specific behaviors which the individual wishes to change. Dustin and George (1977) point out that group discussion can strengthen discrimination learning as members come to compare effective behavior with behavior that does not achieve desired goals.

Most important in this process, group members develop a sense of belonging, and the kind of closeness that develops provides a caring, but challenging environment for personal growth and development. Part of this results from individuals becoming aware of similarities between their problems and the problems of other group members, which leads to decreased feelings of isolation and peculiarity and a sense of commonality with others.

The economic advantages to a group format may be overstated. Many professionals agree that it is generally less expensive when the counselor/leader is able to meet with a number of individuals simultaneously. This is particularly true when the purpose of the group is such that there is material to be learned and common skills to be developed. However, it is important to point out that group approaches are not the answer to limited members of professional personnel or to the limited financial resources of individuals seeking help (Weiner, 1984). Although group settings enable counselors to see more individuals in the same amount of time than would be possible in individual therapy, group experiences are generally less efficient than individual approaches because they cannot be tailored to meet the individual needs of the patient. In addition, group members often need individual sessions from time to time, so that the overall cost of group therapy to individuals is probably close to the cost of individual therapy.

GOALS OF GROUP COUNSELING

Although many professionals in the field of counseling believe that the goals of a particular counseling group should be established by the members and leaders of those groups themselves, there is some agreement in terms of general goals to be accomplished via group settings. Frank (1957) suggested general treatment goals as being (a) to facilitate the constructive release of feelings, (b) to strengthen patients' self-esteem, (c) to encourage patients to face and resolve their problems, (d) to improve their skills in recognizing and resolving both interpersonal and intrapersonal conflicts, and (e) to fortify them to consolidate and to maintain their therapeutic gains.

Later, Kelman (1963) continued the focus on clients' means for improving interpersonal skills by establishing the following goals: (a) to overcome feelings of isolation, (b) to enhance self-esteem and increase acceptance of self, (c) to develop hope for improved adjustment, (d) to help each client learn to be himself and to express his feelings, (e) to accept responsibility for himself and for solving his problems, (f) to develop, practice, and maintain new relationship skills, and (g) to enhance his commitment to change his attitudes and behaviors, and to generalize his insight and skills by implementing them in daily life.

Corey, Corey, Callahan, and Russell (1982) suggest that group leaders should have two kinds of goals in mind for a group: general goals and process goals. General goals have to do with establishing a psychological environment within which individuals can work toward achieving their personal goals. Process goals have to do with clients learning appropriate self-disclosures, being willing to share feelings with other members of the group, being willing to talk about themselves in a personal way, being willing to talk about current feelings, providing feedback to others within the group, learning how to confront with care and respect, and expressing reactions to what is going on in the group.

Perhaps the best list of general goals shared by most counseling groups is one proposed by Corey (1985). These goals include:

1. To learn how to trust oneself and others;
2. To foster self-knowledge and the development of a unique sense of identity;
3. To recognize the commonality of the participants' moods and problems;
4. To increase self-acceptance, self-confidence and self-respect in order to achieve a new view of oneself;
5. To find alternative ways of dealing with normal developmental problems and of resolving certain conflicts;
6. To make specific plans for changing certain behaviors and to commit oneself to follow through with these plans;
7. To learn more effective social skills;

8.   To become more sensitive to the needs and feelings of others;
9.   To learn how to confront others with care, concern, honesty, and directness;
10.   To clarify one's values and decide whether and how to modify them. (p.7)

TYPES OF GROUPS

At various times throughout this book, the term *therapeutic group* is used as a general term for any of a wide variety of groups. By *therapeutic,* it is not meant that the group is used for the treatment of severe emotional and psychological disorders, but rather that the group's overall purpose is to have a positive, healing effect on whatever issues the members of the group may bring to it. These issues may have to do with individuals' wanting to learn more about themselves by increasing their awareness of their feelings, values, and beliefs. Other therapeutic experiences might also include providing information to individuals that will enable them to make more appropriate decisions about the course of their lives, as well as giving them tools necessary to make the kind of changes they would like. As a result, the term *therapeutic group* may be utilized for such diverse counseling groups as growth and development groups, T-groups, encounter groups, awareness groups, sensitivity training groups, consciousness-raising groups, therapy groups, and task-oriented groups, as well as groups where the focus is on specific behavior change and/or the learning of specific new skills.

Before looking at some of the various types of groups that exist, it is important to note that one major difference among the various kinds of groups has to do with the degree of structure of the various group activities. Most growth and development groups utilize minimal structuring in which the direction and progress of the group is generally left to the input and expressed needs of the group members. Only general goals related to the growth and development of those group members are verbalized. Behavior-change groups often provide greater structuring to the group process. Leaders of these groups often convey precisely what they expect of group members, what group members can expect of the leader, how previous group members have been helped through these experiences, and a relatively formalized outline of planned activities. This is done because such groups have very specific kinds of goals to be accomplished as part of the group experience.

Growth and Development Groups

Perhaps the greatest emphasis in counseling groups during the past few decades has been in group experiences that focus on the personal growth of the individual. Such groups are not specifically designed for the rehabilitation of individuals suffering from specific psychological or emotional difficulties, but are intended for relatively normal people who are hoping to enhance their personal living skills particularly as these skills involve relating to others. Such growth-centered groups tend to focus on helping individuals gain specific skills; develop insights into their own sets of values, beliefs, and attitudes; enhance their socialization abilities; and learn how to become more aware of the feelings that they are experiencing. Groups for such growth purposes have been identified by several names depending on the areas of growth which are emphasized.

T-groups, or laboratory training groups, tend to emphasize the development of human relations skills which enable the individual to be more effective in a business organization. Focusing more on group process than on personal growth per se, T-groups emphasize education through experience in an environment in which experimentation can occur while receiving support and feedback from the other members of the group. Individuals are encouraged to try out new behaviors, and those behaviors are analyzed so that the individual learns how his or her behavior is seen by others in the group. T-group members usually increase their sensitivity to the feelings and behaviors of other group members, as well as increase their understanding of group behavior dynamics. Thus, in a sense the T-group provides an opportunity for group members to learn how to learn by discovering that the only real answers in terms of becoming more effective as a leader are answers that are provided by their own experiences and not answers that come from some authority figure. Likewise, T-group members are encouraged to focus on the "here and now" as a means of becoming more aware of what is happening to them at the moment and how they feel about it.

Encounter groups, which are the type of groups most often known as personal growth groups, generally offer an intense group experience in which the emphasis upon personal growth through expanding awareness and the release of dysfunctional inhibitions is utilized as a means of helping relatively healthy individuals gain more effective, valid contact with themselves and others. While such groups are diverse in their methods, in the experiences of their members, and in the styles of leadership involved, their common goal is to teach individuals how to deal with themselves and others in a more open, honest manner. The emphasis is on eliciting emotions and on expressing these emotions fully. Frequent confrontations within the group are often encouraged so that the members of the group learn that such confrontation is not only acceptable but also effective in improving relationships with other people. Thus, encounter groups usually encourage intimacy and sharing, openness, honesty, and intense interpersonal relating, with an emphasis on the spontaneous expression of one's feelings, especially risk-taking expressions and living in the present (Corey et al., 1982).

In addition to the verbal interaction that occurs in an encounter group, nonverbal techniques are often utilized to foster interaction. These may include touching, the use of fantasy, massage, dance, art, meditation, centering, and various encounter games.

Corey (1985) has identified some of the goals of the encounter group as follows:

1. To become aware of hidden potentials, to tap unused strengths, and to develop creativity and spontaneity;
2. To become more open and honest with selected others;
3. To decrease game-playing, which prevents intimacy;
4. To become freer of "oughts," "shoulds," and "musts" and to develop internal values;
5. To lessen feelings of alienation and fears of getting close to others;
6. To learn how to ask directly for what one wants;
7. To learn the distinction between having feelings and acting on them;
8. To increase one's capacity to care for others;
9. To learn how to give to others;
10. To learn how to tolerate ambiguity and to make choices in a world where nothing is guaranteed. (p. 11)

Marathon groups are an intensification of the encounter group experience. Marathon groups meet for a sustained period of time, usually 24 hours or several days, adjourning only to sleep and eat. Inhibitions and defenses break down quickly in such an intense experience as individuals become fatigued and/or learn to trust others quickly, and the process of opening up is accelerated by the continuous contact. Various types of interpersonal communication exercises are frequently used to hasten members' awareness of themselves, to promote contact with the feelings of those members, and to promote increased group participation (Vander Kolk, 1985). In particular, marathon groups focus on individuals' learning more about the mask they wear in daily life, the social facades they present to others, the genuine aspects of themselves that are often hidden by those masks and facades, and how to give up some of these pretenses as they reenter their normal living activities.

Other types of growth and development groups have included sensitivity training, awareness groups, Gestalt groups, and transactional analysis groups. Sensitivity groups generally refer to the kind of experiences provided by both T-groups and encounter groups, but with a particular focus on individuals' becoming more sensitive to their own emotional experiencing as well as to the impact of their behavior on other individuals. Awareness groups, on the other hand, tend to emphasize awareness and expression of one's physical body through movement, spontaneous dance, and other physical activities. Gestalt groups focus on a concept of awareness, in which an expert therapist focuses on one individual at a time, while utilizing other members of the group to provide additional input that will enable the individual on the "hot seat" to become more aware of the total experiencing that he or she is going through. Likewise, transactional analysis (TA) groups provide a framework based on a TA therapeutic model in which members of the group become more aware of their behavior in terms of the ego state they utilize in various interactions with others as well as the kind of interactional patterns they prefer. This is done in such a way that group members examine their pasts, their current ego states, scripts, games, and so forth. Thus, one's psychological and social transactions become the focus of the transactional analysis group experience.

Systematic Human Relations Training

Systematic human relations training is closely related to T-groups, but differs in placing much greater emphasis on specific skill development. It is largely based on the work of Carkhuff (1969), who, expanding on Rogers's work regarding the conditions for therapeutic success, developed a systematic model for training people in various interpersonal skills. Gazda (1978) and Egan (1975) have translated the Carkhuff model to the group experience in such a way that group members are able through experiential learning to develop these skills. Some of the same psychological conditions that exist in the T-group—a small group, feedback, the encouragement of experimentation, psychological safety, and here-and-now focus—are provided so that individuals develop the kind of skills which will enable them to be more effective in their interaction with other persons and thus develop a more satisfying life experience for themselves.

Task Groups

Task-centered groups are those which focus on the successful development of a performance or product through collaborative efforts of the group members, while little effort is used in changing the various group members as individuals. Examples of such task groups would include committees, industrial work groups, conflict resolution groups, community interest groups, and various task forces. These groups are important, not because of the counseling experiences that are provided, but because the successful working of these groups depends on the kind of group dynamics that occur.

Behavior-Change Groups

Behavior-change groups are distinguished from other group approaches in that they specify desirable changes in the behavior of each group member that are to occur as a result of the group experience. Generally, individuals who become part of such a group know in advance what the focus of the group will be and therefore why they are there. While the focus is on the successful change in behavior of the various members of the group, a major aspect or dynamic is support from other group members. Alcoholics Anonymous, Overeaters Anonymous, and Smoke Enders are examples of support groups which exist. Other groups may focus on the development of such specific behaviors as study habits, social interaction skills, and parenting skills.

Learning Groups

Learning groups are those in which the focus is on the acquisition of specific information and knowledge, especially in terms of vocational and academic information. Such groups are typically more structured, with carefully defined goals and more explicit, generally accepted expectations of the group members. Although the focus is on learning specific information, the process involves a great deal of group interaction, with members of the group sharing feelings, attitudes, and values. For example, a group that is focused on developing job-seeking skills, in which participants learn how to find job leads, prepare a resume, prepare for an interview, and present themselves to the employer, will also focus on individuals discussing the kind of fears they have about the total experience. In addition, the members will be continually discussing the kind of internal forces that affect the type of jobs in which they are interested as well as the kind of jobs they will actually seek. Other learning groups might include mid-life career change groups, career exploration groups, work adjustment groups, and various kinds of child-raising groups. One structured group that has received a great deal of attention is parent-effectiveness training, in which parents meet to learn better ways of relating to and managing their children. Group members learn definable skills, while participating in a process that includes group interaction and support.

Psychotherapy Groups

Psychotherapy groups are usually made up of psychiatric patients who are hospitalized as a result of their difficulties and outpatients who have more severe emotional or psychological problems. Generally, therapy groups are aimed at reconstructing the personality, although many people who participate in group therapy do so in an attempt to alleviate specific symptoms or problems, such as depression, anxiety, psychosomatic disorders, eating disorders, chemical dependency, and sexual problems. In such groups, the focus is on identifying and correcting the emotional or psychological difficulties that impede the individual's functioning. Thus the goal may be a minor or a major change in the personality structure both depending on the nature of the difficulty of the individual and the specific theoretical orientation of the therapist.

Psychotherapy groups tend to be of longer duration than the other kinds of groups that have been discussed. Because attention is given to unconscious factors and the influence of past events in the individual's life, a slower process evolves as group members are encouraged to become more aware of those critical events in their lives which may have contributed to the specific dysfunction that has created a problem. In addition, group members are often led to reexperience various traumatic situations in which they have not resolved the particular emotional difficulties that accompanied the problem. By reexperiencing these situations and the accompanying feelings, the individuals are given the opportunity to resolve ''unfinished business'' and to express the kinds of intense feelings that have stayed below the surface for a long period of time. As members become aware of and gain insight into their past, they are able to reconstruct a more healthy emotional attitude about themselves and those experiences and to eliminate the emotional blocking that has interfered with the group members' current functioning.

Many psychotherapy groups utilize psychoanalytic concepts and procedures, such as working with dreams, focusing on the earliest memories of the individual, trying to uncover the unconscious, and symbolically reliving, thus reconstructing, unhappy significant relationships. Other groups may utilize cognitive techniques, behavioral techniques, and other psychotherapeutic modalities to bring about therapeutic change.

It is important to point out that many psychotherapy groups are made up of individuals who are relatively healthy and are not experiencing severe emotional or psychological problems. These individuals participate in group therapy for many of the same reasons that others participate in growth and development groups; that is, to be part of an experience in which a safe climate is provided so that they can become healthier, more effective individuals who live more satisfying lives.

SUMMARY

Although the use of groups to meet counseling needs has existed from the beginning of counseling as a process, there has been an increasing emphasis on the use of group processes during the past two decades.

There are three major types of group activities: group guidance, group counseling, and group therapy. *Group guidance* is a group approach to presenting information about social, personal, vocational, or educational issues, the primary purpose being to provide accurate information for use in improved understanding of self, others, or a particular area of interest. *Group counseling* is focused on personal growth, prevention, and remediation, with attitude change, behavior change, and changes in cognitive processing as examples of potential goals. *Group therapy* is used with individuals suffering from more severe emotional distress and is considered remediative, adjustive, or therapeutic. Where there are differences among the three types, there is also a great deal of overlap.

Group approaches to counseling are particularly valuable. The group becomes a microcosm of the individual's social world, providing a more realistic setting for learning more effective behaviors for relating to others. The resulting psychological environment provides a caring situation for personal growth and development. Group approaches may also be more economical, though this is not always true.

Various types of group experiences exist, with a major difference among them being the degree of structure involved, as well as their primary purpose.

Growth and development groups include T-groups, encounter groups, and marathon groups, and are intended for relatively healthy individuals who are hoping to enhance their personal living skills, particularly as these skills involve relating to others. *Systematic human relations training groups* are similar, but have a much greater emphasis on specific skill development training. *Task groups* are those which focus on the successful development of a performance or product through the collaborative efforts of the group members. *Behavior-change groups* work toward specific desirable changes in the behavior of each group member, while *learning groups* focus on the acquisition of specific information and knowledge, especially in terms of vocational and academic information. *Psychotherapy groups* work on identifying and correcting the emotional or psychological difficulties that impede the individual's functioning.

REFERENCES

BLOCHER, D. H. (1966). *Development counseling.* New York: Ronald Press.

BREWER, J. M. (1942). *History of vocational guidance.* New York: Harper.

CARKHUFF, R. R. (1969). *Helping and human relations.* New York: Holt, Rinehart and Winston.

COREY, G. (1985). *Theory and practice of group counseling* (2nd ed.). Monterey, CA: Brooks/Cole.

COREY, G., COREY, M. S., CALLAHAN, P. J., & RUSSELL, J. M. (1982). *Group technique.* Monterey, CA: Brooks/Cole.

DUSTIN, R., & GEORGE, R. L. (1977). *Action counseling for behavior change* (2nd ed.). Cranston, RI: Carroll Press.

EGAN, G. (1975). *The skilled helper.* Monterey, CA: Brooks/Cole.

FRANK, J. D. (1957). Some determinants, manifestations, and efforts of cohesiveness in therapy groups. *International Journal of Group Psychotherapy, 7,* 53–63.

GAZDA, G. M. (1978). *Group counseling: A developmental approach* (2nd ed.). Boston: Allyn & Bacon.

GEORGE, R. L., & CRISTIANI, T. C. (1986). *Counseling theory and practice* (2nd ed.). Englewood Cliffs, NJ: Prentice-Hall.

GLANZ, E. C. (1962). *Groups in guidance.* Boston: Allyn & Bacon.

KELMAN, H. C. (1963). The role of the group in the induction of therapeutic change. *International Journal of Group Psychotherapy, 13,* 399–432.

MURO, J. J., & FREEMAN, S. L. (1968). *Readings in group counseling.* Scranton, PA: Intext.

VANDER KOLK, C. J. (1985). *Introduction to group counseling and psychotherapy.* Columbus, OH: Charles E. Merrill.

WEINER, M. F. (1984). *Techniques of group psychotherapy.* Washington, DC: American Psychiatric Press.

SUGGESTED ACTIVITIES

In the Classroom

1. With a partner, summarize the types of groups listed in this chapter. Compare your understanding of each of the definitions. Can the two of you think of any additional types of groups?

2. In a small group, discuss the definitions for group guidance, group counseling, and group psychotherapy given in this chapter. What terms caused dis-

agreement in your small group? Why? Are there other areas of disagreement in the small group?

On Your Own

1. Interview a counselor in a setting of interest to you. Attempt to determine how the counselor sees groups within the total job responsibility. How important are groups? Is the counselor doing any? How frequently?
2. Interview a counselor in a setting of your choice. Summarize for the counselor the authors' beliefs about the need for groups. Does the counselor agree? Disagree?
3. Decide how you react to each of Gazda's definitions for group guidance, group counseling, and group therapy.
4. See if you can summarize the definition of a group that the authors are using for this text.

CHAPTER 2
THERAPEUTIC RESULTS OF GROUP COUNSELING

INTRODUCTION

This chapter on therapeutic results is divided into two major sections. In the first the goals and expected results of group counseling according to selected theories will be described. Just what is supposed to happen to members of a counseling group according to these major theories? In the second section, selected outcome studies of group counseling from 1977 to the present will be described. In what areas have groups been successful? To what extent have the theoretical projected results been shown to occur?

THEORETICAL EXPECTATIONS OF SUCCESSFUL GROUP COUNSELING

As a means of understanding the results of group counseling, students can ex-amine what outcomes of successful group counseling have been hypothesized by proponents of selected theories. The brief descriptions of goals of successful group counseling are meant to suggest the flavor and the type of goals that a proponent of each theory might have. The chapter assumes that the reader is already familiar with the basic tenets of each theory. For those readers who are not, some basic readings in each theory are listed. The selected theories are Gestalt, Adlerian, Personal Growth, and Cognitive-Behavioral. Each section is divided into goals of the individual member, interactional goals between members of the group, and overall group goals or group process goals.

Gestalt Groups

Although Frederick Perls was not himself a group therapist, many students may have the impression that Perls was conducting group counseling sessions (Melnick, 1980). Instead, Perl's workshops had only one purpose: to demonstrate his Gestalt techniques. Nevertheless, by examining the writings of other Gestalt writers, it is possible to piece together an approximation of what a Gestalt group counselor might include as a list of expectations for a successful group.

Individual Goals.   The major goal for a Gestalt group leader is to increase the self-awareness of each individual. This increased self-awareness is itself cu-rative according to Gestalt concepts. For the most part, all the goals which follow are either process goals to help increase the self-awareness or they are specific examples of increased awareness.

Additional transparency for each individual is a major goal. Melnick (1980) has described how individuals come to recognize and accept more and more as-pects of themselves and how these individuals also become more willing to com-municate formerly hidden or self-disguised aspects of themselves.

An increase in responsibility for one's self is another goal (Stephenson, 1975).

This frequently comes about through interactions with the group leader and with other group members and can be seen through an increase in "I" statements.

An increased integration of individual conflicts and greater self-reliance are additional goals for the Gestalt approach. Within each individual, inherent conflicts become split into polarities. These polarities are extreme tendencies that individuals hold simultaneously. For example, as one wishes to be loved by a person, there is a tendency to wish to dominate the same person. The top dog–underdog polarity is a commonly used example of such conflict. Increased integration has been called "the overriding objective of Gestalt counseling" (Hansen, Stevic, & Warner, 1982). The split in self-image concepts is gradually reduced as individuals come to accept the divergent, often contradictory, aspects of these images of self. Gradually roles are reduced or eliminated as the person incorporates the other goals listed above. This results in increased integration of the self.

Interpersonal Goals. Members will perform more and more self-disclosure in a Gestalt group as it develops. Increased communication which is focused on the immediate (here-and-now communication) is a goal of a Gestalt group. As individuals become more aware about self, they will increasingly give here-and-now reactions to the group leader and to other group members as well as communicate about themselves in a here-and-now fashion.

As individuals interact within a Gestalt group they will invariably act out sibling rivalries and familial patterns (Smith, 1976). The interactions and the communications of conflict between group members will increase the self-understanding of each group member (For an example, see On Your Own, activity 1 at the end of this chapter.)

Another goal of Gestalt counseling is to stimulate the investigation and exploration of polarities for each individual, mentioned earlier. Much of this exploration occurs as individuals compare and contrast themselves with other group members (Latner, 1973).

Group Process. Group process goals are centered on the climate which is most conducive to individual exploration and growth (Stephenson, 1975). A Gestalt group counselor would be likely to stimulate group exploration of the group's structure and the group's process. As the group facilitator stimulates each member's self-exploration, the counseling group will also be involved in exploration and examination of the group itself.

Just as the growth for individual members occurs through discovery, a group process goal is for the group to make discoveries about its own functioning.

Readers who would like more information on Gestalt Theory could consider these sources:

FAGAN, J. & SHEPARD, I. L. (Eds.) (1970). *Gestalt therapy now.* New York: Harper & Row.
PASSONS, W. R. (1975). *Gestalt approaches in counseling.* New York: Holt, Rinehart, and Winston.
PERLS, F., HEFFERLINE, R. F. & GOODMAN, P. (1951). *Gestalt therapy.* New York: Dell Co.

Adlerian Groups

Much of the writing in Adlerian group counseling currently specializes in groups for elementary-aged children as well as groups for parents. Nevertheless, there are certain general goals which would be hypothesized for any Adlerian group, including groups for younger children (Dinkmeyer, Pew, & Dinkmeyer, Jr., 1979).

Individual Goals.   An Adlerian group counselor helps the client see the beliefs and feelings as well as the motives and goals that determine the individual's life-style. Clients develop insights into their mistaken goals and self-defeating behaviors. They are then helped to develop appropriate life goals.

Group counselors also try to maximize the responsible freedom and personal effectiveness of each individual group member, develop feelings of personal worth in each individual group member, and help each individual consider alternative life-styles and make a commitment towards change.

Interpersonal Goals.   As each group member is encouraged to explore his or her feelings and reactions to other group members, self-understanding is furthered. This goal could be described as providing opportunities for group members to learn about their own style of coping through exploring their interactions with other group members.

In addition, self-understanding is increased by helping each individual member learn how he/she decided to belong to the group. For example, a member might think, "If I join this group I will be able to get out of class."

To develop and to further social interest in group members through their encouraging others and becoming involved with other members' specific life changes is another Adlerian goal (for an example see On Your Own, activity 2.)

Group Process.   Although not emphasized as much as in Gestalt groups, process goals for Adlerian group counseling would include developing an empathic relationship between the group leader and each individual member, encouraging empathy and acceptance by the entire group for each individual member, developing the social interest of individuals through the group climate and the development of an encouraging group, providing a climate of encouragement for individual group members so that they will risk making a commitment to change their behaviors and their life-style, and developing a cooperative climate and norms within the group. Another source for information about Adlerian theory is R. J. Corsini (Ed.), *Current psychotherapies,* Third Edition (Itasca, IL: Peacock Publishers, 1984).

Personal Growth Groups

As was discussed in chapter 1, several types of groups—including human potential, T-groups, and some types of encounter groups—are considered under the general heading of personal growth. Diversity of goals among groups of this type may very well be as large as the diversity of goals for the entire range of counseling theories. Nevertheless, a collection of selected goals representative of personal growth groups follows.

Individual Goals.   As members are given time in the group to relate personal information, self-understanding is an important goal, much as it is for individual client-centered counseling. Furthermore, as individual members are encouraged to explore the meaning of their interactions with other members, self-understanding is said to be increased.

Several specific goals are usually included in personal growth groups. One of these is to increase self-awareness and the awareness of the individual's potential. A second is to increase individual self-exploration and thereby heighten the ability of the individual to achieve greater self-awareness and communicate this awareness. A third goal is to increase individual acceptance of self. As the individual member experiences acceptance from other members of the group and from the leader, self-acceptance then leads to increased self-understanding. As a result, group members are helped to achieve their potential by making choices with which they are faced.

Interpersonal Goals.   Interactions between group members are a means to increasing individual self-understanding. Interactions are explored and examined so that all group members are able to consider their own reactions and to incorporate individual learning. The goal of self-acceptance is furthered as the leader models an accepting individual, even within conflict situations. Individual members are encouraged to be less judgmental and more accepting of each group member. Encouraging the individual's reliance on self as a source of evaluation rather than the reliance on others' appraisal is a major goal as is increasing the frequency of spontaneous reactions and expressions of feelings to other group members.

Group Process.   For some proponents of personal growth groups, the totality of the group's interactions, including changes in group interactions over time, are an important focus. The mutuality of goals for individual members, namely, to foster and to spur individual growth and change, provides an emphasis on certain climate or group process goals.

Another important group goal is to develop a climate of intermember support. The feeling of support from other members encourages individuals to explore and to communicate about themselves (for an example, see On Your Own, activity 3).

To explore, examine, and increase individual awareness of the interdependence of members is still another goal. As individuals are encouraged to learn about themselves, many will offer help to other members and also learn to receive help.

An important group process goal is to create an accepting atmosphere. The reduced fear and self-consciousness in individual members that results is believed to increase self-disclosure and thereby to further individual self-understanding.

Finally, another goal mentioned frequently with growth groups is to increase the group leadership. Increasing self-direction by the group rather than relying heavily on group leaders for direction is seen as a process goal.

Readers wishing further information about personal growth could consider these sources:

GAZDA, G. M. (1984). *Group counseling: A developmental approach* (3rd ed.). Boston: Allyn & Bacon.
JOHNSON, D. W., & JOHNSON, F. P. (1975). *Joining together: Group theory and group skills.* Englewood Cliffs, NJ: Prentice-Hall.

Cognitive-Behavioral Groups

For the purposes of this section, behavioral group counseling does not include instances where a number of subjects are treated simultaneously, as in group relaxation. Although there has been some confusion as to the distinction between groups where interaction among members is encouraged and those where the only interaction is from leader to individuals, this focus on cognitive-behavioral groups is limited to groups in which members have clearly identified changes which they would like to make in their lives outside the group.

Individual Goals.   The central goal of a cognitive-behavioral group is to help individual members make changes in their lives in ways of their choosing. The emphasis is on change outside the group. Such changes would include the decrease of behaviors regarded by the individual as maladaptive and an increase in adaptive behaviors (for an example, see On Your Own, activity 5).

To help an individual practice and receive reinforcement and encouragement would be a major goal so that the individual will succeed with the new behavior outside the group.

Another goal is to help the individual learn techniques to influence his or her own environment. Such techniques might help the individual to set up certain stimuli or change certain stimuli preceding crucial behaviors; to perform designated behaviors; to alter his or her own thinking, and to seek out or otherwise to provide reenforcement for targeted behaviors.

To help individuals examine and carry out changes by interacting with other group members having similar problems is another goal (for example, see On Your Own, activity 6).

Interpersonal Goals.   To provide appropriate models for other group members is a behavioral goal. Use of multiple models could be encouraged so that an individual member could benefit from seeing more than one group member perform designated behaviors.

Increasing the support for individual members through encouragement and social reenforcement is a goal. Interpersonal goals might also include members agreeing to check up with a member, to prompt another member, or to reinforce a member. The opportunity for rehearsal and practice is an important goal of behavioral groups. Members can be especially helpful by being willing to participate in role plays.

An advantage of group counseling lies in the potential for feedback from other individuals. At times this goal will be directly influenced by the group leader's providing training for members in the skill of behavioral feedback.

Group Process.   Although it is often difficult to determine whether group behavioral counseling actually includes group interaction variables such as discussion, sharing feelings, and providing feedback, behavioral group counseling as defined in this section would focus on the group climate. Especially important would be a group climate which would encourage individual exploration and risk-taking which would further the specific goals of the particular group.

At times group members would be trained in certain techniques such as, providing feedback, providing social reinforcement, or providing encouragement. It is desirable that the group provide a climate which seems safe enough for members to share personal concerns and to take risks as they attempt to practice new, and sometimes difficult, behaviors. The group process should be work-oriented. This requires commitment from individual members to stay on a task as well as to offer support and social reinforcement to other members of the group.

Readers who would like additional information about cognitive-behavioral theory could consult with such sources as

BECK, A., RUSH, J., SHAW, B., & EMERY, G. (1979). *Cognitive therapy of depression.* New York: Guilford Press.
ELLIS, A. (1982). *Rational-emotive therapy and cognitive behavior therapy.* New York: Springer.

SELECTED RESEARCH OUTCOMES

Reviewers of research in group counseling have puzzled over the poorly defined terms and concepts (Kaul & Bednar, 1986). They have lamented the lack of effective research methodology (Bloch, Crouch, & Reibstein, 1981). Yet, the professional literature reflects a high interest in this area with long lists of studies and many reviews in many settings.

What follows is a brief look at recent studies in the effectiveness of group counseling and psychotherapy. Because of the infrequent use of comparative studies, the theoretical sections used earlier in this chapter are not used to organize the selected studies here. Instead the categories of goals used for each of the theories provide the organizing headings found later in the review: individual change, interpersonal change, and group process.

Lack of Effective Research

Although a rich and extensive literature exists in the group counseling area, reviewers have consistently complained about the quality of this research. What makes research in group counseling so difficult? A few of the factors are the inability of writers in group counseling to agree upon definitions of terms; the difficulty in comparing theory to theory; complaints that group studies performed in a laboratory with six college sophomores, for example, or for one 20-minute session are not transferable to real groups; and finally, the extreme amount of effort and persistence needed to compare comparable counseling groups in a counseling setting.

When one writer uses a term such as *insight* in a specific way, other writers may very well invent or use their own special meaning for the term insight. When writers from varying theories of group counseling use similar terms, all too often the definitions do not agree. It has been pointed out that many widely used terms in the group area such as self-disclosure and cohesiveness have never had operational definitions which were agreed upon. This lack of operational, agreed-upon definitions, of course, makes comparing results from one study to another virtually impossible. In addition, there has been a tendency in the literature for writers to use *group* in the title or in their introductory paragraph but to never specify exactly what the group consisted of, or what the experience and style of the leader was, what specific interventions were used in the sessions, and whether the same members existed at the end of the group as in the beginning.

In many areas of counseling great strides in research have been gained by looking in the laboratory at very narrow, specific aspects of complicated processes. For example, a study which looked at role taking or, even better, at varying aspects of role taking, might very well result in a hypothesis that could be tested by group leaders in the field or by researchers with the capability to conduct group counseling research in a help-giving setting. However, a lot of the practitioners, and several of the writers in the area of group counseling, have complained violently about the lack of practicality of laboratory studies for the group counseling practitioner.

The significant outcome studies of counseling and psychotherapy have compared counseling of three to five different theoretical backgrounds with one another at the end of counseling. To find on-going, comparable groups at the same time and then to compare results, has been an exceedingly difficult task for group studies. This task has been made even more complicated by the finding that theoretical labels have not differentiated between interventions and techniques used by group leaders. In his thorough review of therapeutic factors in group psychotherapy over a 25-year period, Bloch et al. (1981) confirmed how little definitive research has been done which indicates the effectiveness of various therapeutic factors within groups.

Decision Rule

The studies which were included in the following section do not comprise an exhaustive, thorough list. Rather, studies were selected because they seemed like clear examples of the three headings, namely, individual change, interpersonal change, and group process; or because they were especially effective studies taken from agency or educational settings. Studies were not included which focused on family counseling and psychotherapy, on in-patient groups, or which featured special populations. Studies were included which had been published since 1977.

In the event that a study does feature an in-patient client group or does focus upon a special population, the text will make note of this.

Sample Research

One recent study has been selected as an example which indicates the difficulties of conducting research in group counseling while at the same time providing an effective, exemplary sample. Shadish (1980) conducted an experiment using 49 undergraduates who had volunteered for the study. These subjects were randomly assigned to six groups.

One research difficulty in counseling which is especially troublesome when conducting research in groups is that of design. Shadish assigned his six groups as follows: 10 subjects to a pretested control group, 8 subjects to an unpretested control group, 8 subjects to a pretested verbal group (his treatment), 8 subjects to an unpretested verbal group, 7 subjects to a pretested nonverbal group, and 8 subjects to an unpretested nonverbal group. One of the troubling questions in successful research is that of a control group. This study met this by providing three controls—a pretested control group, an unpretested control group plus the two groups, one in each treatment, which had been pretested along with the other two groups which had not been pretested. This type of design allows the researcher to determine what effect the pretest may have had on the subsequent results of the findings. However in Shadish's study groups of unequal size were used.

All too often, studies do not indicate the experience level of the group leaders. In this study, four pairs of group leaders were made up of clinical psychology graduate students. These pairs were counterbalanced by sex and experience. In addition, all eight group leaders went through an 18-hour educational experience which consisted of didactic and experiential training.

In addition, this experiment used a follow-up. The follow-up in this study was of 3 weeks, not very long, but in our opinion better than no follow-up at all.

One difficulty in conducting research in counseling and psychotherapy is the ability to determine whether the treatment groups, as well as the control groups, actually did contain a treatment or, in the case of the control group, no treatment at all. In this study, Shadish had two senior psychology students observe meetings of the six groups. The two senior students were able to identify correctly whether they were viewing a control group, a nonverbal group, or a verbal group.

The treatment consisted of three 3-hour sessions plus a marathon weekend session. Although no description was given of the control groups or the treatment groups, a sample nonverbal and verbal exercise is described.

Several measures were used in this study. A difficulty of comparing group outcomes is the tendency for researchers to use their own, homemade measures of change. Shadish used standardized instruments. For example, the Personal Orientation Inventory (POI) (Shostrum, 1974) resulted in no differences before the treatment, after the treatment or after the follow-up. The McMillan Affective Relationship Scale (MARS) indicated significant change in the treatment groups.

Individual Changes

In a study described earlier in this chapter, Shadish (1980) looked at changes in members on the POI (Shostrum, 1974) after participation in a weekend marathon and three 3-hour group sessions. The results indicated no significant differences on the POI after the groups, nor at the 3-week follow-up.

Sulzbacher, Wong, McKeen, Glock, and MacDonald (1981) also used the POI as an outcome-measure as well as a self-concept instrument. The treatment was a 3-month intensive resident human growth program with 33 participants. Thirteen members of the participants' families served as the control group. The instruments were administered before the group program, at its conclusion, and at a 1-year follow-up. Highly significant increases were found in self-actualization and self-concept for the participants. These increases were maintained at the end of 1 year. No changes were found at the time of the three testings in members of the control group.

Shapiro, Sank, Shaffer, and Donovan (1982) studied changes in group member depression, state anxiety, trait anxiety and assertiveness. Forty-four enrollees in a health maintenance organization were used as subjects. Of these, 35 completed all assessment inventories. The subjects were described as mildly depressed. Participants were randomly assigned to one of three treatment groups: cognitive behavior therapy, traditional interpersonal process group, and individual cognitive behavior therapy. The cognitive behavior group was given relaxation training and cognitive restructuring practice. The traditional interpersonal group used an unstructured treatment which included elements of insight development, interpersonal feedback, and focus on group process. All three treatments, including the individual treatment, met for 10 weekly sessions (1½ hours for group treatment and 1 hour for individual treatment). All three treatments resulted in reduced depression, less state anxiety, less trait anxiety, and a significant increase in assertiveness. In a 6-month follow-up, the experimenters found maintenance of several changes in the individual participants. Follow-up data was completed on 29 of the original 35 participants. The changes in anxiety and assertiveness were maintained. However, depression had returned towards but did not reach pretreatment levels (Shaffer, Sank, Shapiro, & Donovan, 1982).

Barrera (1979) also studied the effects of group therapy on depression. This study used a subscale of the same measure as Shapiro et al. (Beck Depression Inventory, 1978). The Minnesota Multiphasic Personality Inventory (MMPI) and a personal screening interview were used to diagnose participants as depressed. Twenty subjects were assigned to an immediate treatment group and 20 others to a delayed treatment group. Leaders for both groups were a male and female coleader. At the end of 4 weeks, when the immediate treatment group was completed, and at the end of 8 weeks, when both groups had received treatment, there were no differences between the two groups. At the end of 1 month, the delayed-treatment group was described as much improved on the depression scale. The authors were unable to explain the lack of treatment effect in the immediate treatment group.

In a 1 year follow-up to a study comparing individual and group cognitive behavioral counseling, Kendall (1982) reported significant changes in a study conducted in a school. Teacher ratings of group participants indicated significant behavioral change at the end of the group and at a 1-year follow-up from pretreatment ratings. In addition, group and individual participants in the study were no longer viewed as different from other students by the teachers. However, teacher ratings indicated that the control subjects in the study continued to be rated as different from the majority of the students. The individual treatment and the group treatment were viewed as equally successful in this study.

The final study to be described in this section was conducted with in-patient alcoholics. Olson, Ganley, Devine, and Dorsey (1981) described a 4-year follow-up with 137 participants in a study which compared behavioral versus insight therapy. One hundred thirteen subjects were available from the original 137. The control group received the standard milieu treatment for 1 month. Treatment group 1 received two or three lectures a day plus "traditional group therapy" that focused on feelings. Treatment group 2 received transactional analysis (TA) sessions 3 times a week. Treatment group 3 received behavioral treatment conducted by two therapists. This treatment included covert desensitization—aversiveness, drinking-avoidant behavior and social reinforcement. Treatment group 4 received transactional analysis combined with behavioral treatment under the same leaders. In addition, all treatment groups received bibliotherapy and attended daily Alcoholics Anonymous meetings, individual psychiatric consultations each week, recreational activities, and a weekly family group counseling session.

The follow-ups were conducted on the telephone, with a second interviewer listening on an extension telephone. The reliability of the two interviewers was described as 0.86 and 0.94. No group differences were found 4 years after the treatment, although there was a nonsignificant trend for the TA group to do poorly.

These results, rather than shedding light on differential group treatments causing different outcomes, can better be seen as an example of an outcome study for a treatment setting.

Interpersonal Change

Although interaction and interpersonal communication among group members is commonly described as a reason for group counseling, relatively few research studies in group counseling have focused on interpersonal change (Bloch et al., 1981). Two studies which are representative of writing in this area are described in this section.

Morran, Robison, and Stockton (1985) described a study which focused on feedback among counseling group members. "Interpersonal feedback occurs when one group member shares his or her perceptions of and reactions to another's behavior with that other person" (p. 57).

Earlier studies indicated that effective definitions of feedback must include informational aspects as well as motivational aspects. In addition, group members have been found to accept positive feedback more readily than negative; to respond to positive and negative feedback differently at different stages of group development; and to value behavioral rather than emotional feedback.

This study interrupted the group process in order to devote one session to gathering feedback at either the second, fourth, or sixth group session. Three groups participated in feedback at each of the three sessions (nine treatment groups). Sixty-three subjects participated in 6-week "personal growth groups," meeting 2 hours each week. The nine groups were co-led by male-female or female-female advanced doctoral students who were interns in a counseling agency.

The study was interested in who provided feedback—the members or the leaders; the timing of the feedback—which session it was given in; and positive versus negative feedback. During the special session, group members and the leader completed a form to give feedback to each member. After writing the feedback, each person in the group read his or her feedback to each member. Positive and negative feedback were separated with the order being randomly assigned. Recipients immediately rated the feedback.

Results showed that the sex of feedback givers and receivers was not a factor. Recipients rated positive feedback as more accurate than negative. In addition, feedback in Session 4 was rated as more helpful than feedback in Session 2. Member and leader feedback was rated equally. Feedback from members was more specific when positive, while leader feedback specificity was the same for positive and negative. Negative feedback was less directive the later the session in which it was gathered.

A second example of studies regarding interpersonal change can be found in member attractiveness for the group (cohesion). Falloon (1981) used behavioral group therapy with 76 out-patients described as neurotically depressed or with inadequate personalities who reported having difficulties with their social skills.

Six role rehearsal groups ($n = 6$—10) and three discussion (control) groups were formed. Each group met for 10 weekly 75-minute sessions. The control groups used the same topics, handouts, and homework as the treatment groups. Leaders prompted and praised "constructive discussion and mutual help." The treatment groups were also structured around weekly topics. Patients exchanged information about homework but also participated in deep muscle relaxation, listening to music and other tension relieving activities. Leaders modeled effective behavior each week followed by member rehearsal.

Group attractiveness was greater for the behavioral groups than for control groups ($p < .05$). The authors suggest that cohesiveness can be improved by role rehearsal activities. No differences were found among the behavioral groups. Nor were any differences related to the sex of the leader.

Group Process

The final area of organization for expected goals of theories is group process. Only a few theories focused their expectations on specific group process goals. Likewise the research on group counseling has tended to slight this aspect of groups, an aspect that is unique to group counseling.

Once again, definitions pose a problem in this area. Topics such as member interaction and cohesiveness, treated under interpersonal change above, could be viewed as elements of group process. While some authors focused on "group dynamic processes" (Day, 1981) or "group climate" (MacKenzie, 1981) little research exists on group process changes in the literature.

Interpersonal learning is viewed as an important therapeutic factor by many group writers (Bloch et al., 1981). However this concept is usually measured in any research by obtaining individual group members' self-estimates. In some studies, these measures may be averaged, with the resulting mean seen as an indication of group process change. Such a procedure is not really a group process measure, however. As summarized by Bloch et al. (1981) ". . . there is no evidence of how interpersonal learning occurs or its effect on outcome. . . ." (p. 523). Coche and Dies (1981) point out the overemphasis on group research on the individual.

"The link between total-group cohesiveness and outcome remains largely unexplored" (Bloch et al., 1981, p. 524).

In summary, research in group counseling has exhibited several difficulties including a lack of studies which compare outcomes of groups using different theories, lack of studies which focus on expected outcomes for any theory, lack of agreed-upon definitions or measures, and difficulty in establishing comparable control groups.

Nevertheless, a sample study was shown (Shadish, 1980) which illustrated the type of research which is lacking. In addition, research was described according to the categories used earlier for expected group theory outcomes; namely, individual change, interpersonal changes, and group process.

CONCLUSIONS

All too often, a group theory has been established and practiced totally without regard for empirical findings (Coche & Dies, 1981). Nevertheless, selected theories (Gestalt, Adlerian, Personal Growth Groups, and Cognitive-Behavioral) were described according to their expected goals on the individual, on interpersonal relations, and on group process.

The high quantity of group research sheds little evidence that groups achieve the theoretically proclaimed results. This disappointing finding highlights the need for future research to identify explicitly the therapeutic benefits which are supposed to accrue from each theory of group counseling (Franks & Wilson, 1973). Greater thoroughness is required in future studies (more subjects, more precise description of treatment, standarized instruments of change, and adequate outcome measures) for the questions of the efficacy of group counseling to be satisfactorily answered (Bloch et al., 1981).

REFERENCES

BARRERA, M., JR. (1979). An evaluation of a brief group therapy for depression. *Journal of Consulting and Clinical Psychology, 47,* 413–415.

BECK, A. T., RUSH, A. J., SHAW, B. F., & EMORY, G. (1978). *Cognitive therapy of depression: A treatment manual.* New York: Guilford Press.

BLOCH, S., CROUCH, E., & REIBSTEIN, J. (1981). Therapeutic factors in group psychotherapy: A review. *Archives of General Psychiatry, 38,* 519–526.

COCHE, E., & DIES, R. R. (1981). Integrating research findings into the practice of group psychotherapy. *Psychotherapy Theory Research and Practice, 18,* 410–416.

DAY, M. (1981). Process in classical psychodynamic groups. *International Journal of Group Psychotherapy, 31,* 153–174.

DINKMEYER, D. C., PEW, W. L., DINKMEYER, D. C., JR. (1979). *Adlerian counseling and psychotherapy.* Monterey, CA: Brooks/Cole.

ELLIS, A. (1982). *Rational-emotive therapy and cognitive behavior therapy.* New York: Springer.

FALLOON, I. R. H. (1981). Interpersonal variables in behavioral group therapy. *British Journal of Medical Psychology, 54,* 133–141.

FRANKS, C. M., & WILSON, G. T. (1973). *Behavior therapy: Theory and practice.* New York: Brunner/Mazel.

HANSEN, J. C., STEVIC, R. R., & WARNER, R. W. JR. (1982). *Counseling theory and process* (3rd ed.). Boston, MA: Allyn & Bacon.

KAUL, T. J., & BEDNAR, R. L. (1986). Experiential group research. In S. L. Garfield & A. E. Bergin, (Eds.), *Handbook of psychotherapy and behavior change* (3rd ed., pp. 671–714). New York: John Wiley & Sons

KENDALL, P. C. (1982). Individual versus group cognitive-behavioral self-control training: One-year follow-up. *Behavior Therapy, 13,* 241–247.

LATNER, J. (1973). *The Gestalt therapy book.* New York: The Julian Press.

MACKENZIE, K. R. (1981). Measurement of group climate. *International Journal of Group Psychotherapy, 31,* 287–295.

MELNICK, J. (1980). Gestalt group process therapy. *The Gestalt Journal, 3*(2), 86–96.

MORRAN, D. K., ROBISON, F. F., & STOCKTON, R. (1985). Feedback exchange in counseling groups: An analysis of message content and receiver acceptance as a function of leader versus member delivery, session, and valence. *Journal of Counseling Psychology, 32,* 57–67.

OLSON, R. P., GANLEY, R., DEVINE, V. T., & DORSEY, G. C. JR. (1981). Long-term effects of be-havioral versus insight-oriented therapy with inpatient alcoholics. *Journal of Consulting and Clinical Psychology, 49,* 866–77.

SHADISH, W. R. JR. (1980). Nonverbal interventions in clinical groups. *Journal of Consulting and Clinical Psychology, 48,* 164–168.

SHAFFER, C. S., SANK, L. I., SHAPIRO, J., & DONOVAN, D. C. (1982). Cognitive behavior therapy follow-up: Maintenance of treatment effects at six months. *Journal of Group Psychotherapy, Psychodrama and Sociometry, 35,* 57–63.

SHAPIRO, J., SANK, L. I., SHAFFER, C. S., & DONOVAN, D. C. (1982). Cost effectiveness of individual versus group cognitive behavior therapy for problems of depression and anxiety in an HMO population. *Journal of Clinical Psychology, 38,* 674–677.

SHOSTROM, E. L. (1974). *The Personal Orientation Inventory.* San Diego: EDITS Publishers.

SMITH, E. L. (1976). *The growing edge of Gestalt therapy.* New York: Brunner/Mazel.

STEPHENSON, F. D. (1975). *Gestalt therapy primer.* Springfield, IL: Charles C Thomas.

SULZBACHER, S., WONG, B., MCKEEN, J., GLOCK, J., & MACDONALD, B. (1981). Long-term thera-peutic effects of a three-month intensive growth group. *Journal of Clinical Psychiatry, 42,* 148–153.

SUGGESTED ACTIVITIES

In the Classroom

1. With a partner, review the theories. About which ones do you see yourselves as knowledgeable? If there is disagreement, how could you become more knowledgeable?

2. In a small group, discuss the role that theory should play in successful groups. How can knowledge of a theory help make a leader more effective?

3. In a small group, each of you give some definitions for such terms as "cohesiveness," "insight," and "improved communication." List some of the definitions where each group member can see them. Discuss your definitions in light of the difficulty defining terms as discussed in this chapter.

On Your Own

1. In this chapter it was mentioned that conflicts can result in increased self-understanding. Recall a conflict you had with a sibling or a friend. Can you specify any increase in understanding as a result of this conflict?

2. Select a friend. See if you can decide on a volunteer project or on a good deed you would like to do. Commit to your friend just what you intend to do. After enough time has elapsed, share with your friend your reactions to this example of increasing your social interest.

3. Select someone with whom you spend quite a bit of time. Discuss with this person the feeling of support the two of you receive from each other. There may be differences between the two of you. Discuss how each of you could experience even more support from the other.

4. Check the current time. Now do an exercise about your own awareness of the here and now. See how long you are able to say out loud, "Now I am . . . , now I am aware . . . ." How long were you able to remain in the here and now?

5. Select a negative thought you often have about yourself. Then make an opposite to this negative. Write the opposite on a card and place it in a prominent place—your car, the bathroom mirror or on the refrigerator. Be prepared to discuss with a partner what effect this exercise has had on you.

6. With a partner, identify an area of difficulty that you both have. Each of you set a goal about what you intend to do during the next week to alleviate this difficulty. The two goals may be different. Get together in 1 week to compare how things went. Did you both accomplish your goal?

CHAPTER 3
PERSONAL QUALITIES OF THE EFFECTIVE GROUP LEADER

INTRODUCTION

What the group leader does as part of the counseling process is of major importance in determining the effectiveness of that group. It is also clear that the personal qualities of the group leader are other important determinants of group outcomes. Certainly the personality of the counselor influences strongly the whole therapeutic process, regardless of attempts to be a neutral, therapeutic instrument. The counselor's reactions and interventions are colored by his or her values, personality, and personal needs. Likewise, the character and personal qualities, even the philosophy of life of the leader, are potentially as important as any specific technique in facilitating the group process.

Preconceptions

Napier and Gershenfeld (1983) point out that many individuals subconsciously form a mental picture of what a group leader looks like. They suggest, for instance, that in the T-group sensitivity track, the image is one of a handsome, sexy, six-foot, blue-eyed man with an "ingratiating smile and an even more ingratiating manner" (p. 18). This individual is dressed informally, wearing an assortment of chains around the neck and probably a mustache or beard. Charisma oozes from the individual as his nontraditional, nonauthoritarian style commands attention. Speaking with confidence, but without using big words or getting overly cognitive, this leader is a cross between "Robert Redford and Carl Rogers."

They further describe the organization development image as being a leader who is tall and lean, dressed in the Ivy League tradition, with book-lined walls and an important degree. Such an individual is comfortable with survey data, computer printouts, and research analysis. However, Napier and Gershenfeld go on to suggest that various fantasies tend to have a consistency in that the successful group leader is "male, attractive in his style, has instantaneous charisma, has a natural sense of what to do and how to do it, and leads a group effortlessly—and always successfully" (pp. 18–19). Unfortunately, such an image is all too common, held not only by romantic teenagers, but by all kinds of intelligent, educated individuals. The reality, of course, is that effective group leaders come in all styles and types—male and female, tall and short, black and white, old and young, and charismatic and just normal.

As a result, new counselors often attempt to pattern their behavior after some such fantasy or image that they have of the effective leader. The counselor introduces something that is alien to him or her, making the new behavior more of a gimmick. More important, the group leader, who is "more than the sum total of skills" (Corey et al., 1982, p. 8), must use his or her own personal style and character in a way that is consistent with who he or she is.

CHARACTERISTICS OF EFFECTIVE COUNSELORS

The question of the kinds of personal characteristics and qualities that enable the individual to be most effective has been given as much attention as any other question in the field of counseling. Belkin (1981) points out that such an emphasis is justified. First, he believes that such an emphasis enables counselors to understand the importance of various subtle factors that contribute to counseling success. Second, counselor educators gain important information in helping them make crucial decisions regarding selection and training of potential counselors. Third, aspiring counselors are encouraged to find within themselves, and to strengthen, those qualities that have been indicated as predicters of successful counseling. Finally, trainers and researchers are aided in their attempts to determine the likely outcome of specific counseling interactions, based on tested criteria of counselor effectiveness.

Still, after a number of years and a vast amount of research, theorists are uncertain as to the exact qualities that distinguish an effective counselor from an ineffective one. Often this difficulty is one of semantics, in that words to identify clearly the specific human traits essential in effective counseling intervention are sometimes polluted by their everyday use and thus convey a large variety of meanings. Words such as *accepting, open, warm, genuine,* and *sincere* no longer have specific meanings, but often overlap and are ambiguous. Despite these problems, a great deal is known about these general qualities that significantly contribute to counselor effectiveness.

In 1964, the Association for Counselor Education and Supervision indicated that the counselor should have six basic qualities: belief in each individual, commitment to individual human values, alertness to the world, openmindedness, understanding of self, and professional commitment. Such a position partially resulted from Rogers' (1961) position that the effective counselor had to be an attractive, friendly person, who inspired confidence and trust. In addition, Combs and Soper (1963) had concluded from a study of effective and ineffective counselors that effective counselors perceived their clients as capable, dependable, friendly, and worthy, and perceived themselves as altruistic and nondominating.

Further studies by Combs and his coworkers (1969) led Combs to conclude that the major "technique" of counseling was the "self-as-instrument"; that is, that the self, or personal characteristics, of the counselor and the basic beliefs that counselors had concerning people were major factors in facilitating positive growth in clients. Combs found that effective counselors perceived other people as *able* rather than unable to solve their own problems and to manage their own lives. Effective counselors also perceived people as *dependable, friendly,* and *worthy.* They were also more likely to identify with *people* than things, to see people as having an adequate *capacity to cope* with problems, and to be more *self-revealing* than self-concealing.

In a sense, any analysis of personal characteristics of effective *counselors* must begin with an analysis of the characteristics of effective *persons*. A number of models of human effectiveness have been presented over the years, many of them in the 1962 yearbook of the Association for Supervision and Curriculum Development, entitled *Perceiving, Behaving, Becoming*. In this yearbook, Rogers (1962) listed three characteristics of the "fully functioning" person, presenting them as trends and goals toward which the individual strives. He suggested that the fully functioning person: (a) has an increasing openness to experience, as opposed to defensive reactions to experiences perceived as being incongruent with his or her self-image; (b) is continually moving toward being a process, constantly in change, but fully living each moment in the "here and now"; and (c) has an increasing trust in his own organism.

Combs (1962) provided his description of "adequate, self-actualizing" persons in the same yearbook. Combs described adequate persons as individuals who saw themselves as being liked, wanted, acceptable, and able; as possessing a capacity for identification with others; and as having perceptual fields that are maximally open to experience.

George and Cristiani (1986) present a composite model of human effectiveness that includes the following personal characteristics:

1. Effective counselors are open to, and accepting of, their own experiences.
2. Effective counselors are aware of their own values and beliefs.
3. Effective counselors are able to develop warm and deep relationships with others.
4. Effective counselors are able to allow themselves to be seen by others as they actually are.
5. Effective counselors accept personal responsibility for their own behaviors.
6. Effective counselors have developed realistic levels of aspiration. (p. 15.)

PERSONAL TRAITS OF EFFECTIVE GROUP LEADERS— MODELS

Some writers about group counseling have also attempted to list personal traits of effective group counselors or leaders. Dinkmeyer and Muro (1971) list eight such traits. First, members of the group perceive that the group leader is with them and for them as individuals. Second, the leader is aware of group phases and has the ability to facilitate those phases, knowing when to offer acceptance, confrontation, or cognitive input. Third, the leader has a positive outlook on life. Fourth, the leader is able to help each group member feel that he or she is an important part of the group. Fifth, the leader is professionally knowledgeable and creative. Sixth, the leader's perception of the group is influenced by the relationships that he or she has with the group itself. Seventh, the leader permits participants extensive autonomy. Eighth, their leader's style and work level matches that of the group members.

Corey and Corey (1982) identify some characteristics that they consider to be important elements of the group leader's personhood. Their list includes courage, a willingness to model, a sense of presence, good will and caring, a belief in group process, openness, an ability to cope with attacks, personal power, stamina, a willingness to seek new experiences, self-awareness, a sense of humor, and inventiveness.

Kottler (1983) presents his model for the group leader as being one in which counselors are busy, concerned with the well-being of others and selves, "action-oriented truth seekers" who take risks, and in an ongoing condition of positive change. He describes the effective group leader as being open to self-understanding as the issues of group members unfold, so that in being better able to solve his own personal conflicts, the group leader would become better at working with the problems of the group members. Kottler emphasizes desirable characteristics such as self-confidence, humor, risk-taking, honesty, energetic enthusiasm, and compassion.

PERSONAL CHARACTERISTICS OF THE EFFECTIVE GROUP LEADER

Thus there is general agreement as to the characteristics of an effective leader. Honesty and openness are important in that they imply a willingness to accept feedback and a willingness for the leader to self-examine needs and values to determine their impact on the group. These qualities suggest the leader's interest in personal and professional growth as well as the personal growth of the group members. Such a leader can be nonjudgmental and accepting, can value personal relationships, and can have positive relationships. Without narrow or rigid behavior patterns the effective group counselor takes risks, is flexible and spontaneous, and has a healthy degree of self-confidence and enthusiasm. However, a more thorough look at these qualities is important, so that potential group leaders can evaluate their own personal characteristics in terms of effective and ineffective group leadership.

Self-Awareness

One of the most important traits of effective group leaders is self-awareness. Permitting oneself to be aware of one's experiencing is often a difficult thing for the group leader to do. Paying attention to oneself includes being aware of the emotional reactions that one is having during the group experience. Thus, awareness implies a quality of openness, that is accepting one's feelings as they are, rather than trying to control those emotional reactions.

This quality is difficult to achieve because of the pressure of previous experiences, which teach individuals to deny their feelings. Pressures are applied not to feel depressed or not to be angry or not to be frustrated. Effective group leaders are able to accept within themselves feelings of sadness, anger, frustration, resentment, and other feelings ordinarily considered negative. By being aware of and accepting those feelings as they are, without denying or distorting them, group leaders have greater control over their own behavior. This awareness of their emotional reactions allows leaders to choose how they wish to act, rather than permitting their feelings to affect their behavior without their conscious awareness.

Certainly the effective group leader becomes involved with the experiencing of the group members to the extent that the leader is emotionally touched by the pain, struggles, and joys of others. Some group members may elicit anger in the group leader; while others may evoke pain, sadness, guilt, frustration, or even happiness. When the group leader is afraid of the kinds of emotional reactions that he or she may have during the group setting, there is a tendency to emotionally detach from the experiencing of the group members as an attempt to prevent undesirable reactions. However, effective group leaders recognize that by being aware of their own feelings they can allow themselves to experience those feelings, even for just a few moments. Fully experiencing emotions gives leaders the ability to be compassionate and empathic with the members, while remaining separate persons with their own experiencing.

Group leaders must also be aware of the ways in which group members conform or fail to conform to the leaders' values and beliefs, whether these concern education, morals, or hobbies. When group leaders are aware of their own values and beliefs they are more likely to be tolerant of group members whose life values differ significantly from their own. Also, group leaders must be aware of their own values and beliefs in order to determine to what degree they will expose those values and in what way they will influence the group members.

Genuineness

In our opinion, no other personal quality is more important than that of genuineness. The leader who is authentic, real, congruent, and honest is able to establish a special relationship with group members who recognize that the group leader is not playing a role or hiding behind a facade. Such leaders do not live by pretenses, but are willing to appropriately disclose self and share feelings and reactions to what is going on in the group. Genuine individuals are willing to be themselves and to express, in their words and their behavior, the various feelings and attitudes they hold. They do not need to present an outward appearance of one attitude while holding another attitude at a deeper level. They do not pretend to know the answers when they do not. They do not act like loving persons at moments when they feel hostile. They do not act as though they are confident and full of assurance when they are actually frightened and unsure. On a simpler level, they do not act well when they feel ill.

Such a quality does not mean that the individual counselor must disclose or share all experiencing with the members of the group. Rather, being genuine means that the individual has the choice of whether or not to share with others, but continues to act, verbally and nonverbally, in a way that is congruent with the internal experiencing. This occurs because group leaders who are genuine are comfortable with themselves in all their interactions. They have little need to change when they are with different people, but are able to continue in the same role, regardless of the individual with whom they are interacting.

Genuineness involves spontaneity. While being tactful, effective group leaders do not constantly weigh what they say to members. They do not put a number of filters between their inner lives and what they express to others. They are aware of when they are holding something back as a form of self-protection (for example, because they fear not looking good) and when they are doing it for the member's sake (the group member's reaction would be so strong as to block further exploration). Rogers (1975) points out that being genuine permits the helper to express negative feelings to others only when these feelings persist or when they are interfering with the helper's ability to work with clients in the counseling process.

Ability to Form Warm, Caring Relationships

Effective group leaders are able to develop warm, caring, deep relationships with others because they prize other individuals—their feelings, their opinions, their persons. Such a feeling is a caring that is nonpossessive with little evaluation or judgment; the other person is accepted with few conditions. This warmth or caring is not widespread in our society. Many people experience a certain amount of fear toward allowing themselves to care for other individuals. Their fear is based on the idea that if one freely experiences such positive feelings toward another, the individual may become trapped and therefore vulnerable. Other persons may take advantage; they may make demands that are difficult to reject; they may reject feelings by failing to reciprocate. As a result, many keep their distance, rarely permitting themselves to get close to someone.

Effective group leaders are less vulnerable to such fears because they recognize that the risk involved is worth the value to be gained. They therefore respond to others more freely, developing a close relationship with those who share their interests and values. They have wide freedom of choice in developing such relationships because of their ability to care and their relative lack of fear towards caring. They are not nearly so concerned with how many close friends they have, but with the quality of those friendships.

The ability to form warm, caring relationships is partially based on a trustworthy type of behavior on the part of the group leader. Group members must believe that the group leader is there to promote the well-being of the members, rather than of the leader himself. They must believe that the group leader will maintain appropriate, ethical standards and that they will not be used or taken advantage of in some way.

Corey (1982) suggests some specific ways by which the group leader can increase his or her trustworthiness. These include such things as striking contracts with clients and living up to the provisions of the contract; maintaining confidentiality; being sensitive to the other's needs and feelings; demonstrating genuineness, sincerity, and openness; being realistic, but optimistic about others' abilities to come to grips with their problems in living; using carefully and in the interest of others whatever social-influence power one has; and avoiding behavior that might indicate the presence of such ulterior motives as voyeurism, selfishness, superficial curiosity, personal gain, or deviousness.

In addition, it is important that the effective group leader have a basic trust in the members of the group. As was pointed out earlier, the need to feel little vulnerability in establishing a relationship with the group members is essential in establishing the kind of facilitative environment in which group counseling can be most effective. Certainly, group leaders cannot expect group members to have a basic trust in the leader, unless they perceive that the leader also has a trusting attitude toward them. Trusting behavior itself is defined by Johnson (1981) as "the willingness to risk beneficial or harmful consequences by making oneself vulnerable to another person." In a sense, such trust means that the group leader will not put some type of invisible barrier between self and the group members, keeping them at arm's length so that they will be unable to get a clear view of the leader's personal weaknesses and failures. Without a mutually trusting relationship, little can be achieved in the group counseling situation.

Sensitivity and Understanding

Sensitivity is also a major factor in contributing to counselor effectiveness within the group. Being sensitive involves a cognitive as well as an emotional response to each group member and makes possible a deeper and more spontaneous response to needs, feelings, conflicts, and doubts.

Everyone has some measure of sensitivity to other people. Without this, no one could exist for very long in modern society. Some people develop high degrees of sensitivity as a normal process in their growing up, while others have to work to sharpen their capacities. In either case, counselor sensitivity is so important for the helping process itself, that Rogers named the quality of empathy first among his three "necessary and sufficient conditions" for effective helping relationships.

During the process of group interaction, both the group atmosphere and the emotional being of the various members are continually in a state of flux. Because the group consists of living, responsive organisms, group members are reacting at any given moment to the stimulation of the discussion; whether that stimulation is in the form of verbal responses from the leader, from the group leader's expressions and movements, or from internal, reflective thinking going on in the member's own personal, subjective world. Both the internal processes and the external stimuli have a profound effect on the quality and substance of the interaction among the members of the group, as well as between the members and the group leader. Fortunately, group members do indicate that these changes and responses are occurring in their words, body language, and overall behavioral patterns, as well as by gestures and voice tone. The effective leader is one who is able to discern these minuscule, but nevertheless significant, responses on the part of the group members and to assimilate these changes into his or her own perspectives and understanding of the group (Belkin, 1984).

As suggested, sensitivity is similar to *empathy* as Rogers (1975) described it. His description involved sensing the other's private world as if it were one's own, but without ever losing the "as if" quality. He suggested that to be able to sense the other's anger, fear, or confusion *as if it were one's own,* yet without one's own anger, fear, or confusion getting bound up in it was a necessary condition for therapeutic effectiveness to occur. Thus Rogers specified two critical conditions: The group leader must be able to experience the member's feelings as the member is experiencing them, in the same way, with the same degree of effect and personal meaning; and the group leader must also be able to maintain an individual identity and remain sensitively aware of the differences between self and the member.

Although the communication of empathic understanding as a specific skill or technique to be utilized in facilitating the movement of the group during the counseling process will be discussed in chapter 7, it is important to see this sensitivity and understanding as a personal quality of the individual who is to be effective as a group leader. In this sense, empathy becomes an attitude of the group leader, an attitude that permeates the type of interaction that the leader has with the various group members. Rather than being simply a specific response pattern to a verbal or nonverbal communication by a group member, this type of understanding becomes the basis for various leader behaviors. The group leader is able to decide what kind of intervention he or she wishes to utilize at a given moment in a particular group by being sensitive to the particular dynamics that are occurring in an individual or a group.

Self-Confidence

Self-confidence implies an awareness that one possesses specific skills and knowledge that can be helpful for the members of the group in achieving their individual goals. It does not indicate that the group leader is arrogant, perfectionist, or perfect, but that the group leader is aware of what he or she can do as a leader as well as what he or she is unable to do. Such self-confidence also includes an awareness of the leader's influence on others. This influence does not mean that the leader can dominate and exploit others, which are abuses of power; but that the group leader is aware of the effect he or she has on group participants when encouraging them to get in contact with their own unused power and feelings. Such self-confidence results from the group leader's recognizing that he or she does not need to keep others in an inferior position in order to maintain power.

Sense of Humor

While group counseling is serious business, since the members are there to bring about a change in themselves, there are some humorous dimensions. The ability to laugh at oneself and to see the humor in one's own human frailties can be extremely useful to the group leader. There are times when appropriately used humor can be as helpful as many other types of counselor behaviors, if not more so. At times, people take themselves so seriously that they miss an opportunity to put into perspective the importance of their problems. Occasionally, groups will exhibit a real need for laughter and joking, simply for release of the tension that has built up. Such a release should not be viewed as an escape, but as part of a healing process. The leader who can enjoy humor and infuse it effectively into the group process has an invaluable contribution to make.

Humor, as a therapeutic attitude, is certainly not sarcasm, ridicule, or cynicism. Rather, therapeutic humor stems from empathic listening and reflects a positive outlook on life. Sometimes it results in the leader spontaneously laughing with one or more of the group members; at other times the leader is provoking laughter in others. Such humor is spontaneous and natural, not artificial or contrived. Sometimes it consists of no more than a raised eyebrow, a smile, a gesture. When it occurs therapeutically, it brings the members of the group closer together by establishing an additional bond of genuine caring for each other and confidence in the helping nature of human rapport.

The group leader's sense of humor may allow the leader to take the members' irrational ideas to ridiculous extremes, to reduce them to absurdity, and to employ paradoxical intention as a means of helping those members see the ridicule of their own ideas, not the ridiculousness of themselves. Likewise, humor can be a means of expressing the joy and satisfaction of connecting with and caring about each other.

Such humor, as long as it is not used to derail an important immediate dynamic, to express anger or to ridicule another person, or to conceal a person's deep feelings, has curative value all by itself.

On the whole, humor is an essential part of healthy group life. Group members need to learn to laugh at themselves and at each other. The ability to laugh is not only a valuable skill to be carried into life outside the group, but is also good in and of itself. The visible bubbling-up of joy, of freedom, of well-being, is often the first sign that a group has become truly therapeutic.

Flexibility of Behavior

The ability to be flexible in organizing and responding to the group is essential to the effective group leader. Such flexibility is based on self-confidence, a sensitivity and understanding of the group, and a self-awareness. As such, the flexibility results in the group leader's being able to respond to and with the group members, rather than expecting them to simply follow in the direction that the leader had planned to take.

Such flexibility is most effective when the leader also has the ability to be spontaneously creative, to be able to develop new ways of dealing with problems as they arise. Even the capacity to approach each group with fresh ideas is not easy to maintain, particularly if the counselor leads groups frequently. Group counselors must somehow avoid becoming trapped in ritualized techniques or a systematic presentation of self that no longer is lively and vibrant. By being willing to suspend the use of established techniques and by approaching a group with new ways of doing things, a group leader is unlikely to grow stale.

In many ways flexibility of behavior means that the group leader is letting the group members ''lead'' the direction of the group. By responding to the expressed needs and wishes of the group members as well as to the dynamics of the group as they occur, the group leader is able both to direct the group process and to allow the group to have some say in the experiencing that occurs.

Such willingness to follow the direction of the group largely results from the self-confidence, sensitivity, and self-awareness mentioned earlier, as well as a sense of trust in the group process. Such a sense of trust is based on the belief that when a group is facilitated rather than directed, the group will recognize for itself the unhealthy elements in its process, clear them up or eliminate them, and move on toward more positive processes.

This flexibility does not mean that the leader has no specific goals for a particular group. Rather, the leader trusts the group to participate effectively in finding the direction by which the group goals will be met. Such an approach focuses on establishing a particular type of facilitative environment in which group members can experience and deal with those feelings, attitudes, and behaviors which have been creating problems for them without providing the total direction the group is to take.

Willingness to Self-Evaluate

A crucial leadership attitude is that of continually evaluating one's own contribution to the group process, both during and after each group session. Corey and Corey (1982) point out that leaders need to be able to ask themselves questions such as: What kinds of changes are resulting from the group? What are the therapeutic and antitherapeutic forces in the group? The skill of self-evaluation rests to a large degree on the leader's knowledge of and sensitivity to what is happening in the group. As a personal quality, however, the willingness to self-evaluate means that the group leader is not so wrapped up in looking good that he or she continually distorts the group experiences in his or her own mind so that negative or nonproductive moments are ignored. Rather, the effective group leader is willing to look at the group experience honestly and carefully in an attempt to determine what can be done differently to make the experience more worthwhile for the group members.

SUMMARY

Both what the group leader *does* and *who* he or she is are important to the effectiveness of the group experience. The leader's personal qualities are potentially as important as any specific technique in facilitating the group process.

Although a number of theorists have agreed over the years that the personal qualities and characteristics of the counselor are very important, research has failed to identify clearly just what these qualities are. However, a major difficulty is that different words often have highly similar meanings.

A number of writers have suggested models for organizing the personal traits associated with effective group leadership. A composite model is proposed which includes the following:

1. self-awareness
2. genuineness
3. ability to form warm, caring relationships
4. sensitivity and understanding
5. self-confidence
6. sense of humor
7. flexibility of behavior
8. willingness to self-evaluate

REFERENCES

ALLPORT, G. (1961). *Pattern and growth in personality.* New York: Holt, Rinehart & Winston.

ASSOCIATION FOR COUNSELOR EDUCATION AND SUPERVISION (1964). The Counselor: Professional preparation and role. *Personnel and Guidance Journal, 42,* 536–54.

BELKIN, G. S. (1981). *Practical counseling in the schools* (2nd ed.). Dubuque, IA: Wm. C. Brown.

COMBS, A. (1962). A perceptual view of the adequate personality. In A. Combs (Ed.), *Perceiving, behaving, becoming* (pp. 40–64). Washington, DC: Yearbook Association for Supervision and Curriculum Development.

COMBS, A., & SOPER, D. (1963). The perceptual organization of effective counselors. *Journal of Counseling Psychology, 10,* 222–226.

COMBS, A.; SOPER, D.; GOODING, C.; BENTON, J.; DICKMAN, J.; & USHER, R. (1969). *Florida studies in the helping professions.* Gainesville: University of Florida Press.

COREY, G. (1982). *The skilled helper.* Monterey, CA: Brooks/Cole.

COREY, G. (1985). *Theory and practice of group counseling* (2nd ed.). Monterey, CA: Brooks/Cole.

COREY, G., & COREY, M. S. (1982). *Groups: Process and practice* (2nd ed.). Monterey, CA: Brooks/Cole.

DINKMEYER, D. C., & MURO, J. J. (1971). *Group counseling: Theory and practice.* Itasca, IL: F. E. Peacock.

GEORGE, R. L., & CRISTIANI, T. S. (1986). *Counseling theory and practice* (2nd ed.). Englewood Cliffs, NJ: Prentice-Hall.

JOHNSON, D. W. (1981). *Reaching out* (2nd ed.). Englewood Cliffs, NJ: Prentice-Hall.

KOTTLER, J. (1983). *Pragmatic group leadership.* Monterey, CA: Brooks/Cole.

NAPIER, R. W., & GERSHENFELD, M. K. (1983). *Making groups work.* Boston: Houghton Mifflin.

ROGERS, C. (1975). Empathic: An unappreciated way of being. *Counseling Psychologist, 5,* 2–10.

ROGERS, C. (1961). *On becoming a person.* Boston: Houghton Mifflin.

Rogers, C. (1962). Toward becoming a fully functioning person. In A. Combs (Ed.), *Perceiving, be-having, becoming* (pp. 21–33). Washington, DC: Yearbook Association for Supervision and Curriculum Development.

SUGGESTED ACTIVITIES

In the Classroom

1. With a partner, discuss stereotypes of what a typical group leader looks like. Attempt to identify similarities and differences in your stereotypes. If neither or only one has a stereotype, discuss why you think this is.
2. In a small group, discuss Rogers' description of the characteristics of a fully functioning person.
3. An effective group leader is able to discern minuscule nonverbal responses from group members. Form a small group in order to take turns serving as group leader. Have each group leader focus carefully on member nonverbals as the group engages in a discussion of one of the following:
   a. a student explaining to a support group what it is like to find oneself in the wrong major in college
   b. A person discussing a recent suicide of a best friend
   c. A person explaining to the group a hard test coming up

   After the group leader is able to look for nonverbal reactions, spend some time discussing what the leader saw and how the leader might have reacted.

On Your Own

1. Interview a counselor in a setting of your choice. Have the counselor react to the list of human-effectiveness characteristics given in this chapter. To what extent do the two of you agree about the importance of the characteristics? To what extent do the two of you see group leaders benefiting from each of the listed characteristics? Do the two of you see some characteristics as more important for group leaders than others?
2. Choose the person outside your family whom you believe to be the most effective person in interpersonal relationships. If possible, observe that person; if not, try to recall his or her behavior. Identify those characteristics that enable the individual to be effective. Discuss this individual with a small group of fellow students.
3. Identify and describe the personal strengths you possess that will be helpful in making you an effective group leader. Prepare to discuss in class with one other student your list of personal strengths.

CHAPTER 4
STRATEGIES, SKILLS, AND STYLES OF EFFECTIVE LEADERSHIP

INTRODUCTION

The previous chapter examined the personal qualities of effective group counselors. This chapter describes the strategies, leadership skills, and varying leadership styles of counselors who are effective.

Strategies of a group leader include the thinking that goes on prior to meeting with a group and specific decisions concerning leading the group. What kind of clients will be members of this group? What has been the experience of the group leader with similar groups? What kinds of structure, early group activities, leader involvement, and group norms are desired for this particular group?

In this chapter a selected list of skills or techniques such as leader self-disclosure, leader empathy, and leader feedback are described. While not intended to be an inclusive list, the leadership skills described in this chapter are regarded as highly important for all types of groups.

The third section of this chapter describes different types of leadership styles. Authors have stated that the professed theory of a group leader does not necessarily influence the behavior of the leader (Lieberman, Yalom, & Miles, 1973). Nevertheless group leaders do tend to repeat techniques and interventions across groups. It is important that the group leader begin to recognize his or her own style.

STRATEGIES

It is important for a counselor to consider the goals for a particular group when selecting a strategy for that group. This aspect of group counseling is often overlooked (Masson & Jacobs, 1980).

Groups may be held for purposes that at times will be preventive as well as remedial (Corey, 1981). However, these categories of a group's purposes are too general to offer guidelines to the beginning leader. In addition, many times during the life of a group, activities will be preventive for certain group members while they are remedial for other group members.

Many writers have devised lists of different types of groups. One such list is described here (Masson & Jacobs, 1980). These authors have organized groups into mutual sharing groups, discussion groups, educational groups, problem-solving groups, growth groups, and therapy groups. *Mutual sharing groups* would not likely have a problem orientation. Rather, they would focus on member self-disclosure, providing a chance for members to talk and share ideas, and for universality and mutuality to develop. *Discussion groups* would often have a specific task. They could include orientation groups as well as members getting together to discuss readings. *Educational groups* could include workshops or a group of people receiving certain kinds of training. *Problem solving groups* might be specific task groups or planning groups. However, they also could easily overlap with therapy groups in that members might be working on heterogeneous or homogeneous problems under a certain therapeutic orientation, such as behavioral therapy. *Growth groups* were discussed in chapter 2. For some, this type of group also overlaps with a therapy group having preventive goals. Finally the *counseling* or *therapy group* is viewed by these authors as a specific type of group. This type might be a collection of individuals who seek new approaches and behavior patterns to their life problems.

Also in chapter 2, the reader has seen that different theories suggest different purposes whether they be individual changes, interpersonal purposes, or group process changes. Purposes may be derived from the theoretical orientation of the leader, the characteristics of the prospective members, the setting in which the group is to be offered, the prior experience of the leader, or a combination of several of these. Most important for the beginning group leader is that the purposes be clear. Careful thought will be necessary in order for a leader to obtain clarity in purposes for a group. Most leadership styles would dictate that the purposes for the group which the leader has clearly in mind might be described to group members before or at least early in the life of the group.

What about member-derived purposes of a group? Would it ever be appropriate for a leader to approach a group, say a mutual sharing group, with one of the purposes being to allow the members of the group to develop their own purposes? Group-initiated purposes might have an advantage in member responsibility for the group. This goal may be achieved at the expense of ambiguity and confusion in the early stages of the group.

A second major factor that influences strategies of a group leader is the kinds of members which are in the group under consideration. Several writers have focused on the importance of a group leader's knowing as much as possible about clients in a group (Culpon, 1979; Zamarripa & Krueger, 1983). A prescreening interview has been recommended by more and more authors including Culpon (1979). This issue will be treated in chapter 6. Such a pregroup interaction between a leader and members provides an opportunity to get to know members. Homogeneous groups in which members all identify a certain type of problem for themselves still have highly diverse members. The group leader will be especially interested in knowing the clientele's communication styles, extent of involvement, skills in communications, and other types of information which can best be understood by participating in a group over a period of time. Nevertheless, the purposes of a group usually are determined, at least in part, by characteristics (such as the age of group members) that are readily apparent. This factor is one which influences the strategies a group leader plans.

Another major influence on the strategy which a group leader selects has to do with the leader's self-knowledge. One of the personal characteristics of effective leaders, described in chapter 3, was leader self-awareness. To what extent is the leader able to identify and to own certain traits and certain characteristics? Brutal honesty in assessing one's professional knowledge and expertise about group issues, personal characteristics, and one's own ethical behavior are very important when devising strategies for group leadership. Just as, ethically, the counselor is not to advertise or to make interventions beyond his or her competence, a group leader needs to know his or her own limitations. Zamarripa and Krueger (1983) have stressed the importance of rules for leaders to follow. These rules could easily include an openness on the part of the leader to feedback and to signs of how well the group leader is meeting the preselected goals for the group. The extent to which one is able to know one's self overlaps with the topic of leadership style, which is discussed later in this chapter.

An important aspect of leadership strategies is the extent to which the leader intends to become personally involved. It is one exercise to devise strategies in armchair fashion, as it were, before a group begins; however it is a different task altogether, to influence the group and to implement such strategies. The issue of involvement by the group leader is one that elicits strong disagreement among writers about group counseling. Carl Rogers stresses the importance of a leader's being nonjudgmental. As quoted by Landreth (1984), ''The less judgmental a counselor is, the more likely he [sic] is to produce a climate in which growth will occur'' (p. 325). Although several writers have given the leader almost total responsibility for the energy level of the group (Masson & Jacobs, 1980) as well as for getting the group started and holding the group on the designated focus (Corey, 1981), it still remains an important part of the strategy for each group leader to determine how much personal involvement and personal responsibility the leader intends to take. Is the leader to model certain important group behaviors early in the life of a group? Does the leader prefer to reinforce such important group behaviors after members execute them? On the important issue of trust among members and confidentiality within the group, is it part of the leader's strategy to give direction on these issues or to wait until the group brings them up? A beginning counselor can only attempt to anticipate and develop a strategy with which to meet such questions. The reader can benefit from examining leadership styles which have been developed in the group counseling area. This topic will be addressed after first looking at techniques of group leaders which can lead to effective outcomes for groups.

SKILLS

Regardless of their selected strategy of leadership, effective groups leaders tend to exhibit similar techniques. In this section a representative group of leader skills is described. For each skill, a definition will be followed by a typical example of the skill used by a group leader. The expected purpose for each technique will be described last.

Empathy

Empathy is such an important characteristic of effective counseling that theories either explicitly include its use or indirectly assume that the counselor will be able to communicate empathically with a client. In *group* counseling, empathy takes on a more complex, yet equally important role. Empathy can be viewed as an attitude that a counselor possesses when working with groups, or it can be operationally defined as the accurate communication of understanding in response to a spoken message (Gazda, Asbury, Balzer, Childers, & Walters, 1984). An example of a simple reflection of feeling follows:

GROUP MEMBER (GM):   Sometimes I get confused. I just don't know what you are going to do next.
GROUP LEADER (GL):   It bothers you that you just don't know what to expect.
M: That's right.

Empathy can also be used with the entire group. After a GM has made a self-disclosure, a silence follows. Many of the group members are shifting in their seats and looking at the floor.

GL: It seems that you're all pretty uneasy as to how to respond to what Jim said.
GM: Yes, I don't know what to say.

There are several potential outcomes of group leader empathy. One outcome is that the group leader models understanding responses for the group. Long and Schultz (1973) found that more empathic leaders had group members who communicated higher levels of empathy to each other. Another is that empathic responses deepen the communication and can lead to more group member self-disclosure. Finally, another expected outcome is that empathic responses clarify communication as well as encourage personal exploration.

Nonverbal Attending

Nonverbal attending behaviors are crucial for group leaders. The authors have experienced difficulty when supervising group leaders in getting students to scan the entire group rather than look just at the group member who is speaking. Definitions of nonverbal attending usually include behaviors such as eye contact, leaning towards the speaker, head nods, appropriate gestures, and facial expressions such as smiles (Ivey, 1971).

Although difficult to write, a use of nonverbal attending follows:

While Sally has been talking about her current boyfriend, the group leader looks and nods at her, at the same time watching the entire group.

The expected outcome of nonverbal attending is to demonstrate the lis-

tener's interest and caring. Developing the skill of scanning the nonverbals of the
entire group, no matter who is speaking, is an essential ingredient in the sensitivity
of the group leader. Allen (1982) stated that a group leader who engages in "multiple attending" will increase empathy and trust within the group.

Confrontation

Confrontation is an important technique for many counseling theories and
group leadership strategies. Confrontation has been defined as a statement by a
group leader that has important meaning as well as high emotional investment
for the speaker and the listener (Colangelo, Dustin, & Foxley, 1982). An example
follows:

GL: Jerry, I can't help noticing that you have come late to group consistently. I would
      feel better if I knew what your coming late means both to you and to the group.
      (Jerry responds to the group leader.)

Confrontation can have many purposes: to deepen the communication between the confronter and the person confronted by adding personally emotional
material, to model effective confrontation for the entire group, or to attempt to
change the person being confronted.

Self-Disclosure

When the group leader expresses feelings or opinions to the group, *self-disclosure* occurs.
Examples of leader self-disclosure follow:

GL: I think it is time that we discuss my role in this group
GM: I'm just getting nowhere on my contract that you guys helped me with last week.
GL: It bothers me that you haven't made any progress.

The expected outcomes of leader self-disclosure would include modeling for
the entire group, personalizing the role of the leader within the group, and engaging the group or a member in a personal communication. May and Thompson
(1973) found that group leaders may engage in too much or too little self-disclosure, but that group member perceptions of leader self-disclosure correlated
positively with perceived helpfulness of the group.

Counselor Focus

Ivey and Gluckstern (1976) have defined *counselor focus* as an element of microcounseling. According to their definition, any group leader statement can be
seen to focus on (a) a group member, (b) a group leader, (c) people outside the
group, (d) the group itself, (e) the topic or problem, or (f) cultural-environmental-

contextual factors. The authors say that although ''this type of response is almost totally absent in most theories of helping'' (p. 56), nevertheless some statements could focus on the economic cycle, the national debt or such other factors. Examples of group leader statements which focus on each of the six categories follow:

1. A group member
   GL: Mary, you haven't said anything yet tonight.
2. The group leader
   GL: I'm glad that you said that.
3. Outsiders
   GL: Tell us more about your mother.
4. The group
   GL: You all seem kind of sleepy and laid back tonight.
5. The topic or problem
   GL: So it's more your relationship with your boss than with your wife.
6. Cultural-environmental-contextual factors
   GL: I guess it's the phase of the moon that is responsible for our attitude.

The expected purpose of counselor focus is to help a group leader sharpen his or her awareness of group leader statements. In addition, a leader could intervene by asking the group if they could focus on a particular member or if they could focus on the entire group. The skill or technique of group leader focus seems especially germane to group leader strategies and styles.

Open Questions

Questions that cannot be answered *yes* or *no* have been defined as *open questions*. Open questions can be addressed to individual group members or to the entire group.
Examples of open questions include the following:

GL: Why do you think you feel this way, Jerry?
GL: What is it that is getting in our way?

Asking open questions is an extremely flexible and effective skill. A group leader can change the topic, steer the group, or even confront or reflect feelings through the use of open questions. One common purpose is to draw out another person.

Contracts

Contracts have been defined as oral or written agreements which specify a behavior to be performed by one or more persons. Through experience, group leaders learn to specify and to encourage a paraphrase or a restatement of verbal contracts. In addition, effective contracts will specify which person and which behavior(s) are to be performed. Examples of verbal contracts follow:

GL: Let me see if I understand. You are going to lose three pounds by the next group meeting.

GL: So, the next time I come late to a meeting, we agree that we will discuss the matter again.

The expected purposes of contracts are to clarify and to prevent misunderstandings. Certain strategies of group leadership will make extensive use of contracts between individual members and the group. However, the ability to make clear cut, measureable contracts is a technique which we regard as essential for all group leaders.

Feedback

Feedback is behavioral information about the actions and the impact of those actions on a group member or to the entire group.

Examples of feedback follow:

GL: I think when you come late to the group it disrupts all of us and sometimes gets the group off track.

GM: When you address everyone else in the group except me, it tends to make me feel unwanted.

Feedback is often an important ingredient of confrontation. One purpose of providing feedback is to introduce one or more reactions for the purpose of further discussion and exploration. Another purpose is to increase the awareness of the individual or the group about the impact of their behavior.

Silence

Silence is the omission of verbal statements. In this case it is used by the group leader.

Examples of group leader silence follow:

GM: Does anyone else think that it's annoying when Dick comes late?

GL: Silence—waits for someone else to respond.

GL: Silence—while group members wait and fidget.

The expected purpose of silence is to enable the group leader to make observations. This technique is especially important but tends to be ignored or at least underutilized by beginning group leaders.

Cognitive Restructuring

Cognitive restructuring is the providing of an alternative point of view by the group leader. Frequently this technique is used to put a positive tone to an otherwise negative exclamation.

Examples of cognitive restructuring include:

GL: I think your silence—your not giving a quick response to the question—indicates how seriously you're taking the question.

GM: So I just feel overwhelmed. I have this grant to administer and I'm behind in my writing. Sometimes I just feel useless.

GL: So you feel useless sometimes, but at the same time you seem to be on the verge of a fantastic opportunity.

The intended purpose of cognitive restructuring is to provide an alternative point of view. In so doing, the group leader is able to model one type of help for the entire group.

STYLES OF LEADERSHIP

Leadership style evolves in part from the leader's use of effective skills. No one leader will perform all the skills. Rather the leader's familiarity and acceptance of certain skills will make a difference in skill performance, since some skills are not right for each group leader and may not feel right or comfortable for each leader. Leadership style, as a result, must be highly personal and individual. It follows, then, that leader style has been one of the most vaguely reported variables in all of the group psychotherapy literature (Seemann, 1982). The goal of this chapter is to highlight for the reader the importance of recognizing and developing one's own leadership style. One aspect of style is preplanned strategies. Another is frequency of performance of certain skills.

SELECTED LEADERSHIP STYLES

In 1968, White and Lippitt described three leadership styles which were based upon earlier research they had conducted with Kurt Lewin. The research was based on five member groups comprised of 10-year-old boys.

Authoritarian

The original authoritarian leadership style consisted of a leader who made all policy decisions for the group. All techniques and all activities of the group were decided upon by the leader and communicated to the group member one at a time. Authoritarian leaders tended to make personal remarks which were directed at individuals. These personal remarks included praise. In addition the authoritarian leader remained aloof from the group.

The authoritarian leader gave orders 45 percent of the time, which was by far the highest percentage of the three leadership styles. Members of the groups led by authoritarian leaders tended to react aggressively and with more dependence upon the leader than did members exposed to the other leadership styles. The boys tended to make statements such as "shut up" and "you put them away; you dumped them." These statements were labeled "dominating ascendance."

Democratic

The democratic leadership style featured a leader in which all policies were discussed by the group members. Democratic leadership styles included giving group members the overall goals along with alternative steps and activities to accomplish these goals, then helping the group decide which alternatives to select. Democratic leaders made objective remarks rather than personal remarks and were more likely to participate in the group as a member. Only 3 percent of the democratic leader's style statements were giving orders. In addition, group members were found to work as much as 50 percent of the time and to engage in more friendliness and to exhibit more "group-mindedness."

Laissez Faire

The third leadership style originating from this classic study was laissez faire. This leadership style included minimum participation from the leader. The leader tended to supply materials and then to state that he would give information whenever group members asked. Only 4 percent of the leadership style statements were giving orders. Members of laissez faire groups worked 33 percent of the time, less than those using the democratic leadership style. In addition, the members were less satisfied and seemed less organized than did groups led by leaders with democratic style.

In the many writings which have referred to this classic report in the subsequent years, the impression has emerged that the authoritarian leadership style and the laissez faire leadership style are somehow wrong. Such simplistic conclusions would not be as helpful to a beginning leader as a more specific look at these three classic styles. For example, Scheidlinger (1980) reminds us that no one leadership style will be effective with every group. In addition, the lack of structure under the laissez faire leadership style has some theoretical basis since certain theories of group counseling imply that group members should provide the structure and that group leaders should not make very frequent structuring comments. In the early stages of a group, as members look to the group leader for direction, the leader who provides some structure or who attempts to reduce ambiguity somewhat may not necessarily be the same as an authoritarian leader. Ziff (1980) suggested that structured exercises may be part of a leader's strategy. To further complicate matters, Berman (1982) states that any counselor or therapist is an authority figure in a group counseling situation. No doubt the way in which the structured activity is suggested by a group leader and the extent to which the leader's suggestion can be processed or discussed is an important aspect of leadership style. Those who react quickly to the authoritarian style as somehow undesirable are reminded that a group counselor is in charge, almost always determines the length of the meetings, needs to have a planned agenda, and does have the responsibility for what occurs in the group (Berman, 1982).

A group leader exhibiting rational authority is not necessarily the same as an "irrational authoritarian" (Berman, 1982). What about an important group technique for some theorists, namely, interpretation? When a group leader makes an interpretation to the group or to a group member there is no doubt that the group leader is functioning as an authority. Is interpretation necessarily authoritarian? According to Berman (1982) nonauthoritarian interpretations would be those which are clearly explained so that group members may see the origins and the rationale for the interpretation and which members can respond to and disagree with.

Structured activities or exercises may be suggested to group members, perhaps as an alternative, or they can be ordered and presented to the group with no discussion (Berman, 1982).

Other Styles of Leadership

Two additional leadership styles have been described as of high therapeutic value (Barlow, Hansen, Fuhriman, & Finley, 1982). Leaders using the speculative style speak for themselves and have a here-and-now focus on the meaning of their own or a group member's behavior. Confrontive leadership style includes a here-and-now focus in which leaders reveal the impact of their own behavior on themselves as well as the impact of a group member's behavior on them (Barlow et al., 1982). This leadership style includes a focus on documentation of statements from present as well as previous interactions between the leader and the group member. In a study comparing speculative with confrontive leadership styles, results, as judged by 48 group counseling students, indicated that confrontive leaders were seen as more charismatic and less peer-oriented than were speculative leaders. There were no statistically significant differences on member self-concept changes between members of groups with the two leadership styles (Barlow et al., 1982).

Other authors have focused attention on the charismatic leadership style (Rutan & Rice, 1981). There is a tendency for many group members to look up to the group leader in the early stages of the group. Some members may very well look at the group leader through the irrational eyes of someone undergoing transference in which the leader may become an ego ideal. Rutan and Rice state: "The charismatic situation may be even more devastating for the leaders of therapy groups than for the patients! It is such an intoxicating temptation to be adored, revered, and adjulated by not just a single patient but a whole roomful of patients" (p. 491).

For many group leaders, the strategy has included allowances for at least some members to see the leader in a highly unrealistic fashion. Such leaders will plan to move their structuring behaviors from early responsibility and decisions for the group towards more group discussion and group responsibility for the agenda. Corey (1981) has indicated that the group leader can reduce the level of activity after the first two stages of the group. In the long run, a charismatic leadership style would seem to mitigate against the ultimate autonomy of each individual member (Rutan & Rice, 1981). Even if the group leader intends to harness the charisma from the early group stages, there are two risks each leader must face according to Rutan and Rice (1981). The first is that the leader may become "unconsciously" wedded to the charisma and will not be able to help the group move on. The second risk is that clients who are able to develop a relationship with the leader at early stages will have difficulty or may even attempt to avoid a more mature relationship development with the leader at later stages. As Berman has indicated (1982), it is the transference process that encourages the leader to be seen as charismatic.

IDENTIFYING A LEADERSHIP STYLE

Strategies may not always be performed exactly as planned. In addition, a leader's familiarity with leadership skills and techniques may not always be reflected in the leader's performance. It is a combination of the strategies and the skills which result in a leader's own style. From the very first meeting, group leaders differ in how they communicate and how they are perceived by group members. Even then, different group members will react differently to the group leader (Seemann, 1982). Nevertheless, the way the group leader introduces himself or herself to the group is important. Will most members see the group leader as a trusting individual and as one who is trustworthy? According to Corey (1981), "Talking about matters such as rights of participants, the necessity of confidentiality, and the need for respecting others demonstrates that the leader has a serious attitude toward the group" (p. 33).

The leader's strategy may have included allowing group members to exert more influence and to accept more responsibility over time. Therefore, the leader's style must encourage member's willingness to increase their level of functioning. Covi, Roth, and Lipman (1982) state "as the course of therapy progresses, patients assume increasingly greater responsibility for designing their own assignments" (p. 464).

A perfectly legitimate style for a group leader might include at least some leader ambiguity (Harrison & Cooper, 1976). However, it does not seem possible for the beginning group leader to include ambiguity as an important aspect of style and to also be following the directions of the writers discussed earlier who urged the leader to be active at the earlier stages of group development and for some to even explicitly state the rules and regulations and so self-disclose the leader expectations for members of the group. Although it is necessary to "discover" one's leadership style from feedback and televised observation of actual group leadership, nevertheless certain issues come into focus when a leader plans a strategy that may be contradicted with the techniques or even with other aspects of the preplanned strategy.

Often leaders who include ambiguity as an important aspect of leadership style have the successful working through of member transference as an important strategy. What about other leaders? The discussion of charismatic leadership style indicated that for many group members, the group leader will be viewed at least somewhat irrationally. As members are nervous and concerned about what to expect from the group, the group leader takes on exaggerated importance and can be viewed as having exaggerated strength and wisdom. Therefore, when one or more group members communicate unrealistic expectations or even irrational reactions to the leader, group leaders following certain theories will be ready for the group to begin. What about group leaders with other styles and following other theories? Does the leader style include ignoring such signs of transference? Focusing them upon the group as a whole? While the strategy probably included how a leader intends to develop and to react to relationship issues between the leader and individual group members, the style or the way in which the group leader treats such questions is also a significant aspect of effective group leadership.

Chapter 3 described flexibility of behavior as a personal characteristic of the effective group leader. This flexibility is an aspect of leadership style that almost everyone would agree sounds like a positive trait or behavior. However flexibility has not always been agreed upon by authors in the group area. A ready example would be those writers who urge beginning group leaders to always be active in early stages and phases of the group. Other writers have specified that the group leader must always focus only on individual group members or only upon the group as a whole. In his description of Gestalt theory, Warehime (1981) prefers a leadership style flexible enough so that the leader can choose to focus on the individual, on a pair of group members, or on the whole group.

For Warehime, the "leader develops a group culture in which members are encouraged to take responsibility for their behavior (self-support); express themselves clearly and directly out of their ongoing awareness (authenticity); and . . . support, nourish, and challenge each other" (p. 44).

Some strategies may also require flexibility between emphasizing the cognitive and the affect of the group content. Another aspect of flexibility might include the degree to which the leader is the center of the interaction and the degree to which the interaction remains among the group members. Flexibility seems to imply that certain leadership styles might not always feature only one answer to the above issues.

Although many of the writings, as well as the transcripts, of group counseling would indicate that humor is certainly not to be found in group counseling, one issue of leadership style is certainly that of humor. Is humor always a relief of tension? Must it always signify that the person using the humor is fleeing from the "work" at hand? Rossel (1981) pointed out that humor can add to the tension of a group and that for some groups at least, a competitive and pointed use of humor can be seen in sarcastic putdowns of other members. The awareness of the beginning group leader should at least include how the leader's attempts at humor are perceived by others. It would seem reasonable, for most group leaders at least, that a flexible attitude toward humor would be desirable.

The extent to which the beginning group leader communicates in the moment or the here-and-now; asks other members to communicate in the here-and-now; asks other members to communicate in the here-and-now; focuses remarks and interactions on the here-and-now; and of course, structures the group so that here-and-now statements are held to be desirable goals has to be included in a consideration of leadership style. If lucky, the beginning group leader can receive feedback from professional observers as well as view himself or herself on videotapes in order to judge whether or not the leader is modeling here-and-now communications or whether perhaps the leader is giving contradictory messages between what is expected and what is actually performed. It should also be remembered that for certain strategies of group leadership—ambiguity, for example—here-and-now communications are not always demanded for effective group leadership.

Earlier in this section on leadership style, the confrontive style was described as an effective one. It is important that a leader be aware of the extent to which confrontation is used as an intervention in the group. Does the leader usually confront individuals? If yes, then was such a confrontation part of a strategy? Do the confronted individuals seem to always be of one type or one sex? If the leader tends to confront the group as a whole, then careful observation and recording of the effects of such confrontation upon group development would seem warranted. Rather than getting into evaluation of leadership style, the task here seems to be to raise issues that a leader could choose to consider when attempting to develop and to become aware of the leadership style.

Some strategies will build conflict into an essential ingredient of group development. With other strategies it will seem as though interpersonal conflict never occurs, or at least has not been planned for. Whatever the strategy, the effective group leader needs to be aware of the style of group leading that is performed in conflict situations. Does the leadership style never include leader conflicts with individual members? Does the leadership style seem to place the leader on the fence or in the middle as a mediator between the sources of conflict? It is to be hoped that the leadership style does not indicate a tendency to run from or to defuse prematurely conflicts that will emerge within the group.

Certain theories of group leadership would indicate that strong member reactions as well as most forms of disruptive member behaviors be viewed as resistance. Regardless of the theoretical orientation, effective group leadership style will include a satisfactory and even an effective way of dealing with strong group leader emotions, intervening with disruptive group members, and responding to group leader feelings of defensiveness. Although most strategies will not build in leader defensiveness, and the skills that were treated earlier did not include ways to practice defensiveness, a complete leader style would include how the leader responds when threatened. It would not seem to be effective enough for a group leader to be able to engage in a consistent goal-directed style when things are running smoothly without also attending to the leader's own responses to difficulties within the group.

Descriptions of authoritarian leadership style included the characteristic of making decisions for the group concerning agendas and activities. At the same time, this chapter has indicated that several authors recommend a group leader's structuring early group sessions and taking an active role in the early phases of group counseling. Does a leader who adheres to certain goals in the group or who suggests certain activities for group participation need to engage in an authoritarian leadership style? The reader seems faced with a question of what type of style to seek. Probably the manner in which a leader gives suggestions and the timing of leader suggestions are as important to a perceived leadership style as the suggestion itself. The flexibility called for by Corey (1981)—an effective group leader's being equally comfortable on interpersonal issues as intrapersonal issues—is a desirable characteristic of a beginning group leader's leadership style.

SUMMARY

This chapter identified the strategies, skills, and leadership styles which enable the group leader to be effective when used by an individual who possesses those personal characteristics discussed in chapter 3.

Strategies include the thinking the group leader does prior to the group session and specific decisions regarding the structuring to be done during that session. These strategies are influenced by the purpose of a particular group, the theoretical orientation of the leader, the kinds of members in the group, and the leader's self-knowledge.

Counseling skills that are particularly important for the group leader include empathy, nonverbal attending, confrontation, self-disclosure, counselor focus, open questions, contracts, feedback, silence, and cognitive restructuring.

Various leadership styles have been discussed. Authoritarian leadership involves the leader making all policy decisions for the group. Democratic leadership features a leadership in which all policies tend to be discussed by the group members. The laissez faire style of leadership involves minimal participation from the leader.

Leadership style is a result of the combination of strategies and skills which dominate the leader's behavior. Leader ambiguity, flexibility, humor, focus on the here-and-now, and confrontation are key areas of focus in determining leadership style.

REFERENCES

ALLEN, E. E. (1982). Multiple attending in therapy groups. *Personnel and Guidance Journal, 60*(5), 318–320.

BARLOW, S., HANSEN, W. D., FUHRIMAN, A. J., & FINLEY, R. (1982). Leader communication style: Effects on members of small groups. *Small Group Behavior, 13,* 518–531.

BERMAN, E. (1982). Authority and authoritarianism in group psychotherapy. *International Journal of Group Psychotherapy, 32,* 189–200.

COLANGELO, N., DUSTIN, D., & FOXLEY, C. H. (1982). *The human relations experience: Exercises in multicultural nonsexist education.* Monterey, CA: Brooks/Cole.

COREY, G. (1981). *Theory and practice of group counseling,* Monterey, CA: Brooks/Cole.

COVI, L., ROTH, D., & LIPMAN, R. S. (1982). Cognitive group psychotherapy of depression: The close-ended group. *American Journal of Psychotherapy, 36,* 459–469.

CULPON, F. M. (1979). Studying action sociometry: An element in the personal growth of the therapist. *Journal of Group Psychotherapy, 32,* 122–127.

GAZDA, G. M., ASBURY, F. S., BALZER, F. J., CHILDERS, W. C., & WALTERS, R. P. (1984). *Human relations development: A manual for educators* (3rd ed.). Newton, MA: Allyn & Bacon.

HARRISON, K., & COOPER, C. L. (1976). The use of groups in education: Identifying the issues. *Small Group Behavior, 7,* 259–270.

IVEY, A. E. (1971). *Microcounseling: Innovations in Interviewing Training.* Springfield, IL: Chas. C. Thomas.

IVEY, A. E., & GLUCKSTERN, N. B. (1976). *Basic influencing skills: Participant manual.* North Amherst, MA: Author.

LANDRETH, G. L. (1984). Encountering Carl Rogers: His views on facilitating groups. *Personnel and Guidance Journal, 62,* 323–325.

LIEBERMAN, M. A., YALOM, I. D., & MILES, M. B. (1973). *Encounter groups: First facts.* New York: Basic Books.

LONG, T. L., & SCHULTZ, E. W. (1973). Empathy: A quality of effective group leaders. *Psychological Reports, 32,* 699–705.

MASSON, R. L., & JACOBS, E. (1980). Group leadership: Practical points for beginners. *Personnel and Guidance Journal, 59,* 52–55.

MAY, O. P., & THOMPSON, C. L. (1973). Perceived levels of self-disclosure, mental health, and helpfulness of group leaders. *Journal of Counseling Psychology, 20,* 349–352.

ROSSEL, R. D. (1981). Chaos and control: Attempts to regulate the use of humor in self-analytic and therapy groups. *Small Group Behavior, 12,* 195–219.

RUTAN, J. S., & RICE, C. A. (1981). The charismatic leader: Asset or liability? *Psychotherapy: Theory, Research and Practice, 18,* 487–492.

SCHEIDLINGER, S. (1980). The psychology of leadership revisited: An overview. *Group, 4,* 5–17.

SEEMANN, D. C. (1982). Leader style and anxiety level: Their relation to autonomic response. *Small Group Behavior, 13,* 192–203.

WAREHIME, R. G. (1981). Interactional Gestalt theory. *Small Group Behavior, 12,* 37–54.

WHITE, R., & LIPPITT, R. (1968). Leader behavior and member reaction in three 'social climates.' In D. Cartwright & A. Zander (Eds.), *Group dynamics: Research and theory* (pp. 527–553). New York: Row, Peterson.

ZAMARRIPA, P. O., & KRUEGER, D. L. (1983). Implicit contracts regulating small group leadership: The influence of culture. *Small Group Behavior, 14,* 187–210.

ZIFF, J. D. (1980). Establishing guidelines for differential processing of structured experiences based on self-knowledge theory. *Group and Organization Studies, 5,* 234–246.

SUGGESTED ACTIVITIES

In the Classroom

1. With a partner, summarize the definitions of strategies, skills, and leadership style found in this chapter. Identify questions that the two of you want to raise in class.

2. In a small group, take turns practicing the skills of empathy, nonverbal attending, and self-disclosure. Have the group discuss such topics as
   a. Getting along with a roommate
   b. Being a single parent
   c. Not doing well in a required class

   After one student takes a turn using the skills, have the rest of the group give the "leader" feedback.

3. Take turns serving as a group leader. Each group leader should try to make three or four "here-and-now" statements in response to the discussion. Group members should then give the leader feedback.

4. Take turns serving as the leader for the first meeting of a small group. The strategy of the group leader is to encourage member exploration of their perceptions of their own difficulties. After each "leader," give feedback. Suggested groups:
   a. A group of homogeneous-aged substance abusers. The group is voluntary in nature, will meet twice a week, and has been screened by the leader.
   b. A group of students who have expressed difficulties interacting with faculty members.

5. Have a leader engage in "modeling" in order to show the group members one way to initiate conversation with a member of the opposite sex.
   Give the person doing the modeling some feedback.

On Your Own

1. Interview a counselor from a setting of your choice in order to get some examples of preplanning for groups in that setting.

2. Interview a counselor to determine the counselor's perceptions of his or her own leadership style. Try to determine how the counselor knows or found out about his or her style.

3. Read more about counseling skills. Consider these sources:

EGAN, G. (1982). *The skilled helper* (2nd ed.). Monterey, CA: Brooks/Cole.

GAZDA, G. M., ASBURY, F. J., BALZER, F. J., CHILDERS, W. C., & WALTERS, R. P. (1984). *development: A manual for educators* (3rd ed.). Newton, MA: Allyn & Bacon.

IVEY, A. E., & GLUCKSTERN, N. B. (1976). *Basic influencing skills: Participant manual.* North Amherst, MA: Author.

CHAPTER 5
THERAPEUTIC ELEMENTS IN GROUP COUNSELING

INTRODUCTION

Probably the most important question to be asked about group counseling is, What elements or factors are important in making group therapy effective in helping those individuals who participate? On the one hand, a group approach to counseling individuals is a well-established mode of treatment. At the same time, the question of what it is about the group approach that makes group counseling effective is poorly understood. One part of the difficulty in answering the question results from the fact that any kind of therapeutic change is an enormously complex process and occurs through a multiple interplay of various experiences. Since this process is as complex as it is, efforts have been made to identify the crucial aspects of the group experience which are most important in promoting therapeutic change.

One of the difficulties, however, in studying the literature related to group counseling results from a wide assortment of theories seeking to explain the therapeutic process. Likewise, empirical research sometimes tends to complicate the picture even further, since the research findings are often inconsistent and the quality of the research varies considerably. In addition, some very important questions concerning therapeutic elements have not been put into operation to the degree that they can be fully studied.

One approach to the problem involves the overall concept of therapeutic elements. Researchers such as Frank (1971), Truax and Carkhuff (1967), and Carkhuff and Berenson (1967) have sought to identify and validate that certain elements are consistently related to effective individual counseling. However, there have been only limited efforts made to discover those same kinds of consistent, basic elements in group counseling that constitute the therapeutic process, no matter what theoretical model is being applied. Such research would not only provide a more solid scientific footing for group counseling, but would also enable the group leader to integrate into his or her counseling process those factors that have been shown to be most important in therapeutic change. It is reasonable to believe that the more skillful the group leader is in utilizing therapeutic elements, the more effective the therapy process will be.

The focus in this chapter is on those therapeutic elements which have been tentatively identified. These elements were originally proposed as the result of the group experiences that various individuals encountered. In some cases such elements are included because the observations made were done in a systematic, although not empirical, manner. Where empirical research is available to demonstrate the relationship of a particular therapeutic element to outcome, such research will be briefly summarized. However, as will be seen, such research is limited.

Part of the difficulty in identifying those therapeutic elements results from a tendency among group theorists to use different language and different ideologies to describe the same phenomenon. Successful group leaders frequently attribute their success to the use of certain techniques or strategies. While these techniques and strategies may be extremely important in facilitating the group movement, an analysis of therapeutic elements must go beyond these specific strategies and look at the broader concept of what is happening within the group when such strategies are utilized.

The concept of a therapeutic element is based on the assumption that the group process involves a specific set of elements that can be differentiated from one another as to their exerting specific effects on members of the group, thus facilitating change. These elements, while inherently therapeutic, may be misused by the group leader either because the leader lacks appropriate skill or because a group member is unable to accept that kind of therapeutic factor. With this in mind, a definition of therapeutic element can be proposed. The definition that we are using is that proposed by Bloch (1986). Bloch defines a therapeutic factor as "an element occurring in group therapy that contributes to improvement in a patient's condition and is a function of the actions of the group therapist, the patient, or fellow group members" (p. 679).

This definition takes into account the fact that the means by which therapeutic elements are important varies considerably. The definition also helps to distinguish between therapeutic elements and two other aspects of the group process which are closely related: conditions for change, and techniques. *Conditions for change* are important in the operation of therapeutic elements, but do not in themselves have therapeutic force. For instance, self-disclosure requires listeners, and the actual presence of several individuals to hear that self-disclosure increases its therapeutic effect. Similarly, a technique does not have direct therapeutic effect but is simply a strategy available to the group leader to increase the effectiveness of a therapeutic element. While therapeutic elements, conditions for change, and techniques can be isolated, they often overlap and are interdependent with one another. In addition, none can operate satisfactorily without the others.

HISTORICAL DEVELOPMENT

Corsini and Rosenberg (1955) published the first major effort to produce a unifying classification of those therapeutic elements shared by group counselors of various theoretical persuasions. Basically, Corsini and Rosenberg conducted a "factor analysis" by abstracting the therapeutic factors identified in 300 pre-1955 group counseling articles from which they identified 220 statements reflecting therapeutic factors. They then reduced those to 166 by combining identical statements and then, through a set of hypotheses suggested by a study of those statements, clustered them into nine major categories. Those nine categories (plus a tenth miscellaneous one) formed a classification system for identifying therapeutic factors in group counseling. These categories are

1. Acceptance: A sense of belonging
2. Altruism: A sense of being helpful to others
3. Universalization: The realization that one is not unique in one's problems
4. Intellectualization: The process of acquiring knowledge about oneself
5. Reality Testing: The recognition of the reality of such issues as defenses and family conflicts
6. Transference: A strong attachment either to therapist or to co-members
7. Interaction: Relating within the group that brings benefit
8. Spectator Therapy: Gaining from the observation and imitation of fellow patients
9. Ventilation: The release of feelings and expression of previously repressed ideas

Hill (1957) attempted to take the classification further; he interviewed nineteen group therapists and proposed six therapeutic factors: catharsis, feelings of belongingness, spectator therapy, insight, peer agency (universality), and socialization. The next classification, produced by Berzon, Piovs, and Farson (1963) used group members rather than leaders as the source of information for determining the essential therapeutic elements. Berzon studied eighteen members of two outpatient, time-limited therapy groups which met for fifteen sessions. After each meeting the patients filled out a questionnaire in which they described that incident which was most important to them. As a result, 279 incidents were obtained. Judges then sorted those incidents into nine categories in order of frequency. The resulting nine categories closely resembled those of Corsini and Rosenberg and included

1. Increased awareness of emotional dynamics
2. Recognizing similarity to others
3. Feeling positive regard, acceptance, sympathy for others
4. Seeing self as seen by others
5. Expressing self congruently, articulately, or assertively in the group
6. Witnessing honesty, courage, openness, or expressions of emotionality in others
7. Feeling responded to by others
8. Feeling warmth and closeness generally in the group
9. Ventilating emotions

Notice that the main therapeutic mechanisms were reported to result from the interaction among group members with few of the reports involving the group leader. To a large extent, the major focus was on the interpersonal feedback which group members received, enabling them to modify their self-image and to validate the universality of problems.

Ohlsen (1977) proposed a somewhat different set of therapeutic forces which were based on a series of research conclusions that he summarized. Ohlsen proposed the following fourteen elements which he called "therapeutic forces":

1. Attractiveness of the group
2. Acceptance by the group
3. Expectations
4. Belonging
5. Security within the group
6. Client readiness
7. Client commitment
8. Client participation
9. Client acceptance of responsibility
10. Congruence
11. Feedback
12. Openness
13. Therapeutic tension
14. Therapeutic norms

Such a list differs widely from the previous list that had been proposed in that client attitudes about the group experience are emphasized more strongly. In addition, Ohlsen lists a number of forces which might better be considered as conditions for change.

At approximately the same time, Yalom (1970) proposed his landmark classification of curative factors. Based primarily on a series of research studies which Yalom and his colleagues performed, Yalom emphasized an interactional dimension to the group process and, in particular, highlighted the interaction taking place among the group members themselves. He proposed the term ''interpersonal learning'' as a major curative factor which had two components: input, chiefly through feedback; and output, an actual process whereby the group member attempts to develop more effective modes of relating to others. Yalom also included three new therapeutic factors that had not been earlier proposed: the installation of hope (the member feels optimistic about change as a result of observing progress in others); guidance (the member receives advice from the group leader or from fellow group members); and an existential factor (the member becomes aware that one alone is responsible for the way one lives one's life). Yalom's list of curative factors then included

1. Installation of hope
2. Universality
3. Imparting of information
4. Altruism
5. The corrective recapitualization of the primary family group
6. Development of socializing techniques
7. Imitative behavior

8.   Interpersonal learning
9.   Group cohesiveness
10. Catharsis
11. Existential factors

Finally, Bloch, Reibstein, and Crouch (1979) have sought to exploit the assets of the aforementioned classifications while avoiding the limitations they believed to exist. Their ten-factor classification resembled Yalom's classification but with certain modifications. For instance, they omitted Yalom's existential factor because they believed it did not correspond to their definition of a therapeutic factor; that is, it was not an element of the group process that exerts a beneficial effect. They suggested that the existential factor instead calls for the group member to think about life in a specific way along lines laid down by a particular theory and is therefore better conceptualized as a therapeutic goal. They also omitted family reenactment, since they felt this assumes that the group member should identify a specific cause of his or her difficulties—unresolved family conflict. At the same time, they proposed a new factor of self-understanding which was all-embracing in quality (including both existential and transferential aspects) in the sense that it was based on the members learning about some important aspect of the self. They also made a distinction between two forms of expression: *self-disclosure,* the members revelation of highly personal information reflecting honesty and openness; and *catharsis,* the members release of intense feelings, bringing about a sense of relief. Their final difference from Yalom's was one of emphasis and concerned interaction. Bloch and his colleagues saw interaction as an *attempt* by the member "to relate constructively and adaptively within the group either by initiating a pattern of behavior or by responding to other group members" (p. 682). By titling the factor *Learning From Interpersonal Action,* they were attempting to convey the two interacting aspects: action and cognition. Their resulting product was the following classification of therapeutic factors:

1.   Self-disclosure: revealing personal information to the group
2.   Self-understanding (insight): learning something important about oneself
3.   Acceptance (cohesiveness): sense of belonging and being valued
4.   Learning from interpersonal action: the attempt to relate constructively and adaptively within the group
5.   Catharsis: ventilation of feelings, which brings relief
6.   Guidance: receiving information or advice
7.   Universality: the sense that one is not unique in one's problems
8.   Altruism: the sense that one can be of value to others
9.   Vicarious learning: learning about oneself through the observation of other group members, including the therapist
10. Installation of hope: gaining a sense of optimism about the potential for progress. (p. 681)

THERAPEUTIC ELEMENTS AS WE SEE THEM

In an attempt to build on the work of those individuals whose work we have just summarized, as well as others who have made significant contributions to our understanding of group counseling, we propose a somewhat simpler model for identifying those therapeutic elements which are necessary and sufficient for effective group counseling. Like some of the others who have preceded us, we are basing our ideas concerning therapeutic effectiveness elements on the research that we have reviewed, the conceptual ideas that others have presented, and our own experience in leading various kinds of groups.

From our viewpoint, then, the essential elements that contribute to therapeutic effectiveness in group counseling include the following:

1. Installation of hope
2. Sense of safety and support
3. Cohesiveness
4. Universality
5. Vicarious learning
6. Interpersonal learning

Installation of Hope

This is a therapeutic element through which the group member gains a sense of optimism about his or her progress or potential for progress through actual counseling experience. Although the concept has been emphasized by a number of theoreticians over the years, it has been virtually neglected by those individuals doing empirical research in group counseling. As Frank, Hoehn-Saric, and Imber (1978) have suggested—that hope may act as a placebo factor in psychotherapy generally—it is possible that the installation of hope in a group setting is even more of a placebo effect than in individual therapy since the potential sources of a group member's hope includes all of his or her peers. If future research can somehow prove this placebo effect to be true, the installation of hope will still be an important element since, whether placebo or not, group leaders are only concerned about what it is that helps to bring about therapeutic change among the group members.

Certainly the installation and maintenance of hope is crucial, since hope is required to keep the member in the group so that other therapeutic factors can take effect. When the individual remains within the group, other ''hope-installing'' factors can take place. For instance, other members of the group will have often suffered from some of the same concerns as the individual group member. Such individuals who have had similar problems and have coped with those problems effectively provide hope for others that their own concerns and problems can be resolved. Effective group leaders frequently exploit this factor by calling attention to the improvement that group members have made.

Likewise, if the group members are to possess a sense of hope about the group counseling experience, it is important that the group leader believe in himself and in the efficacy of the group. The belief that the group leader is able to help every member who commits himself to counseling and remains with the group for an appropriate period of time is important for the group leader; sharing this belief with each group member can be an important part of increasing that member's optimism about his group experience.

One of the great strengths of such support groups as Alcoholics Anonymous, Overeaters Anonymous, and Synanon is the fact that the leaders are almost always individuals who have suffered from the same disorders as the current members. These leaders then become living inspirations to the new members, who are able to believe that because the leader was able to overcome his or her problems they will be able to do so also. A major part of the meetings of these groups is dedicated to testimonials from not only the group leader but from the various members of the group. These testimonials are of major importance in the effectiveness of these groups.

Corey and Corey (1977) point out that hope is a belief that change is possible, that "one is not a victim of the past and that new decisions can be made" (p. 185). Such hope comes not only from a sense of identification with other individuals who have solved similar problems, but also emerges from the recognition that one has untapped reserves of spontaneity, creativity, courage, and strength. As individuals recognize and accept that they have the internal resources necessary to direct the course of their lives, their sense of hope greatly increases.

Because individuals enter group counseling with the hope that it will be helpful to them, it is important that the group leader build on that hope so it will block or destroy concurrent feelings of these group members that "maybe nothing can help." One way of maintaining this hope is to develop clear-cut expectations of what will be expected from each member. The more members understand and adopt those expectations—to discuss their problems openly, to work toward specific behavior change, and, when necessary, to confront other group members toward implementing new behaviors—the more those group members will increase their feelings of power and optimism about changing their own lives.

Sense of Safety and Support

The need to feel reasonably secure within the counseling group—where individuals can be themselves, give up their facades, discuss their problems openly, accept other persons' frank reactions to them, and express considerately their own genuine feelings toward others—is a need that is clearly essential to a therapeutic experience within group counseling. Part of this sense of safety and security results from a feeling of genuine acceptance by other group members. This group acceptance not only enhances self-esteem, but provides quality support for various changes in behavior which the individual wishes to attempt. Such acceptance ordinarily involves the affirmation of the individual's right to have his or her own feelings and values and to express them. It also comes from demonstrated caring. This caring is sensed when individuals believe that others are listening to them and have an involvement with their concerns. When group members are able to sense that their concerns are important to others and that they are valued as persons, they are more likely to risk the kinds of changes in their lives that will be therapeutic in the long run. Risking involves opening oneself to others and actively doing those things in the group experience that are necessary for change. As such, this kind of riskiness results in the person's feeling vulnerable to rejection.

Perhaps the key word is *trust*. A sense of safety and support within the group can come only after the individual feels a large level of trust in the group. As Johnson and Johnson (1982) have pointed out, trust is a necessary condition for effective communication. They go on to add, "the higher the trust the more stable the cooperation and the more effective the communication. A group member will more openly express his thoughts, feelings, reactions, opinions, information, and ideas when the trust level is high" (p. 388).

When group members trust the group and feel this sense of safety and support, two particularly important behaviors or effects are likely to occur: self-disclosure and catharsis. A number of studies indicate that successful group members self-disclose (Lieberman, Yalom, & Miles, 1973; Truax, 1968; Truax & Carkhuff, 1965). Self-disclosure has two major effects: (a) a member is able to receive understanding and acceptance from the other group members that will let that member know that he is okay as a person and (b) group members discover that their fellow members whom they may admire have problems as difficult as their own and that they are not giving up. The effect of universality, which will be discussed later, can begin to take effect.

Catharsis—the release of strong feelings, bringing relief—can be therapeutic in that energy is released that has been tied up in withholding certain threatening feelings. Catharsis often permits an individual to realize that negative and positive feelings toward another person or situation may coexist. The relief that results from the individual's knowledge that other people now know about these intense feelings and the situations that brought them about is a major step in that individual's feeling understood and accepted.

Although catharsis has been emphasized by a number of individuals, it has received little attention by those who do empirical research on group counseling variables. One reason for this may be the intrinsic nature of catharsis and the difficulty of measuring its impact. Another reason may be a feeling that catharsis by itself has little value; only when catharsis is complemented by subsequent cognitive reflection does it result in individual growth.

The Lieberman, Yalom, and Miles study (1973) is the major study which has attempted to clarify the value of catharsis *per se*. These researchers asked 210 members of a thirty-hour encounter group to describe the most significant incident that occurred during the course of the group. While experiencing and expressing feelings was frequently selected, this critical incident was not related to positive outcome. Incidents of catharsis were as likely to be selected by group members who showed little change as by those who showed good change. They point out that "catharsis was not unrelated to income; it was necessary but, in itself, not sufficient" (p. 84). They believed that their study showed that individuals who had profited most from their group experience showed a profile of catharsis plus some form of cognitive learning. Thus the open expression of feelings is without question vital to the group therapeutic process. In its absence, the group would flounder in a sterile nonmeaningful exercise. Rather, catharsis is intricately related to cohesiveness and provides the kind of bonding that enables the group to work honestly in the therapeutic change of its members.

Cohesiveness

Although Corsini and Rosenberg (1955), as well as each of the other theorists summarized in this chapter, included the concept of cohesiveness (sometimes called acceptance or belonging) in their classification of therapeutic elements, its precise definition remains elusive. Although acceptance is an element of the sense of safety and support, described earlier, we are including it in this section as part of an individual's feeling that he or she belongs and is part of a particular therapeutic group. This sense of togetherness, which we have labeled group cohesiveness, involves many aspects, including allegiance, agreement with the group's objectives, and attraction to the group leader as well as to peers (Frank, 1957).

Corey and Corey (1977) point out that a group is characterized by a high degree of togetherness at times, providing an environment in which "participants feel free to share problems, try new behaviors, and in other ways reveal the many dimensions of themselves" (p. 155). From a practical standpoint, cohesiveness is important because it has an impact on the attendance of individuals at group sessions as well as their involvement. Thus when a group feels a sense of cohesiveness, they are more likely to take those actions which result in therapeutic change.

A number of research studies have been performed which support the idea that cohesiveness is an important element within group counseling. Dickoff and Lakin (1963), for instance, in a study of former group psychotherapy patients, found that the patients believed that group cohesiveness was of major therapeutic value. They found that over half of those former patients indicated that the primary help they had received in group therapy was the result of mutual support. Also, those patients who perceived their group as cohesive attended more sessions, experienced more social contact with other members, and judged their group as having been therapeutic.

Likewise, a positive association was found by Kapp, Glaser, and Brissenden (1964) in their study of long-term members of discussion and therapy groups. In this study, members rated their own level of change as well as the degree of cohesiveness they perceived in the group. Kapp and his colleagues concluded that cohesiveness may be important in bringing about change. However, a study by Yalom, Houts, and Zimerberg (1967) indicating that patients perceived cohesiveness as positively relating to self-ratings of change, also showed that there was no relationship between the degree of cohesiveness perceived by patients and independent judgments of therapeutic outcome.

In 1977 Jones studied 130 patients who responded to questionnaires at a student mental health service. These patients had attended one of thirty therapy groups offered at the service, consisting of twenty two-hour sessions over a five-month period. Overall, the respondents stated that the most positive aspect of their group experience was the feeling of security and acceptance they had experienced in the group. Jones concluded that the amount of cohesiveness was positively related to the degree of self-reported improvement; that is, that those groups that received high cohesion scores from its members were more likely to have a higher number of patients who improved during the course of therapy.

Yalom (1985) summarized a large segment of the research that has been done in laboratory groups and dyads related to group cohesiveness. He concluded that the overall evidence from this research demonstrates that the members of a cohesive group, in contrast to the members of a noncohesive group, will

1. Try harder to influence other group members;
2. Be more open to influence by the other members;
3. Be more willing to listen to others and more accepting of others;
4. Experience greater security and relief from tension in the group;
5. Participate more readily in meetings;
6. Self-disclose more;
7. Protect the group norms and, for example, exert more pressure on individuals deviating from the norms;
8. Be less susceptible to disruption as a group when a member terminates membership. (p. 68)

Two factors that may contribute to the importance of cohesiveness as part of the therapeutic process are intimacy and empathy. As people experience closeness in a group, an intimacy develops creating a stronger sense of trust in others. Individuals may become aware, as a result of this new sense of closeness to others, of the barriers in their outside lives that have prevented intimacy.

Empathy may also be a part of cohesiveness, since a true sense of empathy involves a deep understanding of the struggles of another individual. In the group setting, commonalities among the individuals emerge that unite them, forming a cohesive bond. The feeling that one is alone lessens with the realization that certain problems—such as fear of rejection, fear of intimacy, loneliness, or hurt resulting from previous experiences—are universal. We have also chosen to include, under the umbrella of cohesiveness, the concept of altruism, which various theorists have proposed as a separate therapeutic factor. In a cohesive group, the individual is more likely to become part of the therapeutic process of offering help to other group members. As a result, the individual is more likely to engage in those activities that will enable him or her to benefit from the realization that he or she can be of value to his or her peers. This results in the realization that, in counseling groups, members receive through giving, not only as part of the reciprocal giving-receiving sequence, but also from the very intrinsic act of giving. Such giving undermines the sense of being demoralized and of having nothing of value to offer others. Thus for the group member, it is a refreshing, self-esteem-boosting experience to find that they can be of importance to others.

Even more important, group members are enormously helpful to one another in the group process itself. By offering support, reassurance, suggestions, insight, and understanding, they provide spontaneous, truthful reactions and feedback, permitting other members to gain insight into how they relate to others.

Carkhuff (1971) pointed out this importance of altruism in the therapeutic process in his comments regarding training as a preferred mode of treatment. His basic concept was that by training individuals to help others, those individuals would receive the greatest degree of help themselves. Perhaps the major reason this occurs was pointed out by Frankl (1969) when he suggested that it is only when we as individuals have transcended ourselves, when we have forgotten ourselves in an absorption in someone or something outside of ourselves, that we obtain self-actualization and meaning in life.

Johnson and Johnson (1982) have suggested several ways by which a group can increase its cohesion. These include

1. Structuring cooperation among members;
2. Successfully meeting the personal needs of members;
3. Maintaining a high level of trust among members;
4. Promoting group norms that encourage the expression of individuality, trusting and trustworthy behavior, and concern and affection among group members.

Universality

Another key element in the therapeutic process of group counseling is that of universality, the sense that one is not unique in one's problems—that others share these problems. Since many clients enter a group setting with some reluctance because they believe that their problems are unique to themselves and have little relationship to the kinds of problems that other people experience, the positive impact that occurs whenever those individuals learn that others do have concerns similar to their own is enormous. A sense of relief often results as these clients hear the self-disclosure of other group members, and a growing insight into the nature of their own problems results. Yalom (1985) reports that clients often indicate that they feel more in touch with the world and see this process of commonality with other group members as one of a "welcome to the human race" experience.

As trainers of counselors, we have often had our counselors-in-training practice an empathy exercise in which each member of the training group would write a secret that he or she would be highly unlikely to share with the rest of the group. After the secrets have been written, they are collected and redistributed, with each member receiving a secret other than his or her own to share with the group. The individual then reads someone else's secret and tries to describe the way he or she believes the other person feels with a secret such as that. Over the years, we have learned that one of the more positive outcomes has been that those who had shared the secrets in the first place discover that their secrets were not devastating to the other group members, but were accepted. In addition, the pattern over the years of those secrets seems to indicate that the kinds of issues which create the major problems for most of us have a great deal in common. Yalom (1985) reports having utilized a similar technique and finding that the most common secret revealed was that of basic inadequacy, followed by a sense of interpersonal alienation.

Thus, as members of the group learn the kinds of feelings, thoughts, and concerns which have disturbed them and made them feel as if they were somehow less than other individuals, they begin to feel a sense of commonality with other people and to lose the sense that something is wrong with them.

Like several other of the therapeutic elements, universality has had little research that demonstrated its importance to group counseling. There has been a growing theoretical interest in it as a concept, especially in the study of self-help groups. Lieberman (1980) suggests that universality is a major feature of the self-help group in providing a supportive effect on the group's members. At about the same time, Robinson (1980) highlighted another dimension: The value of universality as a means of reducing a sense of stigma, so commonly associated with emotional, mental problems. However, the specific therapeutic effects of universality still await empirical research.

Vicarious Learning

Although vicarious learning has been called different things by different theorists, from the very beginning it has been recognized as an important element of group counseling. Corsini and Rosenberg (1955) spoke of "spectator therapy," which they described as gaining from the observation and imitation of fellow patients. George and Cristiani (1986) point out that while clients in groups are focusing on resolving their own interpersonal or intrapersonal difficulties, they are also exposed to interpersonal relationship skills being modeled by both the group leader and the other group members.

In a previous work, we (Dustin & George, 1977) reviewed some of the research that had been done on the effects of imitative learning as part of the group process. We pointed out that modeling can be deliberately used in group counseling sessions as a means of demonstrating desirable behavior before group members try out the new behavior with the group providing feedback. Bandura, Ross, and Ross (1963) have been leaders in the emphasis on social learning as a major therapeutic technique. They demonstrated the power of imitation by successfully treating a large number of individuals with snake phobias by asking them to observe their therapist handle a snake.

The effective group leader, then, is able to utilize this therapeutic element of vicarious learning by bringing into the group process other group members who may be experiencing similar concerns. In doing so, those clients not only gain additional insight into what is occurring with them, but may also learn what does not fit. As Yalom (1985) points out, "finding out what we are not is progress toward finding out what we are" (p. 17).

Jeske (1973) has conducted one of the most important studies of vicarious learning in group counseling. Jeske had each group member who was participating in short-term counseling press a button whenever that individual found himself or herself identifying with another group member. Those patients who showed the greatest improvement recorded twice the number of such identifications as did those who did not improve at all. Jeske concluded that the group leader should promote such intermember identification as a means of facilitating the therapeutic progress.

Interpersonal Learning

Although listed last in this set of therapeutic elements in group counseling, there is little doubt that interpersonal learning plays a major role in the course of group counseling. Several research projects have asked group members to evaluate those factors that have been most helpful to them during the group process. In eight major studies, six of them ranked interpersonal learning among the top three (Yalom, 1985; Weiner, 1974; Rohrbaugh & Bartels, 1975; Butler & Fuhriman, 1980; Long & Cope, 1980; Leszcz, Yalom, & Norden, 1985). Interpersonal learning was ranked among the top five in the other two studies (Flora-Tostado, 1981; Butler & Fuhriman, 1983). In personal growth groups, interpersonal learning is even more highly valued, ordinarily being ranked first by the members of the group.

Bloch (1986) points out that interpersonal learning has two components: input, chiefly through feedback; and output, an actual process whereby the group member attempts to develop more effective modes of relating to others. Certainly the attempt to relate constructively and adaptively within the group becomes an important aspect to many group counseling members as they attempt to develop new ways of interacting in a more satisfying manner with those around them. As gregarious persons who live our lives in a social setting, we are only able to develop self-esteem, a sense of satisfaction, and security from those social contacts that we make. Thus, as a group develops, individuals within the group begin to interact with one another in the same way they interact with others in their lives. Thus, the group becomes a laboratory in which is revealed maladaptive interpersonal behavior and attitudes—arrogance, grandiosity, nonassertiveness, sexualization, overcompliance. As individual group members receive feedback from the other members of the group, the individual learns the effects of his or her behavior on others. When feedback is given honestly and with care, group members are able to understand more clearly the impact they have on others and to learn how often they create the kinds of reactions that they receive from other individuals. As a result, each group member can then decide what to do with this feedback.

As group members become fully aware of the impact of their behavior upon (a) the feelings of others, (b) the opinions that others have of them, and (c) the opinion they have of themselves, they become more aware of their own responsibility for what happens in their interpersonal worlds. Likewise, as each individual fully accepts personal responsibility for that interpersonal world, he or she can begin to struggle with the resulting implication that he or she is the only one thus able to alter that world.

In facilitating the interpersonal learning element of group counseling, the group leader must focus on the present—the here-and-now—of the group interaction. If each group member is to learn as much as possible about the effects of his or her interactions with the group leader and with the other members, the group focus must be upon the immediacy of the interactions occurring in the group. In doing so, the group de-emphasizes the past as well as de-emphasizes the current outside life of each of the members. This does *not* mean that group counseling undermines the importance either of the past or of the current life situation. Rather, it places a focus on the power and efficiency of the interpersonal interactions that are occurring right now.

Such an immediate experience involves both an affective and a cognitive component. That is, group members not only share important emotional experiences, but they also step outside of that emotional experience and examine, understand, and integrate the meaning of that experience they have just undergone. Thus, the most effective here-and-now focus consists of a rotating sequence of affect followed by cognition.

To facilitate both components of the here-and-now requires that the group leader have two different sets of techniques. For the first stage—the stage of emotional experiencing—the leader needs a set of techniques that will plunge the individual, and the group, into an intense awareness of what each is experiencing. This involves the use of the same kinds of techniques that counselors use in individual therapy for helping clients get in touch with their current experiencing. The group leader must be active and continually work toward the shifting of material from the outside to the inside, from the abstract to the specific, from the generic to the personal. In addition, the therapist is often able to encourage a focus on the here-and-now by genuine self-disclosure of his own experiencing.

The second component of the here-and-now—the understanding and clarification of the emotional experience—requires a set of techniques that enables the group to transcend itself in order to examine, explain, and interpret its own experience. This demands reflection, explanation, and interpretation. This phase of group work is called "group process." It refers to what the content of a group discussion or of an individual's comments reveals about the nature of the relationship of the individuals involved in the discussion. In facilitating this cognitive stage of the here-and-now, the group leader must focus on process, listening to the group discussion with an ear toward examining how the words exchanged shed light on the relationships among the participating individuals.

To understand this process, the group leader needs to register all of the available data, both verbal and nonverbal. This includes such simple issues as choice of seats, attendance patterns, being on time, eye contact when talking, and socializing patterns after the group session. However, the most likely productive source of information concerning the group process comes from the group leader's own feelings. If, for example, the group leader feels impatient or discouraged or bored or frustrated, he or she must recognize this as important data about the working of the group and utilize this information to the group's advantage.

OTHER THERAPEUTIC ISSUES

We have chosen to exclude a number of therapeutic elements that others have identified as being essential in the group experience. Some of these are not included because they are more process-oriented, rather than being elements of the group experience itself.

Catharsis

Catharsis, which involves the group member's release of intense feelings bringing about a sense of relief, can be an important process factor within several of the therapeutic elements. Even Yalom (1985), who earlier had defined catharsis as a curative factor in group therapy, points out that catharsis is "intricately interwoven with other therapeutic factors" (p. 4). Certainly, strong expression of emotion is an important aspect of group counseling. It enhances the development of cohesiveness, by binding together members who express strong feelings toward one another. It often results in a sense of relief when the individual learns that his or her expression of intense feelings does not result in rejection by the other group members. Lastly, it provides some immediate relief because the individual has simply "gotten it off my chest."

Imparting of Information

Likewise, we have not included as a therapeutic element what Yalom called "imparting of information." Again we believe that while imparting of information is important as part of the group experience, its function is to be part of various of the therapeutic elements. This aspect of group counseling can include information that is rather specific in its nature, for instance, information about various career issues that might be important to a career counseling group. In addition, a number of self-help groups, for instance Alcoholics Anonymous and Overeaters Anonymous, use guidance and slogans, ("No gain without pain," "One day at a time") as part of the recovery process. Also used is the Serenity Prayer: "Grant me the serenity to accept the things I cannot change, the courage to change the things I can, and the wisdom to know the difference."

Humor

One other therapeutic element that occurs across the others and is therefore not identified individually involves the use of humor in the group counseling process. Although humor can be a negative factor in group situations, especially when it consists of a pseudo-humor which is exercised at the expense of some person or subgroup, humor can become an important healing aspect of the group. As was pointed out in chapter 3, there are some truly humorous dimensions of the human condition. When group leaders possess the ability to laugh at themselves and to see the humor in their own human frailties, the group becomes more likely to do so also. This humor is certainly not sarcasm, ridicule, or cynicism. Rather, spontaneous and natural laughter with one or more of the group members can help establish an additional bond of genuine caring for each other and confidence in the helping nature of human rapport.

The use of humor may allow the group leader to deal with the group member's irrational ideas by taking those ideas to ridiculous extremes or reducing them to absurdity. When this is done, the members are able to see the ridicule of their own ideas, not a ridicule of themselves. Such humor, as long as it is not used to derail an important immediate dynamic to express anger or to conceal an individual's deep feelings, has curative value all by itself.

On the whole, humor is an important aspect of a healthy group. When group members learn to laugh at themselves and each other, they are often able to carry this valuable skill into life outside the group. In many ways, the visible bubbling-up of joy, of freedom, of well-being, is the first sign that the group has become truly therapeutic.

SUMMARY

In order to facilitate a successful group experience, the group leader needs to determine those therapeutic elements which are related to group effectiveness.

A number of theorists have attempted to identify those factors which contribute to improvement in the group member's condition as a result of the actions of the group leader and its members. Based on research findings and therapeutic experiences, these theorists have identified various factors which are therapeutic to the group experience.

We propose a somewhat simpler model for identifying those therapeutic elements which are necessary and sufficient for effective group counseling. These elements include

1. installation of hope
2. sense of safety and support
3. cohesiveness
4. universality
5. vicarious learning
6. interpersonal learning

Other therapeutic factors, which were not included because they are more process-oriented include catharsis, imparting of information, and humor.

REFERENCES

Bandura, A., Ross, D., & Ross, S. (1963). Vicarious reinforcement and imitative learning. *Journal of Abnormal and Social Psychology, 67,* 601–607.

Berzon, B., Piovs, C., & Farson, R. (1963). The therapeutic event in group psychotherapy: A study of subjective reports by group members. *Journal of Individual Psychology, 19,* 204–212.

Bloch, S. (1986). Therapeutic factors in group psychotherapy. In A. J. Frances & R. E. Hales (Eds.), *Annual Review, Vol. 5* (pp. 678–698). Washington, DC: American Psychiatric Press.

Bloch, S., Reibstein, J., & Crouch, E. (1979). A method for the study of therapeutic factors in group psychotherapy. *British Journal of Psychiatry, 134,* 257–263.

Butler, T., & Fuhriman, A. (1980). Patient perspective on the curative process: A comparison of day treatment and outpatient psychotherapy groups. *Small Group Behavior, 11,* 371–388.

Carkhuff, R. R. (1971). Training as a preferred mode of treatment. *Journal of Counseling Psychology, 18,* 123–131.

Carkhuff, R. R., & Berenson, B. G. (1967). *Beyond counseling and therapy.* New York: Holt, Rinehart & Winston.

Corey, G., & Corey, M. S. (1977). *Groups: Process and practice.* Monterey, CA: Brooks/Cole.

Corsini, R., & Rosenberg, B. (1955). Mechanisms of group psychotherapy: Processes and dynamics. *Journal of Abnormal and Social Psychology, 51,* 406–411.

Dickoff, H., & Lakin, M. (1963). Patients' views of group psychotherapy: Retrospections and interpretations. *International Journal of Group Psychotherapy, 13,* 61–73.

Dustin, R., & George, R. (1977). *Action counseling for behavior change* (2nd ed.). Cranston, RI: Carroll Press.

Flora-Tostado, J. (1981). Patient and therapist agreement on curative factors in group psychotherapy. *Dissertation Abstracts International, 42,* 371-B.

Frank, J. D. (1957). Some determinants, manifestations and effects of cohesiveness in therapy groups. *International Journal of Group Psychotherapy, 7,* 53–63.

Frank, J. D. (1971). Therapeutic factors in psychotherapy. *American Journal of Psychotherapy, 25,* 350–361.

Frank, J. D., Hoehn-Saric, R., & Imber, S. D. (1978). *Effective ingredients of successful psychotherapy.* New York: Brunner/Mazel.

Frankl, V. (1969). *The will to meaning.* Cleveland: World Publishing Press.

George, R. L., & Cristiani, T. S. (1986). *Counseling: Theory and practice* (2nd ed.). Englewood Cliffs, NJ: Prentice-Hall.

HILL, W. F. (1957). Analysis of interviews of group therapists' papers. *Provo Papers, 1,* 1.

JESKE, J. O. (1973). Identification and therapeutic effectiveness in group therapy. *Journal of Counseling Psychology, 20,* 528–530.

JOHNSON, D. W. & JOHNSON, F. P. (1982). *Joining together.* Englewood Cliffs, NJ: Prentice-Hall.

JONES, J. (1977). *Group psychotherapy as experiencing interpersonal perceiving and developing of values.* Stockholm: Almquist & Wiksell.

KAPP, F. T., GLASER, G., & BRISSENDEN, A. (1964). Group participation and self-perceived personality change. *Journal of Nervous and Mental Disorders, 139,* 255–265.

LESZCZ, M., YALOM, I., & NORDEN, M. (1985). The value of inpatient group psychotherapy: Patients' perceptions. *International Journal of Group Psychotherapy, 35,* 46–59.

LIEBERMAN, M. A. (1980). Group methods. In F. H. Kanfer & A. P. Goldstein (Eds.), *Helping People Change.* New York: Pergamon.

LIEBERMAN, M., YALOM, I., & MILES, M. (1973). *Encounter groups: First facts.* New York: Basic Books.

LONG, L., & COPE, C. (1980). Curative factors in a male felony offender. *Small Group Behavior, 11,* 389–398.

OHLSEN, M. M. (1977). *Group counseling* (2nd ed.). New York: Holt, Rinehart & Winston.

ROBINSON, D. (1980). Self-help health groups. In P. B. Smith (Ed.), *Small groups and personal change.* London: Methuen.

ROHRBAUGH, M., & BARTELS, B. (1975). Participants' perceptions of 'curative factors' in therapy and growth groups. *Small Group Behavior, 6,* 430–456.

TRUAX, C. B. (1968). Therapist interpersonal reinforcement of client self-exploration and therapeutic outcome in group psychotherapy. *Journal of Counseling Psychology, 15,* 225–231.

TRUAX, C. B., & CARKHUFF, R. R. (1965). Client and therapist transparency in the psychotherapeutic encounter. *Journal of Counseling Psychology, 12,* 3–9.

TRUAX, C. B., & CARKHUFF, R. R. (1967). *Toward effective counseling and psychotherapy.* Chicago: Aldine.

WEINER, M. (1974). Genetic versus interpersonal insight. *International Journal of Group Psychotherapy, 24,* 230–237.

YALOM, I. D. (1970). *The theory and practice of group psychotherapy.* New York: Basic Books.

YALOM, I. D. (1985). *The theory and practice of group psychotherapy* (2nd ed.). New York: Basic Books.

YALOM, I. D., HOUTS, P. S., & ZIMERBERG, S. M. (1967). Prediction of improvement in group therapy. *Archives of General Psychiatry, 17,* 159–168.

SUGGESTED ACTIVITIES

In the Classroom

1. With a partner from class, discuss the following terms. To what extent are the two of you able to make distinctions? Do the two of you believe some of these terms are synonymous?

   a. Acceptance
   b. Sense of belonging
   c. Recognizing similarity to others
   d. Universality

2. Review the discussion on cohesiveness. In groups of four or five take turns with the following:

   Have one member serve as the "target" person. This person could talk about the difficulties of doing without a chemical substance; or talk about the difficulties of a recent divorce; or perhaps, talk about the difficulties of being a single parent.

   Have each person in the small group give "support" statements to the target person.

Next, using the same or different "target," have each person in the small group empathize with the feelings of the target person. Empathy includes accurate communication of the feeling expressed by the target.

As a small group, discuss the similarities and differences of these two types of statements: support and empathy.

3. Select one person to be the leader of a group of three to five people and another person to be the observer. The leader should give a short statement about the importance of any one of the group norms suggested. Then ask for discussion from the group. The observer should pay special attention to the types of questions the group leader uses and how the leader "promotes" discussion, then give the group leader feedback.

4. After doing activity 2 and activity 3 in On Your Own, discuss your findings in a small group. Focus on how similar or dissimilar the identified factors are for counselors and for group members.

On Your Own

1. Interview a counselor who leads groups in a setting of particular interest to you. Determine what the counselor believes is most helpful in groups in this particular setting.

   Review the definition of therapeutic factor (an element occurring in group therapy that contributes to improvement in a group member) and show the extent to which factors identified by the counselor fit this definition. Are these part of the factors identified in the chapter or are they new factors?

2. Interview a counselor who leads groups in the setting in which you are particularly interested. With the counselor, discuss the extent to which the following terms are synonymous:
   a. acceptance
   b. sense of belonging
   c. recognizing similarity to other group members
   d. universality

3. Obtain permission within a setting of particular interest to you to talk with at least two members of a group in that setting. What do the group members think are the most helpful aspects of their group?

   Again, review the definition of a therapeutic factor and show the extent to which factors identified by group members fit this definition. Are these part of the factors identified in the chapter or are they new factors?

CHAPTER 6
GETTING THE GROUP STARTED

INTRODUCTION

This chapter will examine an area that is very important in terms of effective group counseling. The experience of facing a beginning counseling group for the first meeting is probably one of the most exciting occurrences and an event that divides counselors into two groups: those who lead groups and those who don't.

Experienced and inexperienced counselors alike share the challenge of meeting a group for the first time. Examination of this aspect of counseling groups allows the authors to describe some practical, nuts and bolts considerations for the group leader. Areas of discussion in this chapter include forming the group, organizing the group, engaging in the first session, ending the first session, and evaluating the first session.

FORMING THE GROUP

In chapter 4, we discussed the preplanning that is so important in effective counseling groups. What were called ''strategies'' for the group leader would of course include the thoughtfulness entailed in starting a counseling group. An issue central to forming a group is consideration of whether the counselor will be leading the group alone or with a co-therapist.

Cohen and Lipkin (1979) include as advantages of co–group leadership the reduction of a tendency to give a single leader omnipotence by group members, the advantages of modeling disagreements for group members, and the convenience when one group leader is absent. Other advantages include support for the leader, the opportunity to consult with a colleague when issues of ethics or referral arise, and greater flexibility of group leadership, as when Covi, Roth, and Lipman (1982) suggest that one therapist focus on a group member's behaviors while the other group leader concentrates on this same group member's cognitions.

Co-therapy has disadvantages, such as the time-consuming nature of the co-therapy relationship, the tendency for group members to form a subgroup as they tend to identify with one or the other leader, and the common practice of one co-leader being the lead counselor and the other a follower.

Counselors who decide to engage in co-therapy need to be alerted to the greater time which will be necessary for all of the preplanning stages as well as for the planning, evaluating, and referrals or terminations. In our experience, co-leadership has necessitated hours of processing and planning by the two leaders. Attempts to shortcut planning or to abbreviate processing typically result in one dominant leader and another who is relegated to a lesser position.

Counselors who are already leading one or more groups need to preplan how they will manage time and pressures so that they can keep different groups straight. They need to devise a system for making notes in order to chart group progress, follow individual members within different groups, and allow for the multiple groups to be evaluated.

Each group counselor needs to include in preplanning an analysis of the need for supervision. Supervision is a necessity whenever a counselor is leading a group for the first time or for the first time since graduate school. It is strongly advised whenever a counselor will be leading a group for a population with whom the counselor has not had much experience or when a group is planned in a setting which has not commonly had group counseling.

Whenever a counselor has been assigned to lead a group and there has been no discussion about supervision, the counselor must take the initiative to find it. The counselor might, for example, find a colleague willing to share and discuss tapes of the groups each is working with.

Co-therapy has often been recommended as an easy method for counselors to become group counselors, but it is not a substitute for supervision. Even experienced counselors will need to consult with colleagues in certain instances of professional practice. This common sense statement can be seen more clearly through a specific example.

The ethical principles for any counselor include beneficence for clients. The standards, which will be mentioned in chapter 8, include the need for counselors to take responsibility for clients who do not seem to be making satisfactory progress in counseling. It is possible that during a counseling group, the group leader will begin to experience some doubts about the progress of an individual group member. For example, a group member, of the opposite sex from the leader, has publicly disagreed with the leader the last two group meetings. The leader is faced with several choices which might include leader self-disclosure to the group about doubts, a meeting with the particular group member, and termination of the group member from the group. At this point, while the leader is considering courses of action, turning to a colleague with whom a trusting relationship exists is one recommended procedure. Without formalizing a supervisory relationship, each group leader as part of the orientation stage needs to think ahead about which professional would be suitable for consulting when the need arises.

Purpose of the Group

The purpose of the group is an important consideration in the preplanning which goes on before the first meeting. The group leader needs to have in mind a succinct statement of the purpose, preferably in lay person's terms, before sitting down to the first group meeting. It is only reasonable to expect that one or all group members may question the leader at the first meeting about the leader's expectations. Frequently, in our experience, this question may take the form of, "What are we supposed to be doing in here anyway?"

As a step in forming the group, the group leader needs to consider why a group experience would be preferred (over individual counseling) for each potential group member. Because ethics, to be discussed in chapter 8, indicate the need for a counselor to offer alternatives to a prospective client, it is easy to understand why a group leader needs to have this question answered prior to the first group.

The texts from professional training may very well contradict themselves about whether a group leader should simultaneously conduct individual counseling with group members and even whether a group should be formed which includes former clients. The group leader in the process of forming a group, can easily grapple with this issue as the question in the above paragraph is considered. In other words, we believe that specific answers to the question "Why this group for this member" will frequently call for divergent answers.

One practical consideration in forming a group is whether to tailor group membership to meet a set of client needs or whether to select members of a group who fit into a specific group type. Students in group counseling have often said in class that they will be unable to preplan purposes of a group until they get to know the group members and until individual member expectations are clarified. We disagree. Although it is possible to have included in group purposes such objectives as to stimulate group members to clarify their expectations for group counseling or to facilitate group planning and responsibility for the agenda for each meeting, the group counselor needs to clarify the purposes for group meetings. Open-ended groups, in which the group counselor is positive he or she is unable to form specific objectives prior to group meetings, can still come under a purpose statement such as "to develop member responsibility for group counseling procedures." On the other hand, groups frequently are planned around rather homogeneous topics such as "the need to develop social skills" or "difficulties in single parenting." In these instances, the purposes of the group may be made clear, even in written form, and member selection, both by the leader and through member self-selection, may be an important element of group formation.

Selection of Group Members

Consideration of ethical questions invariably leads the students of ethical concern to recognize the importance of the original counseling agreement. Writers in group counseling have begun to converge around the importance of each group leader screening individual members. (See appendix 2.) Common issues covered during screening include stating the qualifications of the group counselor, providing a clear idea for the potential member of what to expect from the group, providing the prospective client with alternatives to the specific group, and giving a chance for the group leader to specify what is expected from each group member. It is important, at least from the standpoint of ethics, for each group member to decide with informed consent whether to join the group. Rose (1977) has indicated the importance of an initial contract being formed between the potential group member and the group leader over and above informed consent. Yalom (1985) indicates the importance of the group leader using screening to look for potential difficulties which certain types of group members present. It is important to note that group members who are in a group against their own will or with confusion about why they are in the group are more likely to experience coercion. In order for the group leader to meet the ethical standard of helping clients and preventing harm, he or she must control which members remain in the group.

In some cases, counselors are in a situation where they have little or no control over the group membership. Inpatient treatment groups for chemical dependency are an example. Usually these groups are ongoing ones, with a continuing turnover of membership. Screening is still valuable in such groups, because it provides an opportunity for the counselor to establish rapport, to clarify norms and expectations of group behavior, and to answer questions the individual may have about the group. This screening may also be useful in assessing whether the potential group member's behavior is so dysfunctional that alternative arrangements for treatment need to be made.

It is not possible to provide a list which would include each attribute of a potential group member which might cause difficulty during the development of a counseling group. In some instances groups will be formed to include quite heterogeneous group members. Perhaps group members who are very assertive will be invited to participate in a group in which several members have stated their desire to work on their own assertiveness. A highly verbal group member, one who is eager to give advice to other group members, might actually prove beneficial in certain groups. Listed below are questions the leader might want to consider when screening potential members. The reader may have others to add to the list.

1. What about a potential member who expresses doubt about the efficacy of groups?
2. What about a potential member who is unable to list satisfying, social relationships?
3. What about a potential member who expresses doubt about being willing to work in a group?
4. What about a potential member who reports being on heavy medication?

Referral procedures will in some cases be very clear and bureaucratized, whereas other instances will force a counselor to develop a method for obtaining potential members for group counseling. Some group leaders are quite successful waiting for individuals to ask to be in groups. Other counselors are presented with a situation where a group has been formed and the counselor is assigned to be the leader. Occasionally counselors are faced with a "group" consisting of members who have been ordered, perhaps by a judge, to attend. Although our position about coercion and the need for voluntary membership in counseling has been made clear, the referral procedures into group counseling are quite diverse. It is best if, before the groups start, members are clear whether new members will be added during the life of the group. When the counselor is satisfied with filling a group through self-referrals, prescreening is still beneficial.

Recently a counseling student was leading a group in a public high school under the supervision of one of the authors. After about six weeks, the student expressed concern about the low motivation and lack of task behavior expressed by the group members. Questions by the supervisor clarified that the high school counselor had formed the group and that the student leader had agreed to proceed. After some discussion, the student decided to take advantage of a closing grading period and to have individual conferences with each member. These individual conferences allowed the student to clarify for group members her expectations and to clarify why the individual high school students had been coming to group. Three high school students decided to end their membership in the group. During subsequent supervision, the student explained she no longer was faced with off-task behaviors as she had been earlier. This example reinforced for the author the importance of a prescreening meeting in which the group leader and the potential member experience deciding whether this particular group will be best.

Authors in some professional texts indicate that they form groups primarily from their own individual client load. Our experience indicates that it is common to fudge the original purposes of a group or to slide around some of the specific needs of a client in order to "help" him or her through the convenience of an ongoing group. The selection of group members does not dictate the purposes of a group nor does an incoming group member necessitate that expectations for all members be changed. Selection of group members is an important, but independent step in the formation of groups.

One of the exciting aspects of including group counseling in a professional role is dealing with the unexpected. Although strategies and preplanning for groups, and for the first group meeting, are necessary, a very important requirement for an effective group leader is flexibility. It needs to be stressed that no matter how much time has been spent planning strategies, selecting group members, and meeting individually with members before the group starts, it will be necessary to think again about the strategies and to adapt group purposes after the first few meetings of the group. Perhaps it looks as though the group will have too few members, or that certain members may need members who will give them support, or that the group leader needs to rethink the group purposes.

ORGANIZING THE GROUP

As time for the first meeting draws closer, the leader needs to consider organizational aspects such as the physical environment for the group and the schedule for individual group sessions.

Physical Environment

The physical setting for counseling groups has often been wherever one could be crammed. In the experience of one of the authors, a drug agency planned group counseling sessions in a hallway between counselor offices and the reception area. When one of the authors was conducting groups in a high school unfamiliar with group counseling, the setting was a janitor's closet. Whatever the realities faced by the group leader, it is important to remember that the physical setting for the group is important. The pleasantness, comfort, and privacy of the setting definitely help set the tone and give new group members an early impression. When group sessions are held in the hallway, every person using the hallway while stepping over and around group members causes an interruption and a temporary disturbance. The author who held groups of ninth graders in the janitor's closet was faced with the frequent disruptions of members playing catch with light bulbs, shaking mops at each other, and pausing while the janitor came in to help himself to various supplies.

In our experience, group members can adjust to seemingly impossible physical environments. Nevertheless, one part of the strategy needs to be consideration by the leader of the setting for the group. With planning, and maybe with luck, ringing phones, office noise, and even pounds and thumps from pipes can be eliminated. No doubt the physical environment can go a long way towards helping the group leader accomplish the planned purposes. Specific purposes may increase the need for diverse physical environments. A study skills group might be enhanced with appropriate materials, perhaps even a computer terminal. A social skills group may require room for members to get up and move around for role plays. A frustration members will experience such as trying to take notes in a group setting where no desks or tables are available can often be avoided through careful leader preparation.

Of course, reality dictates the physical environment for groups. One of the authors, while conducting a group, was startled when a female group member screamed and leaped up out of her beanbag chair. Imagining a psychological break or a psychotic episode, the leader was relieved when he got to the group member to see a cockroach crawling down her blue jeans.

Scheduling Group Sessions

The strategy for a particular group will give strong indications about whether a monthly, weekly, daily, or some other frequency group is optimal. In addition to scheduling group session frequency, the necessity of scheduling the best available physical environment will often dictate preplanning, perhaps well in advance. Scheduling groups is especially an issue if the group leader is conducting other groups simultaneously.

In some situations, the agency or the educational setting will dictate which time period or with which frequency groups will meet. It is important however that the group leader include consideration of scheduling when planning strategies. Certain groups, perhaps social skills groups or assertiveness groups, require more frequent meetings than do other types of groups so that repetition and reinforcement can occur.

The cost to group members may also be a consideration in scheduling group sessions. The counselor may be faced with an agency or system series of fee schedules. Perhaps the group members will be paying different amounts for the same group. The reality of fees in some cases may be a major consideration in group schedules (Rose, 1977).

Before the first group meeting, the group leader can plan certain aspects of the group schedule. The purposes and objectives of the group are important in decisions about scheduling. Members will need to be informed if a regular schedule for the group exists. Members will be able to adjust if each group is to include time to schedule the next group meeting. Another important aspect of group scheduling is the time of termination. Has the group leader considered to what extent the announced time will mark the end of the group? It is more than a characteristic of group leadership style if some groups go 30–45 minutes past the announced quitting time. The consistency of the group leader can quickly be determined by members as they learn the manner in which each group session ends.

THE FIRST SESSION

Initially, the leader is faced with what to do with the results of screening or any other pregroup activities such as testing and assessment. Depending upon the extent to which leader and individual member contact has occurred, the initial minutes of the first group meeting will differ. Some authors have suggested that the purposes of group counseling can more effectively be met if potential group members engage in pregroup training. In keeping with the organization of chapter 4 and the present chapter, group purposes and leader expectations for group membership would have to be clear before a program of pregroup training could occur. If members have undergone training prior to the first group meeting, it is important that every member at the first group meeting has experienced similar training. Because of the importance of first impressions, the first session needs to contain an opportunity for members to recognize the need for their training and be able to perform at least some aspect of their new behaviors.

Even more common than pretraining is the screening interview(s). If assessments were conducted during screening or if other self-report measures were taken, then the potential member has an awareness of the use of such materials. During the first group meeting, the leader will want to be consistent with the member understanding. There may be instances where the first meeting will include feedback and some interpretation to group members about the earlier assessment. Many authors have indicated that the beginnings of orientation to the group can occur in the screening interviews. A group leader who has not begun the process of dealing with member expectations will be forced to spend more time and go into greater detail in the first meeting about the purposes of the group and what is expected of members than will a leader who has already covered much of this material. Where screening has occurred, the first group meeting provides an opportunity for a review and for group members to exchange ideas and to compare their understanding.

Writers have emphasized that one important aspect of the first counseling group meeting is the clarification of member expectations (Corey, 1981). Most writers stress that the first meeting of a counseling group provides an opportunity for the group leader to deal with such issues as member expectations, purposes of the group, and norms. The strategy for the group leader will indicate whether early in this first session the group leader plans time for disclosures about hopes for the group and leader expectations or the delivery of a succinct list of group member expectations. It has been emphasized that early in a counseling group members can benefit from the chance to exchange expectations as well as individual objectives for the group (Johnson & Johnson, 1982).

As indicated in chapter 8, ethical standards dictate that certain aspects of group counseling need to be covered in the first group meeting even if they have been previously covered in a screening interview. Most counseling students in our experience are adamant that they intend to cover the question of confidentiality in both a prescreening interview and again quite specifically during the first group meeting. Other issues suggested by standards for providers include the qualifications of the leader, what group members may expect through participation in the group, and alternatives for potential group members about other methods of receiving services distinct from the specific group. The list seems to grow and grow about all that is to be accomplished during the first counseling group meeting. The content, however, is even less important than the early impression made by the leader. This brings the focus to leadership style.

Implementing Strategies Through Personal Style

Strategies must take into account the purposes and the specific membership for a counseling group. Ideally, the leader's strategy incorporates self-knowledge about the style the leader typically exhibits when conducting group counseling. Certain types of groups, for example those which are very content-filled and quite specific, will feature a different type of discussion of member expectations than will a human potential group or a group for counseling with personal problems. The leader's style, whether it incorporates humor or openendedness, whether it includes a lot of self-disclosure, and whether it includes a lot of leader activity, will heavily influence the first counseling group meeting. Even when members have been told what to expect and told what behaviors will be effective in the group, they will be observing the leader very carefully and attempting to find clues for what the leader wishes from them.

The beginning group leader is at a distinct disadvantage because there has not been an opportunity to learn one's style based on experience with earlier groups. Nevertheless, actually conducting group counseling sessions turns out to be the most effective opportunity for each group counselor to learn about his or her own style.

Certain issues tend to be included in the first group counseling session regardless of the leader's strategies. These issues are listed below. However, it is important to remember that a list of issues tells the reader nothing about all the diversity with which different group counselors cover them.

Frequently, it will be necessary for the leader to provide a means for group members to get acquainted. This may be done through conducting discussions about certain issues and aspects of the counseling group. In other instances, exercises and activities will have been included in the leader's strategy for the first meeting. The group leader may be an active participant in the process of becoming acquainted or may remain removed from the getting acquainted process. This choice, an aspect of leadership style, will be carefully observed by group members.

The question of group norms and the process of combining and changing member and leader expectations for the group is an important one. Counseling students have emphasized to us that certain norms would be dictated to their counseling groups. Common examples include the need for confidentiality and the need to come on time. Other strategies might designate that the gradual establishment of norms by the group will become an important aspect of group development. The strategy, and to a certain extent the style of the leader, will also establish whether this process will be initiated by the leader or whether the leader will tend to react to the introduction of the issue by group members. The Johnsons (1982) have emphasized the necessity of spending time helping members clarify their goals and expectations, perhaps more than any other writers. For them, stagnation of a group or group conflict may result from a failure of group members' being given time to clarify their own individual goals for the group. In our experience, subsequent confusion, or continued milling around and lack of purpose, frequently emanates from the lack of clarity of purpose and expectation both from the leader and from members.

Again, the cautions and warnings that ethical standards indicate as appropriate for group counseling need to be covered in the first group meeting. If somewhat lengthy discussions of individual member expectations are held, then the group leader has a responsibility to respond to differing expectations and to expectations which the leader judges to be unrealistic. Some group members may be expecting miracles or inappropriate results from group counseling. The first meeting, or the earliest that the leader becomes aware of such hopes, would be an optimal time for dealing with the member. Where the group leader may have led one member or group of members to expect something different from other members, these differences will come up in the group. An important preventive alternative for group leaders is to encourage differing expectations to emerge even this early in the group.

Boundaries of the group—whether this group will include personal counseling, whether this is a closed group, limitations on confidentiality, and so forth—

are important for the well-being of clients. As a part of leader strategy, certain boundaries will have been considered by the leader. Usually, it is important to make these boundaries clear to group members. Frequently, the group leader will have undertaken the purposes and strategies for some types of groups which will have a fixed number of sessions. In other cases, the purposes of the group do not include counseling. But, whether dictated by the agency or whether considered in preplanning, it is important for the group leader to set limits, clarify boundaries, and perhaps more important, facilitate member reactions and discussion of these boundaries.

With certain purposes, the leader intends to clarify and facilitate member discussion of their own needs. When done during the first group session, this procedure has many advantages. Frequently, such therapeutic factors, discussed in chapter 5, as universality, installation of hope, and interpersonal learning, can begin at this time. Unless there has been extensive screening, early discussion of member needs allows the leader to identify and to clarify both common needs and divergent needs. In those cases where the first group session has been heavy on the leader's talking, setting boundaries, and covering certain ethical standards and cautions, there will be an acute need for group member discussion. The consideration of why each member is there or what led each member to participate in the group guarantees member discussion, reactions, and questions.

Finally, many group leaders will be depending upon group cohesiveness, either as a main process of accomplishing purposes or even as an important part of the strategy (Rose, 1977). Cohesiveness among group members should begin with the first session. Groups which assume interpersonal learning, or which assume there will be member-to-member advice and feedback, need to become cohesive. Unlike some issues in the first group counseling session, such as confidentiality, or leader expectations, cohesiveness is not something that a group leader can ask for. The strategy will indicate the importance of cohesiveness and hopefully the leadership style will indicate the means by which the group leader intends to facilitate cohesiveness. The need for developing respect and trust among group members begins during the first group session (Corey, 1981).

Establishing Member Responsibilities

The members of each counseling group must learn gradually their own rights and responsibilities as the group develops. While these member responsibilities vary somewhat depending on leader strategies and the purposes of the group, certain commonalties and certain first impressions are established as early as the first group meeting. The clarifying of leader-set boundaries, covering aspects of confidentiality and other ethical standards, and increasing member-to-member interaction all involve individual group member responsibility.

For example, as the leader sets boundaries for the group, certain expectations for group members are implicit. Issues such as informing the group when individual members contact the leader outside the group, sharing with the group any outside contacts between group members, and clarifying what the leader hopes will be the attendance policy all involve member behaviors.

No doubt the reader has decided that accomplishing member-to-member interaction cannot be solely a result of leader talk. Rather, the leader needs to facilitate issues and content that will lead to member-to-member interaction. The establishing of such a norm needs to start as early as the first group. The leadership style is the means through which the leader communicates boundaries, expectations, and responsibilities to members. An important aspect of preplanning is for the leader to account for, and sometimes to compensate for, leader style.

The leader strategy will include whether to cover such basic issues as an in-out group phenomenon, the top-bottom (top dog–underdog) phenomenon and group member difficulties. Deciding whether to cover such issues still does not determine when. Perhaps the leader strategy will indicate that the first group is an appropriate time for such issues. If one group member perceives feelings of being left out of an "in-group," the leader could help members anticipate their responsibility by encouraging a discussion at the first meeting of possible effects on the total group of in-group formation and by indicating to individual members that such feelings of being left out should be brought up in the entire group. Perhaps the top dog–underdog issue is best translated as how to deal with a dominant group member. The group leader can indicate his or her wishes for member responsibility by encouraging members to share their feelings when someone is dominating group time. Likewise, at the first meeting members could be encouraged to discuss possible impact on total group development if a single member, even the leader, tends to dominate early sessions. Finally, members can be told that they have some responsibility for bringing their problems to the group. Their problems may involve reactions to what is happening in the group, feelings about the group leader, or difficulties they are experiencing outside the group.

It is hoped that most leader strategies will allow for the time that it takes for norms to be established, for different group members to accept leader-set boundaries, and for each group member to accept member responsibilities. Whether such issues are included in the first meeting or not, group leaders learn to expect repeated discussions of these important issues in group development.

ENDING THE FIRST SESSION

As can be seen from this rather lengthy discussion of the first group meeting, we believe that group leaders can engage in a lot of thought and preparation. Our students tend to get into a trap concerning the first group meeting. As we supervise inexperienced group leaders, we observe that leaders frequently approach the first session with too much material for the time allotted. This results in a haphazard, slapdash ending to the first group session. It is necessary that planning and leader strategy include how the first session will end. Is the last impression of the first group meeting important to members? We think it is.

At times, beginning group leaders only say good-bye at the end of their first group, inadvertently teaching group members that the group will end late, that leadership style will abruptly change during the last 5 minutes of the group meeting, that there will be no summary or attempt to draw from group members their impressions of each group session, and other unintended lessons. The group process which ends on a positive note at the end of the first meeting will add to cohesiveness, which is frequently defined as attractiveness of a group for its members. Process time at the end also provides an opportunity for leader installation of hope and optimism for subsequent sessions. Leader strategy can also include time at the end to offer advanced organizers to group members about subsequent meetings.

Equally important, evaluation of the first group session needs to include time for the leader to check the members' understanding about the content of the first session.

EVALUATING FIRST SESSION AND PLANNING FUTURE SESSIONS

Although leader strategies can provide risk and even a trap for the group leader, careful preparation and analysis of group purposes are important for an effective group leader. Of equal importance is the necessity for leader flexibility. The reality of the individual members and the physical environment of the first group meeting provide an excellent opportunity for the group leader to loop back through the preplanned strategies as the leader prepares for subsequent group meetings.

As has been indicated in this chapter, if a group leader is working with a co-therapist, this process is more complicated. For example, the two leaders may disagree about what happened during the first session. Changes in the group ideally would be mutually arrived at in co-therapy situations. Even if the group leader is working alone, the possibility of making changes in strategy and strategy implementation can be considered after the first group meeting.

Possible changes may include more realistic goals and purpose statements. Depending upon the use of time at the first meeting, leaders often will scale down their goal statements, thereby scaling down their unrealistic expectations. Another possible change is a leader assessment that other members are needed for the group or that perhaps different group members are needed. An important factor is whether group members have been told that the group is open, and that new members may be added in future sessions. The reader is encouraged to think of other important changes which might be implemented after a first meeting.

Attractiveness of the Group for Members

Cohesiveness has been viewed as a necessary characteristic for effective groups, as an important aspect of effective groups, and as a nonsense term which should be discontinued (Bednar & Kaul, 1978). A definition of cohesiveness which seems useful is the attractiveness of a group for each member. The first group session will either reinforce or discourage members. Evaluation of the first session needs to include leader assessment of the attractiveness of the group for members. A measure taken the first session could be used by the group leader for comparison later in an effort to estimate how group attractiveness has changed for members. Such evaluation therefore offers important data for subsequent planning.

First Impressions

Early evaluation could include written statements by individual group members about their expectations and objectives for the group. Collecting member expectations at a later time would offer additional data regarding the changes members were experiencing. More common, possibly, would be the leader's asking for member impressions either as a summary to the first group meeting or as an activity early in the second group meeting.

The leader needs to form notes and jot down beginning impressions about the group, its accomplishments, and its individual members. Such notes, collected in a folder for each ongoing group, provide a rich source of information later in the group's development.

Yalom (1985) has indicated his frequent use of written summaries. The leader summaries could be distributed to all group members prior to the next group meeting. Group leaders are urged to consider this device as one method of providing focus for the group, initiating discussions and disagreements about reactions to the group, and stimulating individual group members. Whether the informal leader evaluation and impressions of each group session are distributed to all group members or not, these leader notes provide formative evaluation about accomplishments and progress for each group.

Evaluation of Leadership Style

Awareness of leadership style can best be accomplished by direct observation. As a group leader forces himself or herself to watch a videotape of a group meeting, leadership style can be seen directly. The importance of supervision includes the opportunity for a group leader to be directly observed and to receive feedback based upon such observation. Televising of group sessions must be included in leader strategies, rather than impulsively being added, since it potentially raises issues of confidentiality and member privacy. In our experience, counseling groups which are not televised at the first meeting are not likely to be televised subsequently. However, the issues of pressure upon group members and normal member nervousness about a beginning group should not automatically be placed second to the important need for leaders to learn about their leadership style.

Other techniques for increasing leader awareness about style include careful self-observation; periodic assessment from group members; the frequently used open-ended technique of asking members occasionally, "What do you remember that the leader did in today's session?" or "What did the leader do in the past three meetings that was most helpful to you?" or negotiating with group members for an outsider to directly observe the group leader.

At any rate, the implementation of group purposes and all the careful pre-planning finally result in the group meeting for the first time. This beginning leads to consideration of group development, to be discussed in the next chapter.

SUMMARY

The experience of facing a beginning counseling group is a highly exciting one that requires a great deal of planning and organizing.

The first decision in planning frequently involves whether or not to have a co-therapist. The leader must also determine whether supervision is required and arrange for that supervision if deemed necessary. The purpose of the group is also relevant and helps determine how group members are selected.

Organizational aspects in planning for the group include identifying and arranging for an appropriate physical setting in which the sessions can be conducted. In addition, the leader must consider a number of factors in scheduling the group sessions.

The first session is generally considered the most important session of all. The first impressions that members get are very important for the future direction of the group, as the group expectations, purposes, norms, and responsibilities are established.

The first session should end on a positive note, with adequate time for offering advanced organizers to group members as well as for evaluating the session.

REFERENCES

BEDNAR, R. L., & KAUL, T. J. (1978). Experiential group research: Current perspectives. In S. L. Garfield & A. E. Bergin (Eds.), *Handbook of psychotherapy and behavior change* (2nd ed.). NY: John Wiley.

COHEN, R. G., & LIPKIN, G. B. (1979). *Therapeutic group work for health professionals.* New York: Springer.

COREY, G. (1981). *Theory and practice of group counseling.* Monterey, CA: Brooks/Cole.

COVI, L., ROTH, D., & LIPMAN, R. S. (1982) Cognitive group psychotherapy of depression: The close-ended group. *American Journal of Psychotherapy, 34,* 459–469.

Johnson, D. W., & Johnson, F. P. (1982). *Joining together* (2nd ed.). Englewood Cliffs, NJ: Prentice-Hall.
Rose, S. D. (1977). *Group therapy: A behavioral approach.* Englewood Cliffs, NJ: Prentice-Hall.
Yalom, I. D. (1985). *The theory and practice of group psychotherapy* (3rd ed.). New York: Basic Books.

SUGGESTED ACTIVITIES

In the Classroom

1. With a partner from class, discuss whether you would rather be in a homogeneous group or a group of divergent members.

2. In a small group, take turns acting as the leader of a group which is meeting for the first time. The leader should welcome members to the meeting, and briefly, yet clearly, explain the purposes of the group to the new members.
   After each person's turn as leader, give feedback.

3. Form groups of three. One person can be a leader conducting an interview to screen a potential group member. Another person can be a potential group member who has doubts about joining the group. The third person observes the group leader carefully in order to give feedback at the end of the interview about how the leader handled the situation.

On Your Own

1. Select a counselor from a setting of interest to you and interview the counselor carefully about preparations for a new group.

2. Meet with an advanced student in your counseling program, a student who has had practicum or internship. Talk about the first meeting with a counseling group; about how new counseling groups are formed in a particular setting; and about supervision for group counseling.

3. Read the following example carefully. Prepare some notes and come to class ready to discuss your answer.

A 14-year-old female immigrated to the United States 3 months ago. The counselor does not know her at all. However, a recent report indicates that she was arrested for her second shoplifting offense. Teachers report that the female has a good command of English "compared with others like her."

What type of group, if any, should the counselor think about for the client?

CHAPTER 7
ISSUES IN
GROUP DEVELOPMENT

INTRODUCTION

Whereas chapter 6 presented information regarding the steps needed in organizing a group experience, and whereas it analyzed some of the important issues related to the very first session of the group, the early part of this chapter will focus on issues related to the development of that group experience.

STAGES IN GROUP DEVELOPMENT

Four stages are identified: Stage 1 is the *beginning stage,* a stage of exploration, orientation, and development of group goals. Stage 2, the *transition stage,* focuses on establishing a therapeutic environment so that change may occur during a later stage. This stage is characterized by conflict, dominance, resistance, inclusion, confrontation, and rebellion. Stage 3, called the *action stage,* is marked by action. As such, the focus is on cohesiveness, productivity, and mutuality as individuals deal with significant personal issues and work toward bringing about specific change in their behavior, both in the group and outside it. Stage 4, the *completion stage,* works toward completing the group experience through consolidation, termination, follow-up, and evaluation.

Although these stages are identified as separate and will be discussed as if they are completely separate stages in the development of the group, the stages described do not occur in discrete and neatly separated points in the life of a real group. There is considerable overlap between the stages, as groups move from one stage to the other in a somewhat jerky, hesitant manner. As a result, there may be some movement toward the next stage and then regression to the previous stage. Most groups do have these generally clear-cut stages in their development. Thus it is difficult to provide any kind of time sequence as to the length of time spent in each stage; rather, only a description of those stages can be presented.

Stage 1—Orientation Stage

The initial stage of the group is a time of orientation and exploration—determining the nature and structure of this particular group, getting acquainted with one another, exploring other members' expectations, and becoming involved with the workings of the particular group. As the group leader begins the development of a group, a balance of comfort and anxiety should be established early on. Anxiety needs to be reduced to a point where individuals feel reasonably free to participate, so that they are able to look more objectively at themselves and their interactions with others. This reduced anxiety results in an openness necessary for group work. At the same time, a minimal level of anxiety acts to motivate individuals to make positive changes in their lives. The principle involved is much the same as that involved in the relationship between learning and anxiety: modest levels of anxiety are associated with improved learning, while high levels of anxiety act to reduce learning performance.

A major emphasis during this period is that of establishing trust among the group members. Without such trust, group interaction will be superficial, with little self-exploration and little constructive challenging of one another. As a result, the group will operate under the handicap of hidden feelings, and it faces the risk of never moving beyond the first stage. Certainly the key individual in establishing trust is the group leader. By being congruent, by being willing to do what he or she expects the members to do, and by utilizing genuine, appropriate self-disclosure, the group leader establishes the expectation that group members can be trusted. Sometimes the key situation to which the group leader must respond results from group silences and awkwardness. The group's members may be floundering somewhat as they seek to discover how to participate in the group. Thus, the group leader needs to genuinely accept these silences and awkward behaviors as expected and reasonable behaviors on the part of the group members. By accepting even the rough edges of group behavior, the leader makes it easier for group members to take risks in revealing more of themselves to one another.

The early stage is also important in helping group members to identify the goals they have for their group experience. These may be general group goals, which vary from group to group because they are related to the purpose of the group, or they may be group process goals, which apply to most groups (Corey, 1985). In addition to these group goals, members need to establish their own individual goals. Since most have only a vague idea about what they want from a group experience, the leader needs to help in translating these vague ideas into specific and concrete goals with regard to the desired changes and to the efforts the person is actually willing to make to bring about such changes. In doing so, individuals begin this process of sharing important aspects of themselves with other group members.

Stage 2—Transition Stage

Moving from the early phase of beginning the group to a point in the group's development where cohesiveness and action occur requires a transitional period. This intermediate stage involves more open attitudes and feelings, with the resulting conflict, resistance, confrontation, and attempts to dominate. Although each group experiences unique difficulties in its transitional period, almost all groups experience variations of these particular difficulties.

During phase 2, group members test themselves, each other, and the leader. The excitement of expectation concerning the group experience has ended, and most group members are wondering whether or not the group will be useful to them. As members feel freer to criticize each other, some asserting their viewpoints in a judgmental or dogmatic manner, resulting conflicts develop. Some individuals will behave in an inconsistent manner, being aggressive at first and then very quiet. Others will be quiet and share only their "most acceptable" thoughts and feelings with the group. Pressure to conform intensifies and creates conflict, as members attempt to maintain their identities while seeking acceptance from other group members. Thus norms and roles become solidified and those with greater influence establish the guidelines for expected behavior. The roles of the various group members begin to develop and expectations regarding behavior of others form.

A major force in this transition phase is resistance. Resistance may be directed at the subject matter, the group, or the leader, and may take the form of withdrawal, absence from the group, attacking others, or questioning the purpose of the group. While this emergence of hostility may be a struggle for control of the group, the resistance is more likely to have its source in the unrealistic, sometimes magical, expectations which group members have for the group leader. Such expectations are so extreme that the group members are bound to be disappointed by the group leader, no matter how he or she conducts the group. Although this is rarely a conscious process, the group members react to it by showing behaviors of resentment and resistance toward the group's activities and process.

Although a difficult and unpleasant stage for the group leader, the transition stage, with its difficulty in resistance, presents a critical opportunity for the group leader to demonstrate and model the kind of openness to criticism that the leader expects from other group members. By facing the group's attacks and challenges, without retaliation and/or withdrawal, the leader reinforces member behavior of sharing openly their thoughts and feelings about the group workings. If the leader can accept internally that such resistance is a sign that members are working through their attitudes and comfortableness in the group, the leader is more likely to deal with such challenges directly and honestly, to share how he or she is affected by the confrontation, and to encourage continuing open communication.

Stage 3—Action Stage

As conflict and competition decrease and group members drop their preconceptions about the group and learn to accept one another, the group moves into the third stage. This stage, the action stage, in which individuals move toward doing something about changing the way they conduct their lives, is characterized by cohesiveness, productivity, and intimacy. Group members have learned to identify more closely with each other and to lose the sense of isolation they may have experienced in earlier sessions. As they learn that self-disclosure does not result in catastrophe, interpersonal respect and trust develop. Greater closeness and cooperation result, bringing about a greater intimacy among members of the group.

During stage 3, there is an increase in morale, mutual trust, and self-disclosure. Some members now feel free to reveal the "real" reasons they have come for treatment: sexual secrets, long-buried past transgressions, or other hidden secrets. The primary anxieties which individuals feel at the beginning of stage

3 have to do with not being liked, or being close enough to people, or being too intimate.

However, the cohesiveness that is developing results in members' showing greater respect for the statements and concerns of others and listening more carefully to attitudes and feelings as well as to content. As group members express greater understanding of situations, problems, and feelings, communication becomes less defensive, aggressive, or manipulative. Group members become more genuine in what they say and more willing to reveal personally significant material. The therapeutic process maximizes as individual members receive feedback from other group members that their feelings, attitudes, and thoughts are okay.

Although there may be greater freedom of self-disclosure in stage 2, problems sometimes result from the group members' suppressing all expression of negative affect and returning to being too nice to each other. Such group behavior may be supportive and understanding with an examination of one another's problems, but does not allow for confrontation or open expression of negative affect. By trying to facilitate growth with kindness alone, the group faces the danger of reverting to stage 1 in which little meaningful self-disclosure occurs.

A potential problem that may occur during stage 3 results from the group's becoming stuck in the early part of this phase and failing to move into action and behavior change. Such groups may become cohesive and self-explore, care about each other, and even make mild confrontations of one another, but fail to encourage or challenge each other to make changes outside the group. Such group members often enjoy the relationships that have resulted from the cohesive feelings among the group members, but are unwilling to do anything that might jeopardize that closeness. The significant key to this phase is productivity. It is only when group members are willing to explore important aspects of their lives and take action to bring about self-improvement that the group has fully entered stage 3. These attempts at behavior change or new attitudes toward others outside the group, even if unsuccessful, indicate that group members are more willing to take responsibility and less likely to blame others for their problems.

Thus as a result of the developing cohesiveness in stage 3, group members are able to challenge one another toward constructive behavior change. They are able to have more give-and-take discussions. They feel freer to express any feelings without fear of punishment. They are able to work through negative feelings toward each other, instead of avoiding those feelings. They face crises inside and outside the group by discussing them and working them through. Most important, they take on greater responsibility for the behavior and the consequences of it. Thus, stage 3 can make a real difference in the lives of the group members.

Stage 4—Completion Stage

Ending the group experience is a critical and often difficult experience for the group members as well as the leader. In many ways the last session is as important as the first session in its overall effect on the lives of those who participate in the group. Whether the group was an open group or a closed group, members need to anticipate the ending of their experience and work within sessions at the speed and intensity to allow them to accomplish their goals in the allotted time. By handling the ending of the group experience appropriately, the group leader can enhance the probability that group members will have engaged in the cognitive work necessary to make decisions regarding what they have learned about themselves in the group situation and to be able to use that learning in their outside lives.

How members handle ending the group often reflects the degree of growth that has occurred with them during the group experience. A primary example has to do with the way the group members deal with their feelings about the group ending. Sometimes they may be experiencing anxiety over functioning without the group's support and a resulting fear that their lives will regress to a previous level of functioning. There may also be disappointment about never seeing some of the group members again. There may be anger toward members of the group or the leader. Thus anxiety, fear, disappointment, and anger may be present, as well as love, jealousy, and hostility.

In whatever fashion the group members are dealing with these feelings, the group leader can help members face the reality of termination and reinforce their learnings concerning self-disclosure by encouraging them to bring their feelings and attitudes into the open. By having them share their fears or concerns about leaving the group and having to face day-to-day realities without the group's support, the leader can help group members recognize these same behaviors which resulted in the group's being special and utilize them to develop similar relationships outside the group. Thus the emotional aspects of ending the group can be utilized in helping group members make the transition to the outer world. In so doing, the group leader is not denying the sense of loss and sadness that may accompany the ending of the group, but is instead allowing that mourning to become an enriching experience for the members of the group.

A major concern during the completion stage is that of encouraging group members to put into words what they have learned from their group experience and how they intend to apply their increased self-understanding and behavior change to their lives outside the experience. Such an examination must be concrete and specific. Because of the impact that the group has made on the members of the group, the chances will be increased that members will retain and use what they have learned. This experience can be enhanced by utilizing the giving and receiving of feedback skills that members have learned during the group experience. Thus, after members have been asked individually to give a brief summary of how they have perceived themselves in the group, what conflicts have become more clear to them, what the turning points in their lives were, and what they expect to do with what they have learned, others in the group are asked to give feedback concerning how they have perceived that individual as well as their feelings about that person. Such concise and concrete feedback that often relates to the hopes and fears that the individual has expressed can also help members have a sense of closure concerning their group experience.

While feedback from other group members as well as the leader need not be 100 percent positive, the focus should be in that direction. The leader often sets an example by concentrating on individual progress and giving the member ideas as to future work that needs to be done. By minimizing negative feedback, the leader helps to prevent member defensiveness that may lead to discounting the value of the whole experience.

Efforts must be made to provide for follow-up and evaluation of the group experience. As will be discussed in chapter 8, follow-up activities by the group leader are both ethically and legally important and can be particularly useful to both the former group member and the leader. Such follow-up conveys to group members the leader's concern for transferring group learning to real life and the need to function without the group. In addition, such follow-up can become an important part of the evaluation information that is needed in order to improve future group experiences.

ISSUES IN GROUP DEVELOPMENT

Now that four general or generic stages have been described, the rest of the chapter will look at specific issues of group development. Beginning with member issues, the other major topics to be addressed include subgroup formation, conflict, leader efforts to increase member responsibility for the group, group evaluation, termination, and follow-up.

Member Issues

Some of the variations between groups during the developmental stages are to be expected because of the differences in members. At times the lulls in group development can be ended through the introduction of a new member to a group. An important issue is whether the group is open, allowing new members to join, or whether the group is closed. Open groups offer the excitement of a member's "graduating." As members complete their goals and experience less and less need for the group, open groups terminate single members and with a great deal of excitement and sometimes doubt, send the member out into the world. Although all groups will vary among the stages, the important question of whether the group is closed or open is especially relevant as the leader studies issues in group development.

Resistant Member.   The resistant group member is often one who is angry and frustrated. Issues such members present to a group and to the leader can exist in both open and closed groups. As might be expected, the group leader will respond to resistance in the early stage of the group by accepting and treating the resistance as important and worthwhile. Anger and resistance that is expressed in the second stage of group development is viewed by the leader as an example of self-testing, group testing, and leader testing. In order for trust and cohesiveness to develop in the second stage, the leader needs to continue encouraging the group member to express the resistance. If resistance is expressed in the third stage, it can be especially troublesome to a group that is in a cohesive, happy stage of development. Nevertheless, the leader may be able to use the expressed resistance to facilitate the entire group into taking action. The reader has seen that resistance is to be expected in a group. Probably one pitfall all group leaders face is a tendency to label too quickly a single member as resistant or angry. The description of the stages includes member resistance and frustration. It is possible to view a member, not as "resistant," but as an initiator or a lightning rod for group development, in what may be a necessary stage in development.

Manipulative Member.   To label a problem group member as "manipulative" may not be helpful. Perhaps anger is used by a member for manipulative purposes. A member who continually comes late or who is an irregular attender for group sessions presents an important issue to the leader in the group. At the same time, such tardiness or erratic attendance can be labeled manipulative. The reader may believe that all of the member issues, or problem members, which follow could be viewed as manipulative.

Instead, the leader could consider a "reframe." An earlier example was given where the label "angry member" was changed by the leader to one of a member who initiates and anticipates movement which the group needs in order to reach the next stage of development. Often, the anger and frustration of a member can be used to help a group make self-disclosures or to begin to provide feedback to the leader and to individual members.

In many ways the leader can be viewed as manipulating the group. The pacing of leader self-disclosures, the goals of the leader's including exchange of information among members, and the development of cohesiveness may be ways of manipulating the group to bring about effective group counseling outcomes.

For example, the leader may attempt to test expressed resistance by asking, "What do some of you others think?" or "Is this how you others see it?" Some members will begin to self-disclose as they give opinions and feelings and, if appropriate, the leader can help members give feedback as they react to the member expressing the resistance.

Finally, attendance and tardiness are important issues which are connected with trust and cohesiveness. The group leader, usually in the group (depending on purposes of the group and leader style), will need to attempt to change the erratic attendance and the tardiness.

Seductive Member. Issues concerning seductive group members are illustrated by extensive examples in group counseling texts. Often, members of groups will slip into seductive behavior at different times. As the group develops into giving and receiving interpersonal feedback about behaviors in the group, the so-called seductive member can receive the feedback and learn to be responsible for the seductive behavior just as each person in the group is handling other types of behavior. Probably the underlying similarity for each of these member issues is the degree to which they pose a threat to the group leader. Not coming to the group, or resisting the group leader's efforts at introducing activities, can be very threatening. Depending on the leader, open flirtation or open invitations for sex, as in the case of a seductive member, can be very threatening. Certain leadership styles allow the leader to explore doubts and uncertainties about the leader's sexual attitudes and behavior. In such groups, the leader can model an open request for feedback, and, depending on the group stage, can attempt to implement a personal behavior change within the group. However, almost all group leaders, will want to focus on the seductive member, not just the leader. Is the member aware of the behaviors? Can the group help the member explore what the seductive behaviors gain for the member? Is the member open to alternative ways of behavior in order to accomplish the same goals?

Monopolizing Member. The monopolizer has led too many group leaders, especially beginners, to experience discouragement and hopelessness. The reader can see that monopolizing is another effort to manipulate a group leader and the group. "Monopolizers" don't necessarily take over at the beginning stages of a group. It is important for a group leader to allow the monopolizer to perform more than once in order to identify a pattern or a theme of the monopolizing behavior. During the soliloquies of the monopolizer, it is good for a group leader to scan the group and use nonverbal attending to identify reactions from the rest of the group. One overall goal for the leader is eventually to help the member understand when the monopolizing occurs, to explore what possible gain the member may be receiving from all the talking, and to attempt to determine how the member might look for alternative behaviors which would be personally as well as interpersonally rewarding. Once again, if the leader feels threatened by the monopolizer and labels the member as one who is after the leader's power, the leader's thoughts might acerbate the relationship between the leader and monopolizer.

Silent Member. The "silent" group member is viewed quite differently by different group leaders. It is important that the leader observe the silent member long enough to determine whether there is a pattern to the silence. Perhaps the member will respond to direct questions from the leader; or perhaps the silent member will initiate communication near the end of a group session; or perhaps the silent member remains silent in response to direct questions from the leader and from other members. There seems no doubt that silent members may very well be highly involved in the group and may be getting a lot of cognitive and emotional input during group sessions. It also seems reasonable to conclude that members will be different in the amount of dread they experience about self-disclosure in a group. What was described in stage 1 as "typical" or "normal" fear and uncertainties about a new group may remain very real for three or six or eight group meetings for one group member. If the leader can accept the member who is not communicating very much in the group, the leader will get a chance to demonstrate his or her acceptance when someone in the group attacks or intensely questions the silent member. During this exchange (which will occur if the leader gives it time), the leader's acceptance of the silent member while the leader explores the reasons for the silence and learns about how the silence has been affecting other group members, can result in interpersonal learning for the silent member.

All counseling groups contain individuals. The group leader frequently thinks about the members between sessions as members of a group. Certain member-specific issues are the grist for the ongoing growth and exploration of counseling groups. Even in those groups which were formed homogeneously, wide individual differences among the members emerge. The member with the deep dark secret, the member whose sexual preference is divergent from the majority of the group, the member quite different in age from the majority of the group, all represent the individualities that a leader faces and works with as the group develops in personal and interpersonal learning and acceptance.

Subgroups

In the first stage of the group, members will identify similarities and commonalties between themselves and one or more other members. It seems quite natural to expect these members to quickly learn the names of those with whom they identify and to look toward these members for signs of approval or for indications of what kind of member behaviors might be appropriate. It also seems natural for such members to leave group sessions with these similar members or to sit with these members at the next meeting. If the members go to their cars together or make arrangements for social contact between the first and second group meetings, such behaviors seem quite natural and explainable. However we have observed that our students, the beginning group leaders, want to talk about subgroups early, usually in the first group meeting. These students often take the approach that if they tell group members not to have contact between group sessions, this exhortation will prove sufficient. If, despite this, subgroup contacts occur and the beginning leader learns about them, guilt inducement and harangues from the leader follow.

If the reader is able to understand the appeal of subgroup formations, subgroup development can be seen as quite natural and logical, just as the treatment of problem-member issues was described as being within the normal scope of groups. To work to catch group members subgrouping and then to chastise these members probably says more about leadership style than it addresses how members can learn from their own behaviors. Whether the reader expects to address subgroup formation in the first meeting or not, one important issue is the tendency for members to talk one way outside the group or to form secrets about the group and then fail to disclose or fail to talk the same way within the group. Such behavior is a threat to the leader because it undermines the very basis of the group.

Subgroup formation in reaction to a conflict is also to be expected. If the leader is not aware of the subgrouping into pros and cons, most usually at the time of a conflict, this lack of information can undercut the leader's efforts to resolve conflict. The preferred choice is to deal with the need for openness within the group as frequently and as often as the need arises. Do not be surprised if a single group member attempts to form a subgroup with the leader, you. With such an invitation, the response of the leader can model effectiveness for all the group.

For example, "I am going to have to tell the group at our next meeting that you met me today. I think we both need to be willing to tell them what we talked about and be prepared to answer their questions about why we met this way and why you wanted to talk to me alone." Most group theories will include the need for open and honest communication within the group including any communication which occurs outside the group. It is more difficult to find examples of group theory that recommend a group leader's chastising a few of the members of a group.

It is appropriate to remind ourselves that when strong feelings occur, self-disclosures are a way to communicate such feelings. Self-disclosures will take the form of "I" statements rather than chastising and name-calling.

Conflict in the Group

One sign of group development is the first conflict. The reader will recall that stage 2 includes conflict as an expected behavior for the group. However, when any group leader is faced with simmering conflict or the open conflagration of conflict in a group session, the leader tends to emotionalize and personalize the issue. This typical leader reaction, or overreaction, to conflict is almost as predictable as that conflict must occur in order for a group to develop and to grow.

In fact, frequently the first conflict will be leader-caused. The group leader may be unable to tolerate erratic attendance. When a group leader, during a group session, pushes the tardy member for a commitment to a change of behavior, emotional reactions will be engendered among some members. The openness of the leader to explore reactions to the way the tardy member or the member with irregular attendance was treated models how all conflicts can be handled in the group. Certain behaviors or certain conflicts will threaten the very existence of a group. Those caused by one member's attendance or tardiness can be controlled by removing the member from the group. Other conflicts may not fall within the control of the leader. For this reason, the open and thorough exploration of conflicts is a necessary stage of group communication.

The glow among group members after a conflict has been discussed and resolved is a sure sign that the group has moved to the early stages of stage 3. As described earlier in this chapter, ''greater closeness and cooperation result, bringing about a greater intimacy among members of the group.'' Just as surely, the leader can expect a general group effort to keep this glow rather than to allow any hints of subsequent conflicts. Although resolution of conflict may lead to feelings of self-satisfaction which present another issue for the group leader, the patient and open discussion and the facilitating of member-dealing with conflict may comprise the most significant contribution group leaders can make to the group members.

Increasing Member Responsibility

One issue in group development all too often is not accomplished—the importance of looking at the amount of member-initiated activities and the degree of member responsibility during later group meetings. How late in a group's development would it have to be for you, as the group leader, to initiate having members redefine the purposes of a group? For a leader to initiate discussions among members about what they want from their group is to assume that this leader can let go of the original leader-defined and leader-originated purposes. However, member responsibility for their own group and member responsibility for the growth and changes that members can experience while in the group indicate a clear developmental stage.

Readers of chapter 6 in its prepublication stage included two group leaders who objected to the heavy emphasis on leader-invented purposes and leader-invented structure and expectations. These two counseling group leaders said their style was to let members define a group's purposes from the beginning. In such cases, leaders will have already faced this issue.

It is possible that this stage of development does not make sense for open groups, since members who are ready for independence and increased responsibility may have already left the group. But for most groups, the opportunity for a leader to facilitate redirection and increased member responsibility for the life and results of the group offers an exciting risk.

Evaluation

This topic is extremely important. The ethical standards, the growing move for consumer rights in counseling, and the effective development of group leaders all converge upon the importance of the group leader's initiating evaluation of a group's development. In those cases where an agency or the setting for the counseling group initiates group counseling evaluation, it is to be expected that an effective leader would welcome and utilize the system-dictated evaluation. In other cases, it will be necessary for the group leader to conduct the evaluation.

In chapter 6, evaluation was discussed in order to determine the quality of leader behaviors. That discussion emphasized the self-growth that could result from observation and feedback for the group leader about leadership style.

Probably the most effective form of evaluation for the group leader is to gather written information. Certain counseling groups, for example those that emphasize skills or learning, can be evaluated by written content measures about what members have learned and how members have changed. In addition, member impressions can be gathered. Members can describe in what areas they believe they have grown; members can describe how they believe each member of the group has changed; as a further example, members can describe how the group leader changed in later sessions from early ones.

Where the purposes of the group are amenable, observers can present written descriptions of member-to-member interactions, summaries of interactions observed, and summaries of group leader behaviors.

Oral evaluations near the end of a group, while not as objective nor as anonymous, can provide helpful evaluation information. As with any method of evaluation, the leader needs to identify clearly the purposes for the evaluation and the use which will be made of the subsequent evaluation information. A structure supplied by the leader to the group during an oral evaluation may prove helpful.

Finally, the use which the leader makes of the evaluation determines how helpful the process is. While a leader is doing the strategy and preplanning for a counseling group, he or she can obtain important information from the evaluation of earlier groups, leading to improvement and to increased effectiveness. Answers to the following questions would be relevant: At which stage of the group was the leader perceived as the most uncertain? How has the leader performed when leading different types of groups? What are the implications for this upcoming group from such information?

Termination

Earlier, during the discussion of the fourth stage of group development, terminating a group and the completion of a group's work were discussed. The reader is urged to review the fourth stage of group development found earlier in this chapter.

At times, external limitations will dictate a group's ending. Certain groups know of time limitations from their beginning. This advance warning serves notice to the leader and to members as to when termination will occur. The work and the care with which the leader helps the group prepare for termination would apply in such cases.

Frequently, practicum students will be faced with a leader termination while the group continues. One of our students has highlighted strategies for changes in group leadership in the example provided in the box.

A STRATEGY FOR PHASING IN THE NEW GROUP LEADER

There is the chance that somewhere during the life of a therapy group, members will need to face and deal with the transfer of group leadership. In the ongoing therapy group this chance is more likely to become a reality. There are certain strategies that, when implemented, help to make this transfer of leadership as nonthreatening to the group members as possible. I wish to highlight a specific strategy by illustrating the process of transfer of leadership which I have recently experienced with an ongoing therapy group for recovering alcoholics. I will contrast two experiences indigenous to this group which hopefully will aid in establishing a strategy for handling the transfer of group leadership.

When I assumed the leadership of this ongoing therapy group it was without the aid of a transitional period. I was in attendance for the departing therapist's final session with the group. I was introduced as a "visiting observer," and no other attention was paid my visit until the last few minutes of the session when the departing therapist announced: "This is my final session as group leader. Tim will be your new leader beginning next Monday. I have enjoyed my time with you, but it is time to move on. The group is dismissed." The group members left the session that evening confused, angry, and hurt.

The following Monday and several sessions thereafter, the group worked through several issues relating to the transfer of group leadership. The majority of the group members felt abandoned and lost. The person that they had looked to for leadership had "up and left them." Many members were angry because they had not been informed that the group would be getting a new leader. Members were also angry because they felt that they would be wasting their time and money rehashing old group material in order to catch the new leader up on the life of the group. An ongoing group has well-established norms for member and leader actions and interactions. Another point of stress for the group members was the preconception that the new leader would discard all that they had worked on and would redesign the group to fit the leader's goals. It took the group and the leader four sessions to work through these concerns regarding the transfer of group leadership, and to return to the on-task work of the group. What strategy could have been implemented to make this transition more comfortable for both the group members and the new group leader, and to reduce anxieties and tensions?

Six months after assuming the leadership of the group, it was time for me to leave the group. Five weeks before my final group session I announced that the group would be getting a new leader and that I had asked the new leader to attend next week's session in order for the group to meet her, and for her to meet the group. In the next session, the new leader was introduced and the group members took turns making introductions to her. During this session I assumed the responsibility for the leadership of the group, while the incoming group leader remained relatively inactive. In the following two sessions, the new leader gradually took more responsibility for the leadership of the group. By the fourth (and my final) session, the new group leader had assumed full responsibility for group leadership and I remained relatively inactive. During the final ten minutes of the session I said my good-byes to the groups members, they said theirs to me, and the session ended.

During several follow-up conversations with the new group leader, I discovered that the transition had been relatively smooth. While the group did spend some additional time working on issues regarding my separation, group members' anxiety, anger, and feelings of abandonment were kept to a relatively low level. Although transfer of group leadership is an important issue in the life of the group, a strategy can be implemented that aids this process and keeps to a minimum the amount of group time spent on the leadership transfer process.

Source: Timothy R. Ruppert, University of Iowa

It is a rare occurrence for a beginning group leader to be able to get information about how the individual leadership style functions during termination. Frequently the first termination of group counseling occurs for group leaders well after graduation. Even if this "do it yourself" aspect of termination remains typical, students are encouraged to give a great deal of thought to obtaining feedback about their behavior during this important stage in a group's development.

Follow-Up

Editors of journals which feature psychotherapy research are increasingly insisting on follow-up after the psychotherapy research. Ethical codes indicate the gains which can be made from following up clients at some point after counseling and psychotherapy end. Perhaps the most meaningful evaluation material can be gained by a group leader 30 days or more after a group ends. At that time the members are more independent of the leader and perhaps can be more honest in their responses to the evaluation questions. The primary purpose of follow-up is for the group leader to receive information which can help him or her evaluate the leadership of the counseling group.

In addition, new information can be gathered a few months after a counseling group. Questions about the work situation and interpersonal relationships of the client can be answered some time after counseling. One important measure for the group leader is the number of group members who respond to the follow-up. A decision each leader faces is whether or not to call those members who do not respond. The reader is reminded that earlier research (Lieberman, Yalom, & Miles, 1973) showed that group leaders tended to be unaware of negative casualties resulting from counseling groups. This caution indicates the importance of the leader's attempting to contact those members who do not respond to a follow-up.

SUMMARY

The stages of group development follow no set, clear-cut formula. However four basic stages are useful in predicting how a group will move as well as the tasks that a leader will face. The first, or beginning, stage is an important one in the formation of trust and group cohesiveness. The second, or transition, stage can be a stormy one before the resulting therapeutic climate occurs. The action stage is the third, when group cohesiveness and trust result in productivity and significant personal changes for group members. Stage four, the completion stage, provides the setting for solidifying group changes and for group termination.

No two groups are exactly the same. The different members and the different formulations within and among groups make group counseling an exciting aspect of the counselor role. Members who are manipulative, seductive, silent, monopolizing, and resistant present challenges to group leaders.

Evaluation and follow-up of counseling groups are necessary.

REFERENCES

COREY, G. (1985). *Theory and practice of group counseling* (2nd ed.). Monterey, CA: Brooks/Cole.
LIEBERMAN, M. A., YALOM, I. D., & MILES, M. B. (1973). *Encounter groups: First facts.* New York: Basic Books.

SUGGESTED ACTIVITIES

In the Classroom

1. With a partner, discuss the four stages of group development described by the authors in this chapter. Identify any doubts either of you has about any aspect of the four stages. Briefly share your group experiences. At which stage do you recall your group's spending the most time? How far would you say your group progressed? Be prepared to share any questions you have with the course instructor.

2. In a small group, describe your experience with group silence (a characteristic described in stage 1). Discuss how each of you deals with silence.

3. In your small group, role-play situations in which each of you takes turns being tested as leader, with other group members engaging in problem behaviors. Allow time for discussion and group processing about the forms the leader tests take and also the different styles of responding to being tested.

On Your Own

1. Try to find a counselor who uses behavioral contracts or emphasizes action in his or her groups. Interview this counselor or observe this counselor leading a group. How does the group leader implement the action stage?

2. Recall how your practicum supervisor handled members' tardiness or absences. Do you recall any interventions by your supervisor that you would like to include in your leadership skills or style?

In case you have not had a practicum which met as a group, attempt to find other graduate students who have. See if they can complete this exercise with you.

3. Consider carefully your typical reaction to group conflict. Jot down a few notes. Do you respond to conflicts within your immediate family the way you do to a conflict within class, for example? Do you respond differently to work-related conflicts than to conflicts within your personal life?

   See if you can identify what it is about various situations that leads to your different response patterns to conflict.

4. Try to observe a group counseling session either directly or by videotape. Identify the stage of the group you are observing and specify those events that support your judgment.

CHAPTER 8
PROFESSIONAL ISSUES IN GROUP COUNSELING

INTRODUCTION

Group leaders have certain professional responsibilities to the people with whom they work. Certainly group counseling entails more than facilitative skills and attitudes. Group leaders must respond to the complex ethical considerations that have a direct impact on both the delivery of group counseling services and the attitude of the public toward those services. Public acceptance of group counseling as a valued service and of group leaders as respected professionals depends in large measure on an adherence to a high level of ethical and professional behavior. Such acceptance further depends on group leaders' having the education and training to carry out their responsibilities effectively. In addition, professional behavior calls for a continuing evaluation of the service being provided as a means of improving that service.

In this chapter, training, ethics, and evaluation, as they apply to group counselors, are reviewed.

THE EDUCATION AND TRAINING OF THE GROUP LEADER

The issue of whether one is adequately trained to lead a specific counseling group is an ongoing question that faces all professional group leaders. Corey (1985) suggests five questions that the group leader must face:

1. Am I qualified to lead this specific group?
2. What criteria can I use to determine my degree of competence?
3. Perhaps I am "technically qualified," but do I have the practical training or experience necessary to conduct this group?
4. How can I recognize my limits?
5. If I am not as competent as I'd like to be, what specifically can I do? (p.33)

Academic Training

Unfortunately, many professional counselors and psychotherapists have received little or no specific training—especially supervision—in leading therapy groups. Often students are given excellent supervision in their training to do individual counseling, but are later asked to lead counseling groups with no experience and training other than a lecture course in group process. Apparently, many counselor-educators believe that the student will be able, somehow, to generalize from his or her individual counseling training to group counseling.

There are, of course, many ways of becoming a professional group leader. A number of fields of study prepare individuals to become leaders of therapeutic groups. These fields of study include

1. Clinical psychology
2. Clinical social work
3. Counseling psychology
4. Marriage and family counseling
5. Pastoral counseling
6. Psychiatry
7. School counseling

Other disciplines that can help prepare professionals for group work include sociology, philosophy, and the other behavioral sciences. Thus, no one academic discipline holds a monopoly on the training of potential group leaders.

We propose that the group leader should have a thorough grounding in the applied behavioral sciences, placing a heavy emphasis upon interpersonal relations and group dynamics. Courses in personality dynamics, human development, psychopathology, and social psychology are extremely helpful. In addition, a thorough understanding of individual approaches to counseling and psychotherapy are a necessary prerequisite to most successful training in group approaches to counseling. Of course, at least one academic course in the theory and practice of group counseling is essential.

Certainly, a familiarity with the literature in group dynamics is important, so that the potential group leader has some basic information regarding the process of group development, leadership styles and responsibilities, group membership, and the application of theory and techniques to the actual process of group counseling.

Following this general orientation to group dynamics and an orientation to group counseling as a process, the prospective group leader should deal with specific issues and problems of practice. Discussions concerning the techniques and problems of selecting group members, of starting and maintaining a group, of problems of leadership, of issues dealing with subgroup dynamics, of various resisting behaviors of the group members, and of termination of group sessions need to be taken up in this training period.

Thus this basic information foundation which is needed by the group leader includes understanding group dynamics in its broadest social and psychological context, a knowledge of the varieties of theoretical approaches to group counseling in psychotherapy, an awareness of the issues and techniques of leading a group, and at least some familiarity with the approaches to evaluation of the effectiveness of group practice which will be discussed later in the chapter.

Supervised Practice

Although most training programs at the master's level do include a survey course in group counseling procedures, few offer, and even fewer require, supervised experience in group leadership. Whereas few programs would permit degree candidates to complete their program without supervised experience in individual counseling, most do not require a similar experience in working with groups. Corey and Corey (1982) suggest that this experience might be obtained by having a group of leader trainees. In such an experience the trainees could learn a great deal about their own response to criticism, their competitiveness, their need for approval, their anxieties over being competent, their feelings about certain group members, and their power struggles. The prospective group leader then might progress developmentally from group member, to observer, to co-leader, and finally to full leader status.

At each step of the supervision process, the counselor-in-training should be provided with opportunities for integrating content and experience. This integration, done under the supervision of the group leader, can be accomplished by intensive one-to-one supervision by an individual designated for this purpose.

Personal Participation in a Group Experience

While it is not necessary for an individual to have had every human experience in order to be effective in dealing with that problem area, it is difficult to understand how someone can become a sensitive group leader who has not experienced being a member of a group. Participation in a group counseling experience has the positive effect of providing the prospective group leader with a view of the process from the "other side of the room." In addition, increased self-knowledge and insight often result from such an experience. As obvious as it seems, it is important to note that one of the best ways for group leaders to learn how to assist others in their struggles is by working on themselves as members of a group.

We also recommend that group leaders make an effort to have experience in more than one counseling group. This enables them to have a broader perspective of what group participation involves and provides an additional model of group leader behavior, reducing the tendency to try to imitate the behavior and style of the leader instead of developing their own leadership style.

Continuing Education

The effective group leader recognizes that the education and training for leading groups is an ongoing process. Certainly professional group leaders recognize the need to develop both as a person and as a group leader. In order to develop and maintain a high level of competence, group leaders need to engage in various activities to learn new skills as well as to improve current skills. Such activities might include attending professional conferences and workshops designed for in-service training, taking advanced courses in related areas at colleges and universities, and working with colleagues to share knowledge and experience on both a formal and an informal basis. Periodic experiences that combine didactic and experiential learning are also desirable.

Periodic attempts to further one's personal skills as a group leader might also include setting up situations similar to the original supervised experience the group leader had received. By having a continuing supervisory experience as part of one's professional development, the group leader is able to refine his or her skills and to update his or her knowledge in the field.

PROFESSIONAL CREDENTIALING

Because there has been a strong movement in the past decade toward the licensure or certification of the various professional groups within the helping professions, it is important that the professional group leader work toward such credentialing by the professional organization or governmental agency which is most appropriate for his or her own professional training. Such professional recognition of competence by other practitioners within the profession provides greater trust and respect from the public and acts to prevent unqualified individuals from making claims of competence that are untrue.

ETHICAL ISSUES IN GROUP COUNSELING

Group counselors, like all professionals, have ethical responsibilities and obligations. Although the counseling literature contains numerous references to ethics and the legal status of the counselor, group leaders soon learn that the task of developing and maintaining a sense of professional and ethical responsibility is an unending one. For one reason, ethical problems pose particularly difficult situations for individuals in the various helping professions, but especially in group counseling. First, clearcut specific ethical codes that cover adequate guidelines for ethical behavior in every possible situation that can be encountered in counseling relationships have yet to be developed.

Second, counselors are likely to encounter situations where their ethical obligations overlap or conflict. Often the group leader is working simultaneously with several individuals who are involved in their own close interpersonal relationships, whether in the family, the school, or other institutions. In such situations, ethical obligations become exceedingly complex.

Third, the increased number of individuals who participate in a group counseling situation as opposed to one-to-one counseling results in situations where the group leader does not have total control over such issues as confidentiality. Although this issue will be discussed in the next section, it is important to note that while the counselor may have control over what he or she says about a session outside the session itself, the group leader has little control over what other group members may say outside the session, even in slips of the tongue.

The principal rule supporting ethical obligations is that the group leader must act with full recognition of the importance of the rights of each group member, the ethics of the profession, and the relationship of moral standards and values, individual or cultural, in the life of those group members. In fact, the very first sentence of the preamble to the *Ethical Principles of Psychologists* developed by the American Psychological Association (1981) points out this rule by saying, "Psychologists respect the dignity and worth of the individual and strive for the preservation and protection of fundamental human rights" (p.1). In simple terms, the ethical responsibility of the counselor, whether individual or group, is to promote the welfare of those individuals who have entrusted their lives to him or her. Thus any behavior on the part of the counselor that has a negative impact on the welfare of an individual or group of individuals who seek the services of that counselor is considered unethical.

The Nature of Ethical Obligations

Ethics are suggested standards of conduct based on a set of professional values that are accepted by the profession. Thus, a set of ethical standards is an attempt on the part of an aspiring professional group to translate prevailing values into a set of ethical standards that can serve to structure expectations for the behavior of its members in their relationships with the public and with each other. Such standards provide an outline for the implementation of the counselor's responsibility to his or her clients, and they inform those clients of what may be expected from the professional offering service. This includes the responsibility for informing the potential group member of alternatives for help in meeting his or her emotional and psychological needs. These alternatives need to be outlined clearly and to include information about the possible advantages and disadvantages of each for the client.

These guidelines help place specific practices within the framework of the general objectives and goals of the profession, and perhaps limit activities that are contrary to these goals. In addition, such ethical standards offer some protection for the professional by clearly stating the limits of professional practice in particular areas.

Ethical Standards

National professional organizations such as the American Association for Counseling and Development (AACD) (1981) and the American Psychological Association (APA) (1981) have developed sets of ethical standards which have been made available to practitioners. In each case, members who were directly involved in writing the code reviewed and examined a wide range of ethical behavior and problems of professional practice that were of concern to a broadly based membership. Both codes stress adherence to rigorous professional standards and to exemplary behavior, integrity, and objectivity toward clients.

In addition, the Association For Specialists In Group Work (ASGW) (1980) has approved the *Ethical Guidelines for Group Leaders,* which deal with the specific issues and concerns that relate to group counseling. These *Guidelines* are presented in appendix I.

Ethical Guidelines for Group Leaders states clearly that the standards are based on the ethical standards of the American Association for Counseling and Development (formerly APGA) and were intended to complement those AACD standards for group work by "clarifying the nature of ethical responsibility of the counselor in the group setting and by stimulating a greater concern for competent group leadership" (p.1). The *Guidelines* are organized under three categories:

1. The leader's responsibility for providing information about group work to clients.
2. The group leader's responsibility for providing group counseling services to clients.
3. The group leader's responsibility for safeguarding the standards of ethical practice.

The fundamental rule is that the individual must be respected and protected at all times. This can be done only by counselors who manifest honesty, integrity, and objectivity in their behavior toward clients. Unethical behavior consists of group leader's communicating a set of expectations while behaving in a way that is inconsistent with those expectations. For example, the counselor structures the counseling situation verbally or nonverbally, to imply mutual trust, concern, and confidentiality. The counselor upsets these expectations by assigning greater value to another societal role—for example, reporting to the principal that one of the teachers is sexually involved with a student.

In addition, various group theorists have proposed their own sets of guidelines for clarifying the ethical responsibility of the group leader. Hansen, Warner and Smith (1980) propose the following twelve principles:

1. Group leaders have a responsibility to develop a theoretical rationale for group practice which will enable them to identify the goals of their activity.
2. Group leaders have a responsibility to limit their group practice to developed levels of competence and skills, and to reveal these limits to clients.
3. Group leaders have the responsibility to be familiar with the standards and codes of ethical behavior of their parent professional organization and to apply them, where appropriate, to group practice.
4. Group leaders should be relatively congruent and stable individuals, free from gross pathology and with developed insight into their own unique characteristics and needs.
5. Potential group members should be screened to ensure that they are capable of benefiting from the particular experience offered.
6. If participants include individuals whose normal relationships involve extra group contact, such as employment, education, and even personal relationships, safeguards should be taken to minimize the risk of "spillover" from the group experiences.
7. The welfare of participants should be protected by assuring adequate follow-up efforts, which include making available relevant consulting and referral sources. Responsibility for participant welfare does not necessarily end at the point of termination of the group.

8. In general, professionally conducted groups should limit the process to those verbal and nonverbal techniques that do not have the potential to harm participants. Physical assaults, sexual behavior between participants, and excessive verbal abuse are unacceptable.

9. Every effort should be made to insure the maximum privacy of participants in the group process by appropriate discussion of the principles, needs, and implications of the concept of confidentiality. Leaders should frankly confront the fact that they are able to guarantee only their own commitment to the privacy of group discussions.

10. In general, group practice should be limited to volunteer participants who have had ample opportunity to obtain information concerning the process and to evaluate the implications of their own participation, and are thereby able to make a commitment from as fully informed a vantage point as possible.

11. Each participant should have the right to exercise complete freedom of choice with respect to participation in particular group activities or to separation from the group. This right of the individual participant shall be exercised free of undue pressure from the group leader or other group members.

12. Individuals and institutions that offer and support group activities have the obligation to evaluate those activities periodically. Furthermore, those professionals and institutions have an obligation to participate in research activities designed to reform and refine practice and to determine the effectiveness of variations in practice.

Confidentiality

The greatest single source of ethical dilemma in group counseling results from questions of confidentiality. The purpose of confidentiality is to safeguard the client's privacy, and counselors have a moral, ethical, and professional obligation not to divulge information without that client's knowledge and authorization, unless it is in the client's interest to do so. Yet, the ninth principle in the list above points out that the group leader is unable to guarantee that any of the other group members will respect confidentiality. This is particularly troublesome, since groups function best when the members and leader trust one another. Such trust develops when the different individuals believe that what they say will not be repeated outside the group.

It is extremely important that confidentiality be an issue that is discussed in the very first meeting of the group and is reviewed periodically thereafter. This initial discussion of confidentiality between the group leader and the group members is extremely important and may well determine the whole nature of the group experience. Certainly, group members are less likely to discuss personal concerns when they are aware that what they say may become the topic of conversation outside the group. As a result, the group leader and the group members need to discuss what will happen if a member of the group breaks a confidence. Most likely, the best way of approaching this issue is to involve group members in role-playing a hypothetical situation in which a confidence has been broken so that the various group members may achieve an understanding of the kind of personal, emotional impact of such an experience.

Repetition in the discussion of the need for confidentiality is important because most failures to respect the privacy of other group members is done in a nonmalicious way. Our experience has been that deliberate attempts to hurt other group members by talking with people outside the group about those members is a rare occurrence. However, it is human for group members to want to share the nature of their group experience with other people, and in so doing, they sometimes make inappropriate disclosures. Repeated reminders of this possibility are necessary to maximize the respect of privacy.

Follow-Up

Group leaders have the responsibility to provide appropriate follow-up for group members after a group has terminated. In the past decade, there has been increasing concern about the way leaders have handled determination of short-term growth groups, such as the weekend encounter group. Gazda (1984), for example, suggests that group leaders are responsible for these follow-up services:

1. Planning a follow-up session for short-term, time-limited groups.
2. Becoming acquainted with and having a commitment from a qualified professional to whom he or she can refer group participants when the leader cannot continue the professional involvement.
3. Informing the group participants of competent referral sources to whom they will have access provided that such assistance is needed. (p.242)

Although the legal necessity for providing follow-up after a group has terminated is clear, the ethical concern is even more important since the group leader, by agreeing to include individuals within a group for professional help, has agreed to do whatever he or she can to promote the welfare of that individual. Certainly follow-up can be done in a number of ways. Individual sessions, questionnaires, or follow-up sessions can be arranged to determine whether the group experience has initiated some sort of emotional difficulty that needs to be resolved.

The Impact of The Leader's Values on the Group

In our view, a major ethical issue has to do with the group leader's conveying his or her values to the group members. Although some have maintained that the counselor should remain neutral from a value standpoint while counseling and communicate no value orientation to the client, others point out that such scrupulously neutral behavior is neither possible nor desirable. This has been a continuing issue in the area of counseling. As far back as 1958, Williamson called for an abandonment of the neutral position in favor of an open and explicit value orientation in counseling. He suggested that counselor attempts to be neutral in value situations could easily lead the client to believe that the counselor accepted unlawful behavior and even condoned it.

That same year, Patterson pointed out that the counselor's values influenced the ethics of the counseling relationships, the goals of counseling, and the methods employed in counseling. Patterson cited evidence for the assertion that, no matter how passive and valueless the counselor appears, the client's value system was influenced and gradually became more similar to the counselor's value system. At the same time, Patterson suggested that counselors were not justified in consciously and directly imposing their values on clients, for six reasons:

1. Each individual's philosophy on life is different, unique, and unsuited to adoption by another.
2. All counselors cannot be expected to have a fully developed, adequate philosophy on life.
3. The appropriate places for instruction in values are the home, school, and church.
4. An individual develops a code of ethics, not from a single source or in a short period of time, but over a long time and from many influences.
5. No one ought to be prevented from developing her or his own unique philosophy since it will be more meaningful to her or him.
6. The client must have the right to refuse to accept any ethic or philosophy of life. (pp. 216–223)

We take the position that the group leader does not have the right to impose his or her values on the group members. However, the group leader does have the right and the responsibility to *expose* his or her values in those situations where being silent would lead the group members to believe that the leader possesses a set of values that are very different from those which he or she has. In fact, we believe that expressed values are less likely to interfere with the process of a group than are concealed values. Since the ASGW's guideline is "Group leaders shall refrain from imposing their own agendas, needs, and values on group members," it is clear that the imposition of the leader's values is unacceptable. However, the distinction that we are making has to do with the difference between *imposing* and *exposing* one's values. When the leader's values are exposed, not to influence what other individuals accept, but to clarify that leader's beliefs, the impact is positive because it allows the leader to be a role model for other group members in terms of self-disclosure. In addition, it provides the opportunity for the group members to challenge their own thinking against the background of the leader's beliefs, but still make their own choices without being burdened with guilt that they are not meeting the leader's expectations. Most important, we believe that the group leader has the responsibility to help the group members clarify and identify their own values and the priority they put on those values.

Belkin (1984) suggests that the primary value to which counselors must commit themselves is freedom. Freedom is an ideal that propels the individual to certain types of actions. Freedom allows the individual to determine in what direction to move. It allows the individual to be creative, to make choices and to be responsible for them. Freedom also commits the client to assuming responsibility for his or her action and its consequences. This leads to greater autonomy on the part of group members and lessens the likelihood of their becoming dependent on the group leader for instructions on how to live their lives.

THE IMPORTANCE OF EVALUATION

Both as group practitioners and as counselor-educators, we have met few group leaders who had more than a verbal commitment to evaluation. Apparently, evaluation feels too technical, too mechanical, too de-humanistic. The need for precise objectives and goals, the statistical analyses, the need for a defensible research design, and the difficulties involved in gathering data where so many variables are difficult to control—all contribute to the lack of enthusiasm for evaluation in group counseling.

There is an even greater problem for many group leaders—the concern that the evaluation results will indicate that the group leader is ineffective. Certainly, to face the possibility of not being effective is to risk anxiety and to have feelings of uselessness. However, Remer (1981) points out that counselors have an ethical responsibility to both their clients and the public to know the effects and limits of the tools and techniques they use. Although many group leaders are more comfortable with their own self-evaluation of their groups, such self-evaluations are highly subject to distortion and denial of that information which may not be complimentary to the group leader.

Thus, research efforts are necessary to determine the effects that group leaders have on members during group sessions, to ascertain the value of various specialized groups (for example, drug education groups, assertion training groups, children-of-divorced-parents groups) on the behavior of members, to assess the needs of those who are going to become part of a group, and to provide information that may be important in meeting accountability requirements in schools and agencies.

Purposes of Evaluation

Measuring the effectiveness of group counseling continues to be a source of difficulty. Although seen as a threatening process, evaluation is necessary to provide new insights that will help group counselors perform at higher and more professional levels. Since the group experience makes heavy demands on leaders and on group members, both financially and emotionally, it is necessary to determine the values of those services by applying standards. Thus, the major aim of evaluation is to ascertain, within some frame of reference, the current status of the group counseling provided, and then, on the basis of this knowledge, to improve its quality and its efficacy. Thus, evaluation is the vehicle through which one learns whether group counseling is doing what is expected of it.

Difficulties in Evaluation

Although most group leaders agree that evaluation is important in bringing about self-improvement, good evaluation studies of group counseling are relatively rare. A major problem is the difficulty of obtaining agreement on definitions of process and outcome, definitions that permit meaningful evaluations. For one thing, there are almost as many goals and objectives in group counseling as there are group leaders. Some of these goals are almost completely nonoperational: they cannot be easily converted into measurable behaviors. Goals such as developing self-actualization, improving the member's self-concept, or reorganizing the member's self-structure are a bit difficult to translate into measurable terms. Traditionally, member self-reports, counselor judgments of improvement, improved grades, changes in test scores, and indices of behavioral change have been used as criteria for measuring member improvement. Each of these criteria, however, has definite weaknesses, either in terms of validity or in terms of showing long-term changes.

A second problem encountered in measuring or evaluating counseling groups centers on the use of control groups. In any experimental design, an attempt must be made to isolate the effects of the treatment by designating a control group of subjects who are like the experimental group in every way except that they do not receive the treatment. Such control groups are best established by randomly dividing a single population into control and experimental groups. The presumption is that if change occurs in the group receiving treatment and not in the control group, the change can be attributed to the treatment. In counseling research, however, the most relevant characteristics are the hardest to match. The most obvious relevant characteristic is motivation to enter group counseling. Obviously a well-matched control group must contain individuals who also want and need the group counselors' services. At this point a serious ethical issue comes into play. An individual who expresses a need for group counseling does not wish to be assigned to a control group where no counseling help is provided. Such an assignment could well have a negative impact on that individual and perhaps affect the validity of the results. Although this issue is often resolved by utilizing a delaying tactic, wherein the control group subjects are kept on a waiting list while the experimental subjects participate in a group, this is still considered unacceptable by many group leaders. Thus, evaluation which is to be done strictly as a research effort to show a clearer picture of the effects of the group experience must be handled very carefully. Such an effort can be left to the researchers, but evaluation of a counseling group without having a control group for comparison is still important for the group leader.

Another major problem in the evaluation of group counseling is the contamination of treatment effects. When a counseling group lasts for a number of weeks or months, change is likely to occur, whether positive or negative. However, such change may be the result of relationships and events outside the group setting, thereby undermining the evaluative significance of the help the individual has received through the group. In spite of this difficulty, evaluation is important.

Formative and Summative Evaluation

Group leaders need both process and outcome evaluation of what happens during their counseling group. This distinction between process and outcome is similar to that between formative and summative evaluation. *Summative evaluation* is the same as outcome evaluation, its aim being to judge the ultimate results of the group experience. *Formative evaluation,* like process evaluation, focuses on what is happening as the counseling sessions occur so that future sessions can be altered to meet the needs of the group more closely. Thus, formative evaluation requires *ongoing* collection of information regarding the impact of the group sessions. Such information is not an attempt to evaluate the ultimate worth of the total group counseling experience, but rather focuses on specific sessions. Although formative evaluation relies heavily on subjective judgments, it can still be very important in the development of the group.

Methods of Evaluation

Group members can be interviewed to determine if their attitudes have changed, if they have developed new skills, and if they feel the group sessions have been worthwhile. The advantage of interviews is that individuals tend to respond more fully than they do in a questionnaire. However, interviewing a large number of group members requires a great deal of time.

The second method of evaluation is to use trained observers to watch the actual behavior of group members and rate those group members on various desired areas of improvement. These observers can provide objective data as to both the verbal and nonverbal behavior of group members during the sessions to see if any change occurs during the period of time during which group counseling is taking place. These observers, however, must be trained to provide objective data on very specific kinds of counseling goals—whether these be behavioral in nature or be reflective of a particular orientation to counseling growth. For example, the observers can be trained to be sensitive to the kinds of changes that Rogers (1951) has suggested as the goals of client-centered therapy:

1. The individual gradually becomes freer in expressing feelings in verbal and motor channels, and these feelings refer increasingly to the self, rather than to the nonself.
2. The individual gradually changes his or her focus from the "there and then" to the "here and now" of his or her experiencing.
3. The individual gradually becomes aware of experiences that had been denied or distorted previously.
4. The individual's expressed feelings increasingly have reference to the incongruence between certain of his or her experiences and the self-concept.

5. The individual has an increasingly positive self-regard, with a corresponding increase in inner-directed behavior.

Various standardized tests are also used in the measurement of effectiveness. These tests ordinarily are personality tests and include subjective measures, such as changes in the kinds of self-descriptive adjectives the individual uses over a period of time. Personality criteria can also include changes in the scores attained on various personality tests, as well as the Stevenson Q-sort and various true-value-adjustment inventories.

Because of their ease in administration, paper-and-pencil evaluations are the most frequently used. These are not ordinarily measures of behavior, but are methods of allowing group members to describe the changes that have occurred as a result of the group counseling sessions. Such paper-and-pencil evaluations can take the form of open-ended questions, which allow members to record their feelings and opinions without being bound by a structure. These open-ended questions are a good way of getting a broad base of information; however, responses can be so disparate as to preclude any kind of meaningful, objective summary of the information. In addition, the results do not always directly relate to the objectives and goals of the counseling group.

Of course, one way of using paper-and-pencil evaluations and still receiving responses to specific questions is to develop questionnaires which can be geared to the specific goals of the counseling group. Although such questionnaires are easy to administer, their validity is based on how the questions relate to the counseling objectives. Often, such evaluations are a means for the group leader to provide an "appearance" of evaluation—to be briefly glanced at and tossed away. They also have the weakness that the questionnaires are often given to the group members at a time when those members are feeling good and thus tend to provide a "halo effect" about the value of the session(s).

No matter what method of evaluation is used, group leaders need to develop some sort of systematic approach that will give full recognition to the goals and purposes of their counseling groups. In doing so, they may choose not only to include the objective and subjective information provided by the group members, but to include their own subjective report about the effectiveness of the counseling sessions. Certainly, experienced group leaders are able to trust their own judgments about member growth during the group process, and such subjective evaluation can help them determine future courses of action during the group sessions.

SUMMARY

Group leaders must accept professional responsibility for the work they do in order to maintain public acceptance and to emphasize the good for the client.

The education and training of group leaders continues to receive a great deal of attention. Group leaders need a solid foundation in the applied behavioral sciences, including counseling theory and methods. They need an understanding of group dynamics and a supervised experience in group leadership. Finally, they must seek continually to upgrade their skills and knowledge of group work.

Ethical issues in group counseling are especially difficult and important. The group leader must act with full recognition of the importance of the rights of each group member. Knowledge of several sets of ethical standards, and the *Ethical Guidelines for Group Leaders* in particular, can provide the basic information the leader needs about ethical issues. In particular, care must be taken to deal appropriately with the issue of confidentiality and to avoid imposing the leader's values on the group.

Evaluation continues to be difficult for most group leaders. However, evaluation is a professional responsibility, necessary if group leaders have a commitment to work toward providing the most effective group experience possible. Such evaluation can be done with minimal effort if careful planning is utilized in preparing for those group experiences.

REFERENCES

American Association for Counseling and Development. (1981). *Ethical standards.* Washington, DC: Author.

American Psychological Association. (1981). *Ethical principles of psychologists.* Washington, DC: Author.

Association for Specialists in Group Work. (1980). *Ethical guidelines for group leaders.* Falls Church, VA: Author.

Belkin, G. (1984). *Introduction to counseling* (2nd ed.). Dubuque, IA: Wm. C. Brown.

Corey, G. (1985). *Theory and practice of group counseling* (2nd ed.). Monterey, CA: Brooks/Cole.

Corey, G., & Corey, M. S. (1982). *Groups: Process and practice* (2nd ed.). Monterey, CA: Brooks/Cole.

Gazda, G. M. (1984). *Group counseling* (3rd ed.). Boston: Allyn & Bacon.

Hansen, J. C., Warner, R. W. & Smith, E. J. (1980). *Group counseling* (2nd ed.). Chicago: Rand McNally.

Patterson, C. H. (1958). The place of values in counseling and psychotherapy. *Journal of Counseling Psychology, 5,* 216–223.

Remer, R. (1981). The counselor and research: Introduction. *Personnel and Guidance Journal, 59,* 567–571.

Rogers, C. R. (1951). *Client-centered therapy.* Boston: Houghton Mifflin.

Williamson, E. (1958). Value orientation in counseling. *Personnel and Guidance Journal, 36,* 520–28.

SUGGESTED ACTIVITIES

In the Classroom

1. With a partner, share your experience as a group member. Describe for your partner the type of leader you had. What aspects of the leader's style would you like to incorporate in your own?

How important do you and your partner believe a personal group experience is for an effective group leader?

2. In a group of four, discuss alternative means by which a group leader can introduce and/or enforce confidentiality within a counseling group.

    a. Have two members take turns introducing the idea of confidentiality to the group. Give feedback.

    b. Have the other two members each practice one of the following breaches of confidentiality by a group member:

        (1) One member returns and says a friend had teased the member about what was said in the group. The friend had been told by another group member.

        (2) One member complains that the secretary had asked whether or not the member had decided to get a divorce. This member had told no one of the dilemma except the group.

        Give feedback.

3. With a partner, discuss your plans to arrange a supervised practice experience for yourself as a group leader. How difficult is it? How common? Do you and your partner have this practice at your institution?

On Your Own

1. Select an ethical code or a specific ethical guideline relevant to your future plans and examine the code specifically for its guidelines on informal consent for clients in groups. Be prepared to share your findings with the class.

2. Consider the ethical guideline found in appendix I-B-9. Interview a counselor in a setting of your choice about the specific methods you might use to determine to what extent members of your groups meet their personal goals.

3. Consider whether your leadership style deals with your intent to expose or to impose your values. Do you recognize any safeguards in your leadership style characteristics that will help you prevent imposing your values?

CHAPTER 9
GROUP COUNSELING WITH SPECIAL POPULATIONS

INTRODUCTION

Although the group process, practice, and therapeutic elements that we have described are applicable to all groups in all kinds of settings, the application of these concepts may vary according to various stages of human development or the particular needs of a specific group. Thus in this chapter, we will discuss special needs and implications for group leaders who work with children, adolescents, and older adults, as well as those who work with couples and families. In addition, information is provided for working with various other groups, especially groups who are dealing with problems of chemical dependency, eating disorders, and career choice. Finally, we will provide some guidelines related to the use of groups in career counseling.

GROUPS FOR CHILDREN

As was stated in the previous paragraph, basic principles of group counseling apply to all ages. However, the group counselor must adapt his or her techniques to the clients' social, emotional, and intellectual development, as well as their ability to communicate verbally. In adapting group techniques for children, then, certain considerations need to be addressed: for example, the younger the children, the shorter the session. Group leaders working with children must judge the attention span of the children and adapt the time of the session to meet the children's needs.

A second difference that is important in working with children has to do with the size of the group. Since younger children are just learning to function in groups outside their immediate families, the younger the group, the smaller the group needs to be, with a recommended size of four to six for children under age 10. Such younger groups also need greater structure, and are often more responsive to play counseling or therapy. Since younger children are obviously unable to comprehend fully the nature of personal adjustment problems and normal developmental issues, the group leader must provide opportunities other than just talking for those children to express what is happening with them.

Ginott (1968) suggests that members for groups of younger children be selected from among children with dissimilar problems and needs, so that they will have the opportunity to relate to children who are both different and complementary. By mixing passive children with more assertive children, each learns from the other—the quiet learn from the verbal, while the verbal learn from the quiet. Ginott also suggests that it is best to have members span an age range of only 12 months, with less mature children in the same age group being assigned to a younger group. Mixing boys and girls in groups is an issue where different theorists disagree. Whereas Ginott (1968) has recommended that preschool children be placed in mixed-sex groups and school-age children separated by sex,

Gazda (1984) believes that there is little need to separate the sexes until the age of 9 or 10. At the same time, Ohlsen (1977) prefers that groups include both boys and girls, since he feels that the counseling group may be "the safest place in which boys and girls can learn to cope with the problems with which they are faced as a consequence of their differing rates of social-sexual development" (p.161).

Another issue in using group approaches to counseling children is the issue of trust. Children seem to trust the counselor more readily than do either adults or adolescents and are therefore more willing to communicate their thoughts and feelings. Their ability to communicate this information, however, is less developed. Thus, to communicate effectively with children (even more than with adults), the group leader must understand the vocabulary, language development, and family background. He must be sensitive to the child's search for words to express himself, must be able to listen empathically, and must help teach children the vocabulary for self-expression.

Likewise, working with children involves a recognition that there are differences in child-child and therapist-child relationships. Although subgroups form and disassociate, individuals within this group may still often choose to play by themselves. Thus, group interaction provides an opportunity for children to learn to give and receive and develop relationships.

Adapting Group Techniques to Children

Vander Kolk (1985) suggests eight aspects of a therapeutic approach for group therapy with children:

1. Total acceptance of the child
2. A simple invitation to play without explanations, goals, reasons, questions, or expectations
3. Helping the child learn to express himself and to enjoy respect
4. Permitting, but not encouraging, regressive behavior early in therapy
5. Permissiveness of all "symbolic behavior" with limits on destructive behavior
6. Prohibiting children from physically attacking each other
7. Enforcing limits calmly, noncritically, and briefly, mentioning limits only as necessary
8. Empathy (p. 304)

Dinkmeyer and Muro (1979) believe that children can be given an orientation to the purpose for the group and that the children need to discuss or work on agreed areas of concern. They suggest puppets or a media presentation to help explain the nature of the group experience. While they believe that group members will initially be awkward, silly, and perhaps engage in horseplay, the process will be important in helping the group members gain the maximum benefit from their group experience. At the same time, Dinkmeyer and Muro believe that play approaches are extremely important, and they list useful items for permitting the child optimal expression. They suggest using open shelves which have a wide variety of toys and games. These will permit the child to express feelings toward her or his world, releasing aggression and enhancing self-concept. Through a relationship approach to such media, the group leader expresses understanding of feelings, without interpreting those feelings for the child. Thus this play media is utilized to bring out feelings and attitudes, with the group leader's acceptance reinforcing attitudinal and behavioral changes.

Developmental Issues

In developing goals for children, group leaders must have knowledge of developmental tasks in coping behavior for determining a child's progress or lack thereof. Gazda (1984) suggests seven basic areas of human development that are important in assessing the potential needs of children in group counseling. In addition, he suggests developmental models for understanding those seven areas. These include:

1. Psychosocial—represented by the work of Tyron and Lilienthal (1950), Havighurst (1972), and Erikson (1963)
2. Vocational—as presented by Super and Associates (1957)
3. Cognitive—as provided by Piaget (Flavell, 1963; Wadsworth, 1971)
4. Physical-sexual—as presented by Gesell, Ilg, Ames, and Bullis (1946)
5. Moral—represented by Kohlberg (Duska & Whelan, 1975)
6. Ego—represented by Loevinger (1976)
7. Emotional—represented by Dupont (1979)

Gazda (1984) provides an excellent summary of these developmental tasks and the corresponding coping behaviors for the seven areas of human development. His charts, which divide the various developmental tasks according to the seven areas, list the various tasks for each of those areas according to age, task characteristic, and coping behavior. The information that he provides gives group leaders guideposts for evaluating a child's total developmental progress and allows that leader to spot potential problems so that intervention can be utilized as a means of rectifying the problem. Even more important, the developmental tasks and coping behaviors that Gazda summarizes provide the lifeskills trainer an outline of the kinds of information and skills a child needs and the time when he or she would be most ready and receptive to receive and utilize them. In addition, Gazda lists acceptable behavioral characteristics, as well as behavioral characteristics showing minimal and extreme psychopathology for the child and parent(s).

Most group leaders who work with children emphasize behavioral goals and the use of cognitive-behavioral techniques for attaining these goals. Thus, in addition to play media, the use of role-playing, behavior rehearsal, coaching, and various cognitive approaches with older children are particularly effective as part of the group process. Group leaders who will be working with children are encouraged to do further reading regarding the specific application of group techniques to this age group. Some major contributions to the area include

1. *Play Therapy* (Axline, 1969).
2. *Developmental Groups for Children* (Duncan & Gumaer, 1980).
3. *Group Counseling: Theory and Practice* (Dinkmeyer & Muro, 1979).
4. *Group Psychotherapy With Children: The Theory and Practice of Play Therapy* (Ginott, 1961).
5. *Windows to Our Children: A Gestalt Approach to Children and Adolescents* (Oaklander, 1978).

GROUPS FOR ADOLESCENTS

Probably no other age group creates more frustration, more feelings of impatience, and more "throw-up-my-hands-and-quit" feelings than does the adolescent age group. In spite of the common statement that adults make that "being a teenager is the best years of one's life," adolescence is an extremely difficult period, characterized by paradoxes. Adolescence is a period when individuals are in the process of achieving their independence, but are still trapped by dependence on their parents for financial assistance, as well as for emotional support and guidance. Adolescents strive for closeness, but often fear intimacy and seek to avoid it. Adolescents want direction and structure, but rebel against control. Expected to act like mature adults, adolescents are not given complete autonomy and are typically self-centered and preoccupied with their own worlds. They are asked to deal with reality—a reality of stress, frustration, and feelings of inadequacy—and are tempted to escape those unpleasant experiences through avenues considered unacceptable by the adult world: sex, alcohol, other drugs, and fantasy.

Thus, the adolescent period is a time of searching for identity, of establishing oneself in an adult role, and of developing a system of values that will influence the course of one's life. Adolescents, more than any other age group, are desperate for feelings of group acceptance, for believing that they are part of an important group. This need for group belonging ties in well with the corresponding need to experience success that will lead to a sense of self-confidence and self-respect.

As a result of the conflicting messages that adolescents often receive and the intensity of their needs to belong and to feel important, adolescents often experience a great deal of loneliness and isolation. In fear of rejection, the adolescent often fails to disclose those feelings and thoughts that might be unacceptable to others. Adolescents frequently withdraw or put on a facade of bravado in which they pretend that no problems exist at all.

McCandless (1970) suggests that many adolescent problems involve frustrations in achieving major goals: status, adequate sexual adjustment, and self- and socially-fulfilling values and morals. Status is important as adolescents are pressured to succeed, they are expected not only to perform up to the level of their parents, but in many ways are expected to exceed their parents' own performance, as parents work toward making their child have a better life than they have had. Sexual conflicts are also a major part of this period as adolescents attempt to establish a meaningful guide for their sexual behavior as well as for their sex role identification. Most have real difficulty in clarifying what it means to be male or female, and what kind of man or woman they want to become. Likewise, the development of values and morals and the importance that adolescents place on these is likely to be more important than anything else in determining the quality of their lives. Such morals and values frequently determine the kind of lifestyle these adolescents will have, including educational goals, family roles, and societal roles.

Ohlsen (1977) points out that the adolescent is trying "to determine who he is, what he would like to do, what he can do, and to develop the will and self-confidence to do it" (p. 176). At the same time, the adolescent is becoming more and more concerned about the attitudes and beliefs of his or her peers, and giving less emphasis on family attitudes. Thus, the resulting conflicts between the adolescent and his or her family heighten the tension and anxiety that occurs during this age period.

Developmental Needs

Gazda (1984) summarizes the needs to be met during adolescence as statements of general goals for group counseling of adolescents as follows:

1. Search for identity by defining meaningful goals for various facets of life.
2. Increased understanding of one's interests, abilities, and aptitudes.
3. Improving skills for identifying opportunities and for evaluating them in terms of one's own interests, abilities, and aptitudes.
4. Increasing interpersonal skills and self-confidence to recognize and solve problems.
5. Improving interpersonal skills and self-confidence to recognize when decisions are required, how to make them, and how to implement them.
6. Increasing sensitivity to others' needs and improving skills for helping others satisfy their needs.
7. Improving communication skills for conveying one's real feelings directly to relevant persons, and with consideration for their feelings.
8. Independence to examine what one believes, to make one's own decisions, to take reasonable risks, to make one's own mistakes, and to learn from one's mistakes.
9. Improving interpersonal skills to deal with authority figures in a mature manner, for example, employers, police, government officials, as well as parents and teachers.
10. Meaningful participation in developing and maintaining limits on one's own behavior.

11. Growing knowledge and skills for coping with one's physical and emotional changes associated with maturation.
12. Improving skills for living adult roles. (pp. 177–178)

Dealing with Age-Related Issues

Because of this increasing concern about peers, as well as the number of adolescent needs that involve the improvement of specific skills, group approaches to counseling have the potential to be particularly effective in helping adolescents deal with the age-related issues that confront them. Of course, to do so involves certain inherent difficulties. For example, many adolescents feel a lack of motivation for counseling. Either they do not believe they have problems or else they prefer to deny those problems. Often, even those who are willing to admit that they do have problems would prefer not to discuss them with others. Adolescents often feel a stigma in participating in group counseling. A second difficulty often results from the possibility of unacceptable group norms that may develop within an adolescent group. Such groups may reinforce deviant behavior and punish appropriate behavior, unless the leader is able to intervene in such a way as to encourage acceptable behavior with a reward system for appropriate behaviors. Often including a highly respected peer in the group not only increases the motivation for participating in group counseling, but also increases the importance of appropriate group behavior. Likewise, adolescents are often reluctant to share their feelings, thoughts, and attitudes with their peers. When adolescent group members refuse to discuss personal problems, share experiences, or even role-play the types of problems that adolescents face, the group leader can reinforce those who do self-disclose. Contracts with individual members of the group can help in preventing this reluctance to self-disclose from becoming a continuing problem. Finally, a typical adolescent behavior is that of blaming others for his or her problems. The effective group leader can point this out to the group, set a rule against it, or discuss the importance of each individual taking responsibility for his or her own behavior.

Group leaders who are new to facilitating adolescent groups often report a great deal of frustration in terms of group control. Many of these problems result from poor communication skills. Adolescents are more likely to provide harsh feedback, to interrupt others, to engage in disruptive behavior, and to demonstrate insensitivity. Thus, part of the work involved in forming an adolescent group includes teaching adolescents appropriate communication skills. In many ways such communication training can be highly important as a framework for the therapy sessions, building on the idea from chapter 8 that training individuals to be facilitative to others is often the best way of providing treatment for their own problems. In addition, the improvement of communication skills is important because of the need for adolescents to communicate more effectively in the outside world if their lives are to be more productive and satisfying.

In spite of such difficulties, however, adolescent groups can be highly successful. Feedback from peers is often accepted far more readily than feedback from adults. Learning that other peers are having the same kinds of experiences that they are is facilitative to adolescents who are highly concerned about their own experiences being normal. Learning new skills that are important in relating to other individuals can improve the quality of their lives outside the group itself to the extent that adolescent group members can become highly excited and enthusiastic about their experiences. Thus, the group counseling experience provides two highly important elements: Genuine acceptance and encouragement of peers, and a trustworthy adult who seems to trust and respect the adolescent.

Individuals who will be working with adolescents in groups are encouraged to read the following:

1. *Group Counseling* (Ohlsen, 1977).
2. *Group Counseling* (Gazda, 1984).
3. *Groups: Process and Practice* (Corey & Corey, 1987).
4. *Introduction to Group Counseling and Psychotherapy* (Vander Kolk, 1985).

GROUPS FOR OLDER ADULTS

We are including a special section on older adults because of their unique characteristics and needs, which group leaders must consider in working with this population. As an increasingly greater percentage of our population belongs to the older adult age group, there has been, and will continue to be, an increasing concern for meeting the needs of this age group. While the counseling profession has shown an interest in the elderly for some time, only a small percentage of programs in counselor education offer courses in counseling the elderly (Salisbury, 1975) and only a very small percentage of the elderly receive outpatient treatment (Busse & Pfeiffer, 1973).

Unique Characteristics of Older Adults

The most accurate statement to be made in regard to characteristics of older adults is that there is a lack of universal characteristics and that variability is highly evident. Nevertheless it is possible to enumerate some prevalent characteristics. Older adults are more likely than individuals in other age groups to be struggling with some particular themes: loneliness; social isolation; feelings of loss (either of individuals or of physical capabilities); poverty; feelings of rejection; dependency; feelings of uselessness, hopelessness, and despair; fears of death and dying; depression; and regrets over past events. Older adults have a high incidence of alcohol and other drug abuse. They have high levels of suicide. The fear of growing older and losing their independence, their intellectual capacities, and their physical abilities often leads to despair. For many, the need for a self-identity separate from their occupations and work-related activities presents an extremely difficult problem with which to cope (George & Cristiani, 1983).

Someone working with older adults via group counseling faces some obstacles which are specific to this age group. Older adults are often more resistant and sceptical about the effectiveness of group counseling than are other age groups. Many have shorter attention spans as the result of physical or psychological difficulties, and require a slower pace within the group process. Their ability to concentrate and to fully experience the group activity may be hampered by medications, by tendencies to return to the past in their thinking, and, for some, by advanced stages of senility. In addition, older adults often have more difficulty in being regular with group session attendance because of a variety of factors that may interfere with their attendance.

Meeting Older Adult Needs

In leading counseling groups composed of older adults, the counselor needs to exhibit greater activity or direction. Providing ground rules, building positive expectancies, and setting goals provide adequate focus for older adults with reality orientation intact and major hearing impairment absent. One method that is particularly useful is to use taped presentations dealing with the expressed needs of the group members—for instance, health, finance, role changes, reminiscence, attitudes of self and others toward aging, and relationships with spouse, peers, family, and others.

A general goal in group counseling with older adults is to help each feel more in control of his or her life. A climate of support and encouragement, more than confrontation, helps older adults explore options and alternatives and make decisions with regard to the future. Likewise, older adults have a great need to be listened to and understood, since they frequently feel that their ideas and feelings are discounted and ignored because of their age. Thus the goal of counseling groups is oriented toward making life in the present more meaningful and satisfying to the older adult.

Further reading about groups for older adults can be done in the following:

1. *The Aged Patient* (Ernst & Glazer-Waldman, 1983).
2. *Group Counseling* (Gazda, 1984).
3. *Introduction to Group Counseling and Psychotherapy* (Vander Kolk, 1985).
4. *Groups: Process and Practice* (Corey & Corey, 1987).

GROUPS FOR COUPLES

Although we prefer to do marriage counseling by seeing only the individual couple, there has been a recent trend toward seeing couples in a group setting. Ohlsen (1979) describes this approach in his *Marriage Counseling in Groups*. His approach is based on the learning model and places an emphasis on the prevention of major problems, the diagnosis of early characteristics of self-defeating behaviors, and the substitution of desirable behaviors for less desirable ones. Ohlsen sees this trend in using groups in marriage counseling as a way for couples to improve their relationships skills, try new behaviors, and obtain feedback from others on newly attempted behavior.

Vander Kolk (1985) suggests that improvement is more likely to result from exploration and self-revelation of couples in groups because of the following factors:

1. Other couples are more likely to see through the unproductive games.
2. Similar experiences can be the basis for giving helpful feedback.
3. Distressed couples can gain support from others with similar problems.
4. Other couples can insist on learning new and more positive behaviors.
5. Individuals can act as models for certain types of productive behaviors.
6. It can be easier to learn how to gain support without being dependent.
7. Others' growth can be encouraging. (p. 341)

Within a group setting, spouses appear to be more likely to accept responsibility for talking openly about their own concerns, rather than simply criticizing their mates. They also seem to make greater progress in learning to listen to their spouse, to communicate, to make requests, and to share warmly private feelings. In addition, marriage counseling clients within a group learn to recognize the early signs of conflict, to help each other reveal early what is annoying, and to cooperate with each other in resolving conflicts.

The group setting helps to reduce some of the difficulty that results from a triad counseling model. Just as parents have learned that a third child brought into a play relationship with two others greatly intensifies potential conflicts and difficulties, psychologists have known that whenever three people work together, two often pair up against the third. Even when this pairing does not occur, an individual who believes that the other two have developed this alliance, will act as though the pairing has resulted. In traditional marriage counseling, in which a single counselor works with one couple, great care must be taken to prevent either of the spouses from believing that the counselor is siding with the other spouse. This is difficult when one of the two is greatly lacking in self-confidence and/or is convinced that others really don't care what he or she feels. Though this difficulty can be overcome, the time and effort needed to prevent such a problem is unnecessary for the most part in group approaches to marriage counseling.

Besides the obvious benefit of couples's learning that other pairs are having many of the same difficulties they are, the group setting presents an excellent opportunity for feedback from other married couples. This feedback often results in couples's learning more about the way they interact with others than would be possible in a traditional marital counseling experience. In addition, other couples can suggest ways they have dealt with problems, and that may be of some value.

Vander Kolk (1985) suggests that role-playing is an effective technique in marital group counseling. He suggests that role-playing forces clients to act out their feelings, attitudes, and perceptions of others, giving the group an opportunity to view member behavior firsthand. Behavior and feelings that have not been expressed in the group will surface as role-players act out feelings rather than holding them in or talking about them. As a result, group participants see the behavior and get a more accurate picture of the problem with greater accuracy in perception and reaction. Likewise, couples may see behavior that relates to their own marital relationship and gain insight as to the nature of their own difficulties. Vander Kolk goes on to suggest three specific role-playing techniques:

1. The couple may role-play themselves.
2. The couple may role-play each other.
3. Other members of the group may role-play a target couple.

Thus, counseling groups for couples provide opportunities for individuals in intimate relationships to examine the quality of their relationship, to determine what issues are preventing genuine intimacy, to make decisions concerning how they would like their lives together to be changed, and to explore those conflicts which have a continuing effect on their lives together. In doing so, couples are likely to learn that in order to keep their relationship a satisfying one they must be committed to working hard at it, making that relationship among their highest priorities. They must be willing to share their concerns and fears with each other, learning that the risk of creating a problem within the relationship is not nearly as great from sharing those concerns as it is from not sharing those concerns and letting the problem continue to develop. Finally, couples are likely to learn the importance of providing flexibility for the spouse to think, feel, or value differently, without that difference being a threat to the relationship.

Individuals wishing to use group counseling with married couples are urged to read:

1. *Marriage Counseling in Groups* (Ohlsen, 1979).
2. *Group Counseling* (Ohlsen, 1977).
3. *Introduction to Group Counseling and Psychotherapy* (Vander Kolk, 1985).
4. *Groups: Process and Practice* (Corey & Corey, 1987).
5. *Group Counseling* (Gazda, 1984).

GROUP COUNSELING IN SPECIAL AREAS

Chemical Dependence

During the 1980s, a major thrust in counseling has been in providing help for victims of chemical dependence. Rapidly increasing numbers of individuals have sought help in treatment centers, as well as in outpatient treatment programs for dealing with their alcohol and drug usage problems. Although many of the programs that provide treatment are "self-help" programs which will be discussed later, there has been an increasing need for counselors to be familiar with the specific problems inherent in those who are chemically dependent. In addition, group approaches to treating chemical-dependent victims are by far the most utilized treatment methods. Very little one-to-one counseling is provided because, traditionally, professionals in the field have believed that the group setting is the most potent way of treating those with this problem. The influence of Alcoholics Anonymous, which consists of self-help groups, has contributed to this emphasis on a group setting.

In addition to a knowledge and skill base that is relevant in all group counseling, group leaders who work with those who are chemically dependent must also have a knowledge of the basic psychological factors and needs that relate to the disease. This knowledge permits the group leader to place a focus in the group on those issues that require major emphasis. By being aware of the kinds of psychological problems that substance abusers are likely to experience, the group leader can more easily cut through the verbiage and get to the heart of the difficulty.

Probably the most important psychological issue is denial. Few substance abusers readily admit that they have a problem in their use of alcohol and other drugs. They tend to make rationalizations or excuses for their usage, to minimize the amount of usage that they have, or to place a focus on the usage of other individuals in an attempt to take the focus off themselves. The first step the group leader must take with a new individual or a new group is to confront this tendency toward denial directly and then work toward the individuals' openly admitting that they have a problem in the usage of chemical substances.

Other psychological issues have been clearly linked to the misuse, or abuse, of mood-altering chemicals. Drug abusers have been characterized as having an external locus of control—that is, the belief that their lives are controlled by external forces such as fate or chance (Williams, 1973). These individuals have also been shown to have lowered self-esteem and increased anxiety and depression. Most professionals in the field believe that individuals who have become chemically dependent have major defects in their psychological defenses, so that they experience feelings of hurt, anger, shame, loneliness, aggression, and depression in a much stronger way than these feelings are ordinarily experienced. These individuals turn to mood-altering chemicals in the hopes of diminishing their painful emotions (at least temporarily) and coping better. The group leader must thus be aware that the ordinary empathic response must be intensified in its expression, if such individuals are to feel that they are truly understood in their suffering.

Anger needs special consideration. Individuals who are chemically dependent tend to have a great deal of anger bottled up inside. In spite of some aggressive behavior that would suggest that they have found more violent means of expressing anger, they have generally repressed that anger except when drinking or using a chemical substance. The group setting offers a unique opportunity to allow these individuals to express their anger and to learn that such expression can be accomplished without losing self-control and physically harming someone.

Even more important than with other types of group members, chemically dependent individuals require a strong therapeutic alliance at the very beginning of group treatment. Especially if the group leader is not a recovering chemical-dependent himself, the group leader must show some understanding of the nature of the problem as well as the difficulties involved in staying clean and dry. The group leader must become quite active in communicating an attitude of interested, supportive empathy, even though confrontation may be provided as well. Cynical or moral judgments on the part of the leader will destroy the group before it ever begins. Because the chemically dependent individual has been experiencing a life that is out of control, major emphasis during the early part of group counseling must be on providing structure, even if that structure deals primarily with what is to be accomplished as part of the group process. Setting goals, establishing norms, setting boundaries (e.g., no one allowed in the group who has been drinking or using), and establishing expectations for the individual behavior within the group are important in allowing group members to realize that at least one aspect of their life will be under control.

There are several important components of the counseling process which must be considered and utilized during this group counseling process. These include

1. Continued attendance to patient motivation, aimed at developing self-motivation, to replace external pressures;
2. Education about the nature and course of chemical-dependency, its effects on the family, and the dangers of dependency;
3. Increasing self-knowledge, particularly concerning the role of mood-altering chemicals in the individual's life: as psychoactive drug, as medicine, as weapon, as excuse, and as substitute for other satisfactions;
4. Opening new options for handling life problems without alcohol, using social support systems and improved interpersonal relationships;
5. Developing a carefully thought-out emergency plan—including telephone numbers to call and a pre-arranged way to establish a temporary safe environment—for use in case of unexpected emotional distress which might otherwise lead to relapse. (Blume, 1984, p. 342)

To these might be added two more important components: One is the development of coping skills, including assertiveness, decision-making, and relationship-building. The second is education regarding steps to be taken to improve the individual's physical health, including diet and exercise.

Unfortunately, relapses are an integral part of the history of chemical dependency, and they must be handled firmly in order to minimize the length of the drinking or using episode as well as the associated psychosocial features. While it is often difficult to determine what "caused" the return to usage, important possibilities should be explored. The relapsing member should attempt to describe the kind of emotional and cognitive patterns that were occurring just prior to the relapse. In addition, the group leader must try to reduce the feelings of guilt and personal failure on the part of the relapsing individual as well as process the effects on the other group members who may feel threatened, angry, or frustrated. It is important, though often difficult, for group leaders to remember that individuals are responsible for their own behavior, including the maintenance of an abstinent state.

Confrontation, various cognitive techniques, and techniques for helping individuals become more aware of the emotions that they are experiencing are particularly important in working with those who are chemically dependent. It has been very useful to help these individuals label cognitively the feelings of anxiety, depression, or anger that had been conditioned to the experience of alcohol and other drug cravings. In addition, individuals can be helped to look at the kind of irrational, illogical thinking that has supported their use of mood-altering chemicals and justified them.

Members of a counseling group focusing on problems in the use of alcohol and other drugs often need to develop new ways to structure leisure time and to handle feelings and situations that were previously dealt with by drinking. Thus, according to the individual member's needs, counseling focuses on trying out new behaviors, from practicing self-assertion to learning patience, from controlling one's temper to expressing anger. Most important, individuals need to learn how to relax, to enjoy the pleasures of living, and to express affection without a drink or drug. Thus, the identification and discussion of feelings and aspects of self-care must receive prominant attention.

Individuals planning to work in the area of chemical dependency counseling can get further information by reading

1. *Loosening the Grip* (Kinney & Leaton, 1983).
2. *Group Counseling* (Gazda, 1984).
3. *Essentials of Chemical Dependency Counseling* (Lawson, Ellis, & Rivers, 1984).
4. *Intensive Psychotherapy of Alcoholism* (Forrest, 1984).

Eating Disorders

As in the area of chemical-dependency, but at a lesser rate of occurrence, there are an increasing number of individuals who are seeking help for eating disorders. These include anorexics (individuals who have suffered severe weight loss, have severe body image disturbances, and who are preoccupied with an exaggerated goal of thinness), bulimics (individuals who have an intense desire for thinness, but who engage in binge eating and who utilize vomiting, excessive use of laxatives, or excessive exercise in an attempt to rid themselves of the calories gained from the binge eating), and compulsive overeaters (individuals who cannot control the amount of eating that they do). Because the psychological characteristics and needs of anorexics tend to be somewhat different from the characteristics and needs of bulimics and compulsive overeaters, working with these individuals in groups requires two basic sets of information.

Individuals suffering from anorexia nervosa have been described as being very difficult to treat in group therapy. Despite a restoration of body weight, the anorexic often remains withdrawn, anxious, rigid, egocentric, and preoccupied with body weight and food, having extreme difficulty in identifying and expressing feelings (Hall, 1985). Anorexics often attempt to be the ''perfect'' patient, describing the feelings they believe the group leader wants them to have rather than their actual feelings. Such characteristics do make group therapy difficult, since facing a whole group of such individuals is a highly demanding task for the group leader. However, such individuals do tend to respond better to group therapy than to individual therapy. In particular, those who are most likely to benefit from a group include

1. Those who are not severely ill, but are gaining weight or are relatively stable;
2. Those who are highly motivated;
3. Those who have benefited psychologically from other treatments;
4. Those who are not totally isolated or withdrawn;
5. Those in whom denial or intellectualization is not predominant and who show some capacity for psychological-mindedness, ability to reveal feelings, and sensitivity to others;
6. Those for whom another treatment approach (e.g., family therapy) is not indicated or where a combination of other treatment with group therapy is practical;
7. Those who are liked by the group leader and have the potential to be liked by other group members. (Hall, 1985, p. 220)

Anorexics, however, do share with bulimics many characteristics that can be approached in group sessions. These characteristics include (a) a feeling of being unable to control the direction of their lives or of all important relationships; (b) an inability to know what they really want or who they really are, including a sense of constant mental turmoil and confusion at having to wear a mask of happiness for the sake of others; (c) relatedly, an obsession with the way they look, a strong fear of getting fat, and a state of chronic depression over their eating patterns; (d) an overriding feeling of obligation toward or protectiveness for certain other family members; and (e) an orientation toward poor extremes of faking, affect, and behavior (Schwartz, Barrett, & Saba, 1985, p. 285).

With these issues in mind, the group leader who conducts a group for individuals with eating disorders needs to focus on many of the same issues that are found for individuals who are chemically dependent. Denial, anger, a lack of coping skills, and a sense of life's being out of control are commonly found with individuals having eating disorders. Thus the same caring, supportive approach that intertwines understanding and confrontation is necessary in being facilitative with such individuals.

Further reading that will be helpful for those who plan to work in the area of counseling those with eating disorders can be done in

1. *Anorexia Nervosa and Bulimia: A Handbook For Counselors and Therapists* (Neumann & Halverson, 1983).
2. *Handbook of Psychotherapy for Anorexia Nervosa and Bulimia* (Garner & Garfinkel, 1985).
3. *Anorexia Nervosa* (Selvini-Palazzoli, 1974).
4. *The Golden Cage* (Bruch, 1978).

Career Counseling Groups

In recent years, schools and agencies have increasingly used group procedures for working with individuals who are dealing with some aspect or another of career development. The advantages of such an approach, extending beyond the obvious economic consideration, include peer support, the opportunity to compare one's perceptions about particular jobs with the perceptions of others in the group, and the opportunity to learn and practice those social and communication skills that may be important in various careers. In addition, the group leader's ability to observe each individual in a social setting can lead to the remediation of some problems affecting the individual's work, because work is often a social activity.

Career counseling groups can be designed to meet various needs. To some extent, the design will reflect the leader's theoretical orientation to career development as well as the factors he or she considers significant in each individual's career development. Thus, one step in becoming a career counseling group leader is to study the major theories of career development and to determine which of those theoretical approaches is most consistent with his or her ideas. By establishing a strong theoretical base, the group leader has a foundation on which to base the activities and interaction of the group sessions.

Content areas of career counseling groups tend to be similar, although some programs emphasize certain areas over others. Vander Kolk (1985) writes that the career counseling group will ordinarily include aspects of the following categories: self-appraisal, identification of work values, vocational exploration, decision-making skills, and the development of a career plan. In addition, some career counseling groups may focus on job placement, in which the emphasis will be on the development of a resume, the completion of an application, the identification of jobs, the contacting of employers, and the development of interviewing skills.

During the past decade there has been an increased need for career counselors to deal with special issues. One of these is mid-life career changes, Many individuals have either been forced by technological change to seek a new career or have chosen to seek a new career that provides the opportunity for greater job satisfaction. A second area with increased emphasis involves the ''displaced homemaker.'' These individuals are typically women who reenter the job market after a number of years of not being employed outside the home. Often these individuals face a real sense of uncertainty and frustration in determining what direction job choices might take. Related to this issue is that of dual-career marriages, which, while giving couples many increased opportunities, also increases the stress of their daily lives. Each partner's role may change. Differences in the division of responsibilities within the home may change. Males may find that their careers are no longer the determining factor in decisions about where the couple lives and the lifestyle in which they engage. Females may experience severe distress trying to balance traditional and nontraditional roles. Demanding work schedules can also decrease the amount of time that the two individuals have for each other.

Skilled group leaders in career counseling must also learn how to integrate group experiences and the use of various informational packages that are available. With the arrival of computer software packages that complement vocational development, individuals are able to catalog and call up information about the world of work almost instantaneously. In addition, there are a number of career testing and career information materials that are helpful in career development. Likewise, various structured approaches to career counseling have been developed: the Vocational Exploration Group (Daane, 1972), the PATH System (Figler, 1979), the Job Seeking Skills program (Bakeman, 1971), and the Job Club concept (Azrin & Besalel, 1980).

Individuals using group approaches to career counseling are encouraged to read further, including such books as

1. *Career Counseling: Models, Methods, and Materials* (Crites, 1981).
2. *Career Counseling: Theoretical and Practical Perspectives* (Weinrach, 1979).
3. *Introduction to Group Counseling and Psychotherapy* (Vander Kolk, 1985).
4. *Groups: Process and Practice* (Corey & Corey, 1987).

SUMMARY

Some groups have unique characteristics and needs, requiring the group leader to have specialized knowledge in order to facilitate their growth and development.

Group experiences for children must be organized with the need for shorter sessions and smaller groups in mind. In addition, individual goals have even greater importance for children than for adults. Using various play approaches and showing extra sensitivity to deal with the child's feelings and attitudes enables the leader to be more effective.

Adolescents present a particular challenge to the group leader as they are desperate for feelings of group acceptance and belonging. Their needs to achieve status, adequate sexual adjustment, and values and morals leave them vulnerable to strong feelings of failure and inadequacy. However, their eagerness for peer approval makes a group approach potentially powerful in working through problems.

The special needs of older adults are becoming more apparent as the median age in the United States continues to climb. Their special needs and concerns must be considered, and greater structure provided, if group counseling is to be successful.

In addition, there are specific considerations in dealing with other groups, such as groups for couples, for those who are chemically dependent, for those who have eating disorders, and for those who seek career counseling. Recognizing the emotional and psychological needs of these individuals enables the group leader to utilize a group approach in an effective, facilitative way.

REFERENCES

AXLINE, V. (1969). *Play therapy* (rev. ed.). New York: Ballantine Books.

AZRIN, N. H., & BESALEL, V. A. (1980). *Job club counselor's manual.* Baltimore: University Park Press.

BAKEMAN, M. (1971). *Job seeking skills: Reference manual.* Minneapolis: Multi-Resource Center.

BLUME, S. B. (1984). Psychotherapy in the treatment of alcoholism. In L. Grinspoon (Ed.), *Psychiatry Update: Vol. III.* (pp. 338–346). Washington, DC: American Psychiatric Press.

BRUCH, H. (1978). *The golden cage.* Cambridge, MA: Harvard University Press.

BUSSE, E. W., & PFEIFFER, E. (Eds.). (1973). *Mental illness in later life.* Washington, DC: American Psychiatric Association.

COREY, G., & COREY, M. S. (1987). *Group counseling: Theory and practice* (3rd ed.). Monterey, CA: Brooks/Cole.

CRITES, J. O. (1981). *Career counseling: Models, methods, and materials.* New York: McGraw-Hill.

DAANE, C. (1972). *Vocational exploration group: Theory and research.* Washington, DC: U.S. Department of Labor.

DINKMEYER, D. C., & MURO, J. J. (1979). *Group counseling: Theory and practice* (2nd ed.). Itasca, IL: F. E. Peacock.

DUNCAN, J. A., & GUMAER, J. (Eds.). (1980). *Developmental groups for children.* Springfield, IL: Charles C Thomas.

DUPONT, H. (1979). Affective development: Stage and sequence. In R. L. Mosher (Ed.), *Adolescents' development and education* (pp. 163–183). Berkeley: McCutchan.

DUSKA, R., & WHELAN, M. (1975). *Moral development: A guide to Piaget and Kohlberg.* New York: Paulist Press.

ERIKSON, E. H. (1963). *Childhood and society* (2nd ed.). New York: W. W. Norton.

ERNST, N. S., & GLAZER-WALDMAN, H. R. (Eds.). (1983). *The aged patient.* Chicago: Yearbook Medical Publishers.

FIGLER, H. E. (1979). *PATH: A career workbook for liberal arts students.* Cranston, RI: Carroll Press.

FLAVELL, J. H. (1963). *The developmental psychology of Jean Piaget.* New York: D. Van Nostrand.

FORREST, G. G. (1984). *Intensive psychotherapy of alcoholism.* Springfield, IL: Charles C Thomas.

GARNER, D. M., & GARFINKEL, P. E. (Eds.). (1985). *Handbook of psychotherapy for anorexia nervosa and bulimia.* New York: Guildford Press.

GAZDA, G. M. (1984). *Group counseling* (3rd ed.). Boston: Allyn & Bacon.

GEORGE, R. L., & CRISTIANI, T. (1983). Improving communication with older adults. In N. S. Ernst & H. R. Glazer-Waldman (Eds.), *The aged patient* (pp. 31–40). Chicago: Yearbook Medical Publishers.

GESELL, A., ILG, F. L., AMES, L. B., & BULLIS, G. E. (1946). *The child from five to ten.* New York: Harper.

GINOTT, H. G. (1961). *Group psychotherapy with children: The theory and practice of play therapy.* New York: McGraw-Hill.

GINOTT, H. G. (1968). Group therapy with children. In G. M. Gazda (Ed.), *Basic approaches to group psychotherapy and group counseling* (pp. 176–194). Springfield, IL: Charles C Thomas.

HALL, A. (1985). Group psychotherapy for anorexia nervosa. In D. M. Garner & P. E. Garfinkel (Eds.), *Handbook of psychotherapy for anorexia nervosa and bulimia* (pp. 213–239). New York: Guilford Press.

HAVIGHURST, R. J. (1972). *Human development and education* (3rd ed.). New York: Longman.

KINNEY, J., & LEATON, G. (1983). *Loosening the grip* (2nd ed.). St. Louis: C. V. Mosby.

LAWSON, G. W., ELLIS, D. C., & RIVERS, P. C. (1984). *Essentials of chemical dependency counseling.* Rockville, MD: Aspen.

LOEVINGER, J. (1976). *Ego development: Conceptions and theories.* San Francisco: Jossey-Bass.

McCANDLESS, B. R. (1970). *Adolescents: Behavior and development.* Hinsdale, IL: Dryden.

NEUMANN, P. A., & HALVERSON, P. A. (1983). *Anorexia nervosa and bulimia: A handbook for counselors and therapists.* New York: Van Nostrand Reinhold.

OAKLANDER, V. (1978). *Windows to our children.* Moab, UT: Real People Press.

OHLSEN, M. M. (1977). *Group counseling* (2nd ed.). New York: Holt, Rinehart & Winston.

OHLSEN, M. (1979). *Marriage counseling in groups.* Champaign, IL: Research Press.

SALISBURY, H. (1975). Counseling the elderly: A neglected area in counselor education. *Counselor Education and Supervision, 14,* 237–238.

SCHWARTZ, R. C., BARRETT, M. J., & SABA, G. (1985). Family therapy for bulimia. In D. M. Garner & P. E. Garfinkel (Eds.), *Handbook of psychotherapy for anorexia nervosa and bulimia* (pp. 280–307). New York: Guilford Press.

SELVINI-PALAZZOLI, M. (1974). *Anorexia nervosa.* London: Chaucer.

SUPER, D. E. (1957). *Vocational development: A framework for research.* New York: Teachers College Press.

TYRON, C., & LILIENTHAL, J. W. (1950). Developmental tasks: I. The concept and its importance. In ASCD, *Fostering mental health in our schools: 1950 Yearbook* (pp. 46–63). Washington, DC: Author.

VANDER KOLK, C. J. (1985). *Introduction to group counseling and psychotherapy.* Columbus, OH: Charles E. Merrill.

WADSWORTH, B. J. (1971). *Piaget's theory of cognitive development.* New York: Longman.

WEINRACH, S. G. (Ed.). (1979). *Career counseling: Theoretical and practical perspectives.* New York: McGraw-Hill.

WILLIAMS, A. F. (1973). Personality and other characteristics associated with cigarette smoking among young teenagers. *Journal of Health and Social Behavior, 14,* 374–380.

SUGGESTED ACTIVITIES

In the Classroom

1. With a partner, discuss the following

   a. Is it rare to find group goals in group counseling for children?

   b. Is group cohesion important in group counseling with children?

   c. How permissive should the leader of a children's group be?

2. With a partner, examine and check out from an educational library a group kit which includes a puppet or materials for elementary children. Make arrangements with your instructor to briefly show the puppet or materials to your class.

3. In a small group, discuss your comfort level in handling discussion topics on human sexuality with adolescents. Take time to role-play adolescents asking the group leader specific questions about orgasm, birth control, and AIDS.

4. In a small group, take turns as the group leader to introduce a role-play exercise of one's choice to a group of couples. Have the couples (the small group members) then give each leader feedback about his or her directions and instructions.

On Your Own

1. Make arrangements to observe counseling groups with children and/or with older adults. Be prepared to share your observations with the rest of the class.

2. Make arrangements to interview an experienced counselor in substance abuse. During your conversation check out some of the ideas from this chapter, such as the tendency of patients to engage in denial, the tendency of group members to blame others or factors outside themselves for their problems, the need for empathy to be intensified with such clients, and the need for special focus on anger.

3. Read at least one of the books suggested for extra reading and be ready to summarize its major contributions in class.

APPENDIX I
ETHICAL GUIDELINES FOR GROUP LEADERS (1980 REVISION), APPROVED BY THE ASGW EXECUTIVE BOARD, NOVEMBER 11, 1980

PREAMBLE

One characteristic of any professional group is the possession of a body of knowledge and skills and mutually acceptable ethical standards for putting them into practice. Ethical standards consist of those principles which have been formally and publically acknowledged by the membership of a profession to serve as guidelines governing professional conduct, discharge of duties, and resolution of moral dilemmas. In this document, the Association for Specialists in Group Work has identified the standards of conduct necessary to maintain and regulate the high standards of integrity and leadership among its members.

The Association for Specialists in Group Work recognizes the basic commitment of its members to the Ethical Standards of its parent organization, the American Personnel and Guidance Association and nothing in this document shall be construed to supplant that code. These standards are intended to complement the APGA standards in the area of group work by clarifying the nature of ethical responsibility of the counselor in the group setting and by stimulating a greater concern for competent group leadership.

The following ethical guidelines have been organized under three categories: the leader's responsibility for providing information about group work to clients, the group leader's responsibility for providing group counseling services to clients, and the group leader's responsibility for safeguarding the standards of ethical practice.

A. RESPONSIBILITY FOR PROVIDING INFORMATION ABOUT GROUP WORK AND GROUP SERVICES

A-1. Group leaders shall fully inform group members, in advance and preferably in writing, of the goals in the group, qualifications of the leader, and procedures to be employed.

A-2. The group leader shall conduct a pre-group interview with each prospective member for purposes of screening, orientation, and, insofar as possible, shall select group members whose needs and goals are compatible with the established goals of the group; who will not impede the group process; and whose well-being will not be jeopardized by the group experience.

A-3. Group leaders shall protect members by defining clearly what confidentiality means, why it is important, and the difficulties involved in enforcement.

A-4. Group leaders shall explain, as realistically as possible, exactly what services can and cannot be provided within the particular group structure offered.

A-5. Group leaders shall provide prospective clients with specific information about any specialized or experimental activities in which they may be expected to participate.

A-6. Group leaders shall stress the personal risks involved in any group, especially regarding potential life-changes, and help group members explore their readiness to face these risks.

A-7. Group leaders shall inform members that participation is voluntary and that they may exit from the group at any time.

A-8. Group leaders shall inform members about recording of sessions and how tapes will be used.

B. RESPONSIBILITY FOR PROVIDING GROUP SERVICES TO CLIENTS

B-1. Group leaders shall protect member rights against physical threats, intimidation, coercion, and undue peer pressure insofar as is reasonably possible.

B-2. Group leaders shall refrain from imposing their own agendas, needs, and values on group members.

B-3. Group leaders shall insure to the extent that it is reasonably possible that each member has the opportunity to utilize group resources and interact within the group by minimizing barriers such as rambling and monopolizing time.

B-4. Group leaders shall make every reasonable effort to treat each member individually and equally.

B-5. Group leaders shall abstain from inappropriate personal relationships with members throughout the duration of the group and any subsequent professional involvement.

B-6. Group leaders shall help promote independence of members from the group in the most efficient period of time.

B-7. Group leaders shall not attempt any technique unless thoroughly trained in its use or under supervision by an expert familiar with the intervention.

B-8. Group leaders shall not condone the use of alcohol or drugs directly prior to or during group sessions.

B-9. Group leaders shall make every effort to assist clients in developing their personal goals.

B-10. Group leaders shall provide between-session consultation to group members and follow-up after termination of the group, as needed or requested.

C. RESPONSIBILITY FOR SAFEGUARDING ETHICAL PRACTICE

C-1. Group leaders shall display these standards or make them available to group members.

C-2. Group leaders have the right to expect ethical behavior from colleagues and are obligated to rectify or disclose incompetent, unethical behavior demonstrated by a colleague by taking the following actions:

    a. To confront the individual with the apparent violation of ethical guidelines for the purposes of protecting the safety of any clients and to help the group leader correct any inappropriate behaviors.

    b. Such a complaint should be made in writing including the specific facts *and dates* of the alleged violation and all relevant supporting data. The complaint should be forwarded to:

        The Ethics Committee,
        c/o The President
        Association of Specialists in Group Work
        Two Skyline Place, Suite 400
        5203 Leesburg Pike
        Falls Church, Virginia 22041

The envelope must be marked "CONFIDENTIAL" in order to assure confidentiality for both the accuser(s) and the alleged violator(s). Upon receipt, the President shall (a) check on membership status of the charged member(s), (b) confer with legal counsel, and (c) send the case with all pertinent documents to the chairperson of the ASGW Ethics Committee within ten (10) working days after the receipt of the complaint.

c. If it is determined by the Ethics and Professional Standards Committee that the alleged breach of ethical conduct constitutes a violation of the "Ethical Guidelines," then an investigation will be started within ten (10) days by at least one member of the Committee plus two additional ASGW members in the locality of the alleged violation. The investigating committee chairperson shall: (a) acknowledge receipt of the complaint, (b) review the complaint and supporting data, (c) send a letter of acknowledgment to the member(s) of the complaint regarding alleged violations along with a request for a response and relevant information related to the complaint and (d) inform members of the Ethics Committee by letter of the case and present a plan of action for investigation.

d. All information, correspondence, and activities of the Ethics Committee will remain confidential. It shall be determined that no person serving as an investigator on a case have any disqualifying relationship with the alleged violator(s).

e. The charged party(ies) will have not more than 30 days in which to answer the charges in writing. The charged party(ies) will have free access to all cited evidence from which to make a defense, including the right to legal counsel and a formal hearing before the ASGW Ethics Committee.

f. Based upon the investigation of the Committee and any designated local ASGW members one of the following recommendations may be made to the Executive Board for appropriate action:
    1. Advise that the charges be dropped.
    2. Reprimand and admonishment against repetition of the charged conduct.
    3. Notify the charged member(s) of his/her right to a formal hearing before the ASGW Ethics Committee, and request a response be made to the Ethics Chairperson as to his/her decision on the matter. Such hearing would be conducted in accordance with the APGA Policy and Procedures for Processing Complaints of Ethical Violations, "Procedures for Hearings," and would be scheduled for a time coinciding with the annual APGA convention. Conditions for such hearing shall also be in accordance with the APGA Policy and Procedures document, "Options Available to the Ethics Committee, item 3."
    4. Suspension of membership for a specified period from ASGW.
    5. Dismissal from membership in ASGW.

APPENDIX II
ETHICAL STANDARDS, AMERICAN ASSOCIATION FOR COUNSELING AND DEVELOPMENT

PREAMBLE

The American Personnel and Guidance Association is an educational, scientific, and professional organization whose members are dedicated to the enhancement of the worth, dignity, potential, and uniqueness of each individual and thus to the service of society.

The Association recognizes that the role definitions and work settings of its members include a wide variety of academic disciplines, levels of academic preparation and agency services. This diversity reflects the breadth of the Association's interest and influence. It also poses challenging complexities in efforts to set standards for the performance of members, desired requisite preparation or practice, and supporting social, legal, and ethical controls.

The specification of ethical standards enables the Association to clarify to present and future members and to those served by members, the nature of ethical responsibilities held in common by its members.

The existence of such standards serves to stimulate greater concern by members for their own professional functioning and for the conduct of fellow professionals such as counselors, guidance and student personnel workers, and others in the helping professions. As the ethical code of the Association, this document establishes principles that define the ethical behavior of Association members.

SECTION A: GENERAL

1. The member influences the development of the profession by continuous efforts to improve professional practices, teaching, services, and research. Professional growth is continuous throughout the member's career and is exemplified by the development of a philosophy that explains why and how a member functions in the helping relationship. Members must gather data on their effectiveness and be guided by the findings.

2. The member has a responsibility both to the individual who is served and to the institution within which the service is performed to maintain high standards of professional conduct. The member strives to maintain the highest levels of professional services offered to the individuals to be served. The member also strives to assist the agency, organization, or institution in providing the highest caliber of professional services. The acceptance of employment in an institution implies that the member is in agreement with the general policies and principles of the institution. Therefore the professional activities of the member are also in accord with the objectives of the institution. If, despite concerted efforts, the member cannot reach agreement with the employer as to acceptable standards of conduct that allow for changes in institutional policy conducive to the positive growth and development of clients, then terminating the affiliation should be seriously considered.

3. Ethical behavior among professional associates, both members and nonmembers, must be expected at all times. When information is possessed that raises doubt as to the ethical behavior of professional colleagues, whether Association members or not, the member must take action to attempt to rectify such a condition. Such action shall use the institution's channels first and then use procedures established by the state Branch, Division, or Association.

4. The member neither claims nor implies professional qualifications exceeding those possessed and is responsible for correcting any misrepresentations of these qualifications by others.

5. In establishing fees for professional counseling services, members must consider the financial status of clients and locality. In the event that the established fee structure is inappropriate for a client, assistance must be provided in finding comparable services of acceptable cost.

6. When members provide information to the public or to subordinates, peers or supervisors, they have a responsibility to ensure that the content is general, unidentified client information that is accurate, unbiased, and consists of objective, factual data.

7. With regard to the delivery of professional services, members should accept only those positions for which they are professionally qualified.

8. In the counseling relationship the counselor is aware of the intimacy of the relationship and maintains respect for the client and avoids engaging in activities that seek to meet the counselor's personal needs at the expense of that client. Through awareness of the negative impact of both racial and sexual stereotyping and discrimination, the counselor guards the individual rights and personal dignity of the client in the counseling relationship.

SECTION B: COUNSELING RELATIONSHIP

This section refers to practices and procedures of individual and/or group counseling relationships.

The member must recognize the need for client freedom of choice. Under those circumstances where this is not possible, the member must apprise clients of restrictions that may limit their freedom of choice.

1. The member's *primary* obligation is to respect the integrity and promote the welfare of the client(s), whether the client(s) is (are) assisted individually or in a group relationship. In a group setting, the member is also responsible for taking reasonable precautions to protect individuals from physical and/or psychological trauma resulting from interaction within the group.

2. The counseling relationship and information resulting therefrom [must] be kept confidential, consistent with the obligations of the member as a professional person. In a group counseling setting, the counselor must set a norm of confidentiality regarding all group participants' disclosures.

3. If an individual is already in a counseling relationship with another professional person, the member does not enter into a counseling relationship without first contacting and receiving the approval of that other professional. If the member discovers that the client is in another counseling relationship after the counseling relationship begins, the member must gain the consent of the other professional or terminate the relationship, unless the client elects to terminate the other relationship.

4. When the client's condition indicates that there is clear and imminent danger to the client or others, the member must take reasonable personal action or inform responsible authorities. Consultation with other professionals must be used where

possible. The assumption of responsibility for the client's behavior must be taken only after careful deliberation. The client must be involved in the resumption of responsibility as quickly as possible.

5. Records of the counseling relationship, including interview notes, test data, correspondence, tape recordings, and other documents, are to be considered professional information for use in counseling and they should not be considered a part of the records of the institution or agency in which the counselor is employed unless specified by state statute or regulation. Revelation to others of counseling material must occur only upon the expressed consent of the client.

6. Use of data derived from a counseling relationship for purposes of counselor training or research shall be confined to content that can be disguised to ensure full protection of the identity of the subject client.

7. The member must inform the client of the purposes, goals, techniques, rules of procedure and limitations that may affect the relationship at or before the time that the counseling relationship is entered.

8. The member must screen prospective group participants, especially when the emphasis is on self-understanding and growth through self-disclosure. The member must maintain an awareness of the group participants' compatibility throughout the life of the group.

9. The member may choose to consult with any other professionally competent person about a client. In choosing a consultant, the member must avoid placing the consultant in a conflict of interest situation that would preclude the consultant's being a proper party to the member's efforts to help the client.

10. If the member determines an inability to be of professional assistance to the client, the member must either avoid initiating the counseling relationship or immediately terminate that relationship. In either event, the member must suggest appropriate alternatives. (The member must be knowledgeable about referral resources so that a satisfactory referral can be initiated.) In the event the client declines the suggested referral, the member is not obligated to continue the relationship.

11. When the member has other relationships, particularly if an administrative, supervisory and/or evaluative nature with an individual seeking counseling services, the member must not serve as the counselor but should refer the individual to another professional. Only in instances where such an alternative is unavailable and where the individual's situation warrants counseling intervention should the member enter into and/or maintain a counseling relationship. Dual relationships with clients that might impair the member's objectivity and professional judgment (e.g., as with close friends or relatives, sexual intimacies with any client) must be avoided and/or the counseling relationship terminated through referral to another competent professional.

12. All experimental methods of treatment must be clearly indicated to prospective recipients and safety precautions are to be adhered to by the member.

13. When the member is engaged in short-term group treatment/training programs (e.g., marathons and other encounter-type or growth groups), the member ensures that there is professional assistance available during and following the group experience.

14. Should the member be engaged in a work setting that calls for any variation from the above statements, the member is obligated to consult with other professionals whenever possible to consider justifiable alternatives.

SECTION C: MEASUREMENT AND EVALUATION

The primary purpose of educational and psychological testing is to provide descriptive measures that are objective and interpretable in either comparative or absolute terms. The member must recognize the need to interpret the statements that follow as applying to the whole range of appraisal techniques including test and nontest data. Test results constitute only one of a variety of pertinent sources of information for personnel, guidance, and counseling decisions.

1. The member must provide specific orientation or information to the examinee(s) prior to and following the test administration so that the results of testing may be placed in proper perspective with other relevant factors. In so doing, the member must recognize the effects of socioeconomic, ethnic and cultural factors on test scores. It is the member's professional responsibility to use additional unvalidated information carefully in modifying interpretation of the test results.

2. In selecting tests for use in a given situation or with a particular client, the member must consider carefully the specific validity, reliability, and appropriateness of the test(s). *General* validity, reliabilty and the like may be questioned legally as well as ethically when tests are used for vocational and educational selection, placement, or counseling.

3. When making any statements to the public about tests and testing, the member must give accurate information and avoid false claims or misconceptions. Special efforts are often required to avoid unwarranted connotations of such terms as *IQ* and *grade equivalent scores.*

4. Different tests demand different levels of competence for administration, scoring, and interpretation. Members must recognize the limits of their competence and perform only those functions for which they are prepared.

5. Tests must be administered under the same conditions that were established in their standardization. When tests are not administered under standard conditions or when unusual behavior or irregularities occur during the testing session, those conditions must be noted and the results designated as invalid or of questionable validity. Unsupervised or inadequately supervised test-taking, such as the use of tests through the mails, is considered unethical. On the other hand, the use of instruments that are so designed or standardized to be self-administered and self-scored, such as interest inventories, is to be encouraged.

6. The meaningfulness of test results used in personnel, guidance, and counseling functions generally depends on the examinee's unfamiliarity with the specific items on the test. Any prior coaching or dissemination of the test materials can invalidate test results. Therefore, test security is one of the professional obligations of the member. Conditions that produce most favorable test results must be made known to the examinee.

7. The purpose of testing and the explicit use of the results must be made known to the examinee prior to testing. The counselor must ensure that instrument limitations are not exceeded and that periodic review and/or retesting are made to prevent client stereotyping.

8. The examinee's welfare and explicit prior understanding must be the criteria for determining the recipients of the test results. The member must see that specific

interpretation accompanies any release of individual or group test data. The interpretation of test data must be related to the examinee's particular concerns.

9. The member must be cautious when interpreting the results of research instruments possessing insufficient technical data. The specific purposes for the use of such instruments must be stated explicitly to examinees.

10. The member must proceed with caution when attempting to evaluate and interpret the performance of minority group members or other persons who are not represented in the norm group on which the instrument was standardized.

11. The member must guard against the appropriation, reproduction, or modifications of published tests or parts thereof without acknowledgment and permission from the previous publisher.

12. Regarding the preparation, publication and distribution of tests, reference should be made to:

   a. *Standards for Educational and Psychological Tests and Manuals,* revised edition, 1974, published by the American Psychological Association on behalf of itself, the American Educational Research Association and the National Council on Measurement in Education.

   b. The responsible use of tests: A position paper of AMEG, APGA, and NCME. *Measurement and Evaluation in Guidance,* 1972, 5, 385-388.

   c. "Responsibilities of Users of Standardized Tests," APGA, *Guidepost,* October 5, 1978, pp. 5-8.

SECTION D: RESEARCH AND PUBLICATION

1. Guidelines on research with human subjects shall be adhered to, such as:

   a. *Ethical Principles in the Conduct of Research with Human Participants,* Washington, D.C.: American Psychological Association, Inc., 1973.

   b. Code of Federal Regulations, Title 45, Subtitle A, Part 46, as currently issued.

2. In planning any research activity dealing with human subjects, the member must be aware of and responsive to all pertinent ethical principles and ensure that the research problem, design, and execution are in full compliance with them.

3. Responsibility for ethical research practice lies with the principal researcher, while others involved in the research activities share ethical obligation and full responsibility for their own actions.

4. In research with human subjects, researchers are responsible for the subjects' welfare throughout the experiment and they must take all reasonable precautions to avoid causing injurious psychological, physical, or social effects on their subjects.

5. All research subjects must be informed of the purpose of the study except when withholding information or providing misinformation to them is essential to the investigation. In such research the member must be responsible for corrective action as soon as possible following completion of the research.

6. Participation in research must be voluntary. Involuntary participation is appropriate only when it can be demonstrated that participation will have no harmful effects on subjects and is essential to the investigation.

7. When reporting research results, explicit mention must be made of all variables and

conditions known to the investigator that might affect the outcome of the investigation or the interpretation of the data.

8. The member must be responsible for conducting and reporting investigations in a manner that minimizes the possibility that results will be misleading.

9. The member has an obligation to make available sufficient original research data to qualified others who may wish to replicate the study.

10. When supplying data, aiding in the research of another person, reporting research results, or in making original data available, due care must be taken to disguise the identity of the subjects in the absence of specific authorization from such subjects to do otherwise.

11. When conducting and reporting research, the member must be familiar with, and give recognition to, previous work on the topic, as well as to observe all copyright laws and follow the principles of giving full credit to all to whom credit is due.

12. The member must give due credit through joint authorship, acknowledgment, footnote statements, or other appropriate means to those who have contributed significantly to the research and/or publication, in accordance with such contributions.

13. The member must communicate to other members the results of any research judged to be of professional or scientific value. Results reflecting unfavorably on institutions, programs, services, or vested interests must not be withheld for such reasons.

14. If members agree to cooperate with another individual in research and/or publication, they incur an obligation to cooperate as promised in terms of punctuality of performance and with full regard to the completeness and accuracy of the information required.

15. Ethical practice requires that authors not submit the same manuscript or one essentially similar in content, for simultaneous publication consideration by two or more journals. In addition, manuscripts published in whole or in substantial part in another journal or published work should not be submitted for publication without acknowledgment and permission from the previous publication.

SECTION E: CONSULTING

Consultation refers to a voluntary relationship between a professional helper and help-needing individual, group or social unit in which the consultant is providing help to the client(s) in defining and solving a work-related problem or potential problem with a client or client system. (This definition is adapted from Kurpius, DeWayne. Consultation theory and process: An integrated model. *Personnel and Guidance Journal,* 1978, 56.)

1. The member acting as consultant must have a high degree of self-awareness of his-her own values, knowledge, skills, limitations, and needs in entering a helping relationship that involves human and-or organizational change and that the focus of the relationship be on the issues to be resolved and not on the person(s) presenting the problem.

2. There must be understanding and agreement between member and client for the problem definition, change goals, and predicted consequences of interventions selected.

3. The member must be reasonably certain that she/he or the organization represented has the necessary competencies and resources for giving the kind of help that is needed now or may develop later and that appropriate referral resources are available to the consultant.

4. The consulting relationship must be one in which client adaptability and growth toward self-direction are encouraged and cultivated. The member must maintain this role consistently and not become a decision maker for the client or create a future dependency on the consultant.

5. When announcing consultant availability for services, the member conscientiously adheres to the Association's *Ethical Standards*.

6. The member must refuse a private fee or other remuneration for consultation with persons who are entitled to these services through the member's employing institution or agency. The policies of a particular agency may make explicit provisions for private practice with agency clients by members of its staff. In such instances, the clients must be apprised of other options open to them should they seek private counseling services.

SECTION F: PRIVATE PRACTICE

1. The member should assist the profession by facilitating the availability of counseling services in private as well as public settings.

2. In advertising services as a private practitioner, the member must advertise the services in such a manner so as to accurately inform the public as to services, expertise, profession, and techniques of counseling in a professional manner. A member who assumes an executive leadership role in the organization shall not permit his/her name to be used in professional notices during periods when not actively engaged in the private practice of counseling.

   The member may list the following: highest relevant degree, type and level of certification or license, type and/or description of services, and other relevant information. Such information must not contain false, inaccurate, misleading, partial, out-of-context, or deceptive material or statements.

3. Members may join in partnership/corporation with other members and-or other professionals provided that each member of the partnership or corporation makes clear the separate specialties by name in compliance with the regulations of the locality.

4. A member has an obligation to withdraw from a counseling relationship if it is believed that employment will result in violation of the *Ethical Standards*. If the mental or physical condition of the member renders it difficult to carry out an effective professional relationship or if the member is discharged by the client because the counseling relationship is no longer productive for the client, then the member is obligated to terminate the counseling relationship.

5. A member must adhere to the regulations for private practice of the locality where the services are offered.

6. It is unethical to use one's institutional affiliation to recruit clients for one's private practice.

SECTION G: PERSONNEL ADMINISTRATION

It is recognized that most members are employed in public or quasi-public institutions. The functioning of a member within an institution must contribute to the goals of the institution and vice versa if either is to accomplish their respective goals or objectives. It is therefore essential that the member and the institution function in ways to (a) make the institution's goals explicit and public; (b) make the member's contribution to institutional goals specific; and (c) foster mutual accountability for goal achievement.

To accomplish these objectives, it is recognized that the member and the employer must share responsibilities in the formulation and implementation of personnel policies.

1. Members must define and describe the parameters and levels of their professional competency.
2. Members must establish interpersonal relations and working agreements with supervisors and subordinates regarding counseling or clinical relationships, confidentiality, distinction between public and private material, maintenance, and dissemination of recorded information, work load and accountability. Working agreements in each instance must be specified and made known to those concerned.
3. Members must alert their employers to conditions that may be potentially disruptive or damaging.
4. Members must inform employers of conditions that may limit their effectiveness.
5. Members must submit regularly to professional review and evaluation.
6. Members must be responsible for inservice development of self and-or staff.
7. Members must inform their staff of goals and programs.
8. Members must provide personnel practices that guarantee and enhance the rights and welfare of each recipient of their service.
9. Members must select competent persons and assign responsibilities compatible with their skills and experiences.

SECTION H: PREPARATION STANDARDS

Members who are responsible for training others must be guided by the preparation standards of the Association and relevant Division(s). The member who functions in the capacity of trainer assumes unique ethical responsibilities that frequently go beyond that of the member who does not function in a training capacity. These ethical responsibilities are outlined as follows:

1. Members must orient students to program expectations, basic skills development, and employment prospects prior to admission to the program.
2. Members in charge of learning experiences must establish programs that integrate academic study and supervised practice.

3. Members must establish a program directed toward developing students' skills, knowledge, and self-understanding, stated whenever possible in competency or performance terms.

4. Members must identify the levels of competencies of their students in compliance with relevant Division standards. These competencies must accommodate the para-professional as well as the professional.

5. Members, through continual student evaluation and appraisal, must be aware of the personal limitations of the learner that might impede future performance. The instructor must not only assist the learner in securing remedial assistance but also screen from the program those individuals who are unable to provide competent services.

6. Members must provide a program that includes training in research commensurate with levels of role functioning. Para-professional and technician-level personnel must be trained as consumers of research. In addition, these personnel must learn how to evaluate their own and their program's effectiveness. Graduate training, especially at the doctoral level, would include preparation for original research by the member.

7. Members must make students aware of the ethical responsibilities and standards of the profession.

8. Preparatory programs must encourage students to value the ideals of service to individuals and to society. In this regard, direct financial remuneration or lack thereof must not influence the quality of service rendered. Monetary considerations must not be allowed to overshadow professional and humanitarian needs.

9. Members responsible for educational programs must be skilled as teachers and practitioners.

10. Members must present thoroughly varied theoretical positions so that students may make comparisons and have the opportunity to select a position.

11. Members must develop clear policies within their educational institutions regarding field placement and the roles of the student and the instructor in such placements.

12. Members must ensure that forms of learning focusing on self-understanding or growth are voluntary, or if required as part of the education program, are made known to prospective students prior to entering the program. When the education program offers a growth experience with an emphasis on self-disclosure or other relatively intimate or personal involvement, the member must have no administrative, supervisory, or evaluating authority regarding the participant.

13. Members must conduct an educational program in keeping the current relevant guidelines of the American Personnel and Guidance Association and its Divisions.

APPENDIX III
ETHICAL PRINCIPLES OF PSYCHOLOGISTS

This version of the Ethical Principles of Psychologists (formerly entitled Ethical Standards of Psychologists) was adopted by the American Psychological Association's Council of Representatives on January 24, 1981. The revised Ethical Principles contain both substantive and grammatical changes in each of the nine ethical principles constituting the Ethical Standards of Psychologists previously adopted by the Council of Representatives in 1979, plus a new tenth principle entitled Care and Use of Animals. Inquiries concerning the Ethical Principles of Psychologists should be addressed to the Administrative Officer for Ethics, American Psychological Association, 1200 Seventeenth Street, N.W., Washington, D.C. 20036.

These revised Ethical Principles apply to psychologists, to students of psychology, and to others who do work of a psychological nature under the supervision of a psychologist. They are also intended for the guidance of nonmembers of the Association who are engaged in psychological research or practice.

Any complaints of unethical conduct filed after January 24, 1981, shall be governed by this 1981 revision. However, conduct (a) complained about after January 24, 1981, but which occurred prior to that date, and (b) not considered unethical under prior versions of the principles but considered unethical under the 1981 revision, shall not be deemed a violation of ethical principles. Any complaints pending as of January 24, 1981, shall be governed either by the 1979 or by the 1981 version of the Ethical Principles, at the sound discretion of the Committee on Scientific and Professional Ethics and Conduct.

PREAMBLE

Psychologists respect the dignity and worth of the individual and strive for the preservation and protection of fundamental human rights. They are committed to increasing knowledge of human behavior and of people's understanding of themselves and others and to the utilization of such knowledge for the promotion of human welfare. While pursuing these objectives, they make every effort to protect the welfare of those who seek their services and of the research participants that may be the object of study. They use their skills only for purposes consistent with these values and do not knowingly permit their misuse by others. While demanding for themselves freedom of inquiry and communication, psychologists accept the responsibility this freedom requires: competence, objectivity in the application of skills, and concern for the best interests of clients, colleagues, students, research participants, and society. In the pursuit of these ideals, psychologists subscribe to principles in the following areas: 1. Responsibility, 2. Competence, 3. Moral and Legal Standards, 4. Public Statements, 5. Confidentiality, 6. Welfare of the Consumer, 7. Professional Relationships, 8. Assessment Techniques, 9. Research With Human Participants, and 10. Care and Use of Animals.

Acceptance of membership in the American Psychological Association commits the member to adherence to these principles.

Psychologists cooperate with duly constituted committees of the American Psychological Association, in particular, the Committee on Scientific and Professional Ethics and Conduct, by responding to inquiries promptly and completely. Members also respond promptly and completely to inquiries from duly constituted state association ethics committees and professional standards review committees.

PRINCIPLE 1
RESPONSIBILITY

In providing services, psychologists maintain the highest standards of their profession. They accept responsibility for the consequences of their acts and make every effort to ensure that their services are used appropriately.

a. As scientists, psychologists accept responsibility for the selection of their research topics and the methods used in investigation, analysis, and reporting. They plan their research in ways to minimize the possibility that their findings will be misleading. They provide thorough discussion of the limitations of their data, especially where their work touches on social policy or might be construed to the detriment of persons in specific age, sex, ethnic, socioeconomic, or other social groups. In publishing reports of their work, they never suppress disconfirming data, and they acknowledge the existence of alternative hypotheses and explanations of their findings. Psychologists take credit only for work they have actually done.

b. Psychologists clarify in advance with all appropriate persons and agencies the expectations for sharing and utilizing research data. They avoid relationships that may limit their objectivity or create a conflict of interest. Interference with the milieu in which data are collected is kept to a minimum.

c. Psychologists have the responsibility to attempt to prevent distortion, misuse, or suppression of psychological findings by the institution or agency of which they are employees.

d. As members of governmental or other organizational bodies, psychologists remain accountable as individuals to the highest standards of their profession.

e. As teachers, psychologists recognize their primary obligation to help others acquire knowledge and skill. They maintain high standards of scholarship by presenting psychological information objectively, fully, and accurately.

f. As practitioners, psychologists know that they bear a heavy social responsibility because their recommendations and professional actions may alter the lives of others. They are alert to personal, social, organizational, financial, or political situations and pressures that might lead to misuse of their influence.

PRINCIPLE 2
COMPETENCE

The maintenance of high standards of competence is a responsibility shared by all psychologists in the interest of the public and the profession as a whole. Psychologists recognize the boundaries of their competence and the limitations of their techniques. They only provide services and only use techniques for which they are qualified by training and experience. In those areas in which recognized standards do not yet exist, psychologists take whatever precautions are necessary to protect the welfare of their clients. They maintain knowledge of current scientific and professional information related to the services they render.

a. Psychologists accurately represent their competence, education, training, and experience. They claim as evidence of educational qualifications only those degrees obtained from institutions acceptable under the Bylaws and Rules of Council of the American Psychological Association.

b. As teachers, psychologists perform their duties on the basis of careful preparation so that their instruction is accurate, current, and scholarly.

c. Psychologists recognize the need for continuing education and are open to new procedures and changes in expectations and values over time.

d. Psychologists recognize differences among people, such as those that may be associated with age, sex, socioeconomic, and ethnic backgrounds. When necessary, they obtain training, experience, or counsel to assure competent service or research relating to such persons.

e. Psychologists responsible for decisions involving individuals or policies based on test results have an understanding of psychological or educational measurement, validation problems, and test research.

f. Psychologists recognize that personal problems and conflicts may interfere with professional effectiveness. Accordingly, they refrain from undertaking any activity in which their personal problems are likely to lead to inadequate performance or harm to a client, colleague, student, or research participant. If engaged in such activity when they become aware of their personal problems, they seek competent professional assistance to determine whether they should suspend, terminate, or limit the scope of their professional and/or scientific activities.

PRINCIPLE 3
MORAL AND LEGAL STANDARDS

Psychologists' moral and ethical standards of behavior are a personal matter to the same degree as they are for any other citizen, except as these may compromise the fulfillment of their professional responsibilities or reduce the public trust in psychology and psychologists. Regarding their own behavior, psychologists are sensitive to prevailing community standards and to the possible impact that conformity to or deviation from these standards may have upon the quality of their performance as psychologists. Psychologists are also aware of the possible impact of their public behavior upon the ability of colleagues to perform their professional duties.

a. As teachers, psychologists are aware of the fact that their personal values may affect the selection and presentation of instructional materials. When dealing with topics that may give offense, they recognize and respect the diverse attitudes that students may have toward such materials.

b. As employees or employers, psychologists do not engage in or condone practices that are inhumane or that result in illegal or unjustifiable actions. Such practices include, but are not limited to, those based on considerations of race, handicap, age, gender, sexual preference, religion, or national origin in hiring, promotion, or training.

c. In their professional roles, psychologists avoid any action that will violate or diminish the legal and civil rights of clients or of others who may be affected by their actions.

d. As practitioners and researchers, psychologists act in accord with Association standards and guidelines related to practice and to the conduct of research with human beings and animals. In the ordinary course of events, psychologists adhere to relevant governmental laws and institutional regulations. When federal, state, provincial, organizational, or institutional laws, regulations, or practices are in conflict with Association standards and guidelines, psychologists make known their commitment to Association standards and guidelines and, wherever possible, work toward a resolution of the conflict. Both practitioners and researchers are concerned with the development of such legal and quasi-legal regulations as best serve the public interest, and they work toward changing existing regulations that are not beneficial to the public interest.

PRINCIPLE 4
PUBLIC STATEMENTS

Public statements, announcements of services, advertising, and promotional activities of psychologists serve the purpose of helping the public make informed judgments and choices. Psychologists represent accurately and objectively their professional qualifications, affiliations, and functions, as well as those of the institutions or organizations with which they or the statements may be associated. In public statements providing psychological information or professional opinions or providing information about the availability of psychological products, publications, and services, psychologists base their statements on scientifically acceptable psychological findings and techniques with full recognition of the limits and uncertainties of such evidence.

a. When announcing or advertising professional services, psychologists may list the following information to describe the provider and services provided: name, highest relevant academic degree earned from a regionally accredited institution, date, type, and level of certification or licensure, diplomate status, APA membership status, address, telephone number, office hours, a brief listing of the type of psychological services offered, an appropriate presentation of fee information, foreign languages spoken, and policy with regard to third-party payments. Additional relevant or important consumer information may be included if not prohibited by other sections of these Ethical Principles.

b. In announcing or advertising the availability of psychological products, publications, or services, psychologists do not present their affiliation with any organization in a manner that falsely implies sponsorship or certification by that organization. In particular and for example, psychologists do not state APA membership or fellow status in a way to suggest that such status implies specialized professional competence or qualifications. Public statements include, but are not limited to, communication by means of periodical, book, list, directory, television, radio, or motion picture. They do not contain (i) a false, fraudulent, misleading, deceptive, or unfair statement; (ii) a misinterpretation of fact or a statement likely to mislead or deceive because in context it makes only a partial disclosure of relevant facts; (iii) a testimonial from a patient regarding the quality of a psychologists' services or products; (iv) a statement intended or likely to create false or unjustified expectations of favorable results; (v) a statement implying unusual, unique, or one-of-a-kind abilities; (vi) a statement intended or likely to appeal to a client's fears, anxieties, or emotions concerning the possible results of failure to obtain the offered services; (vii) a statement concerning the comparative desirability of offered services; (viii) a statement of direct solicitation of individual clients.

c. Psychologists do not compensate or give anything of value to a representative of the press, radio, television, or other communication medium in anticipation of or in return for professional publicity in a news item. A paid advertisement must be identified as such, unless it is apparent from the context that it is a paid advertisement. If communicated to the public by use of radio or television, an advertisement is prerecorded and approved for broadcast by the psychologist, and a recording of the actual transmission is retained by the psychologist.

d. Announcements or advertisements of "personal growth groups," clinics, and agencies give a clear statement of purpose and a clear description of the experiences to be provided. The education, training, and experience of the staff members are appropriately specified.

e. Psychologists associated with the development or promotion of psychological devices, books, or other products offered for commercial sale make reasonable efforts to ensure that announcements and advertisements are presented in a professional, scientifically acceptable, and factually informative manner.

f. Psychologists do not participate for personal gain in commercial announcements or advertisements recommending to the public the purchase or use of proprietary or single-source products or services when that participation is based solely upon their identification as psychologists.

g. Psychologists present the science of psychology and offer their services, products, and publications fairly and accurately, avoiding misrepresentation through sensationalism, exaggeration, or superficiality. Psychologists are guided by the primary obligation to aid the public in developing informed judgments, opinions, and choices.

h. As teachers, psychologists ensure that statements in catalogs and course outlines are accurate and not misleading, particularly in terms of subject matter to be covered, bases for evaluating progress, and the nature of course experiences. Announcements, brochures, or advertisements describing workshops, seminars, or other educational programs accurately describe the audience for which the program is intended as well as eligibility requirements, educational objectives, and nature of the materials to be covered. These announcements also accurately represent the education, training, and experience of the psychologists presenting the programs and any fees involved.

i. Public announcements or advertisements soliciting research participants in which clinical services or other professional services are offered as an inducement make clear the nature of the services as well as the costs and other obligations to be accepted by participants in the research.

j. A psychologist accepts the obligation to correct others who represent the psychologist's professional qualifications, or associations with products or services, in a manner incompatible with these guidelines.

k. Individual diagnostic and therapeutic services are provided only in the context of a professional psychological relationship. When personal advice is given by means of public lectures or demonstrations, newspaper or magazine articles, radio or television programs, mail, or similar media, the psychologist utilizes the most current relevant data and exercises the highest level of professional judgment.

1. Products that are described or presented by means of public lectures or demonstrations, newspaper or magazine articles, radio or television programs, or similar media meet the same recognized standards as exist for products used in the context of a professional relationship.

PRINCIPLE 5
CONFIDENTIALITY

Psychologists have a primary obligation to respect the confidentiality of information obtained from persons in the course of their work as psychologists. They reveal such information to others only with the consent of the person or the person's legal representative, except in those unusual circumstances in which not to do so would result in clear danger to the person or to others. Where appropriate, psychologists inform their clients of the legal limits of confidentiality.

a. Information obtained in clinical or consulting relationships, or evaluative data concerning children, students, employees, and others, is discussed only for professional purposes and only with persons clearly concerned with the case. Written and oral reports present only data germane to the purposes of the evaluation, and every effort is made to avoid undue invasion of privacy.

b. Psychologists who present personal information obtained during the course of professional work in writings, lectures, or other public forums either obtain adequate prior consent to do so or adequately disguise all identifying information.

c. Psychologists make provisions for maintaining confidentiality in the storage and disposal of records.

d. When working with minors or other persons who are unable to give voluntary, informed consent, psychologists take special care to protect these persons' best interests.

PRINCIPLE 6
WELFARE OF THE CONSUMER

Psychologists respect the integrity and protect the welfare of the people and groups with whom they work. When conflicts of interest arise between clients and psychologists' employing institutions, psychologists clarify the nature and direction of their loyalties and responsibilities and keep all parties informed of their commitments. Psychologists fully inform consumers as to the purpose and nature of an evaluative, treatment, educational, or training procedure, and they freely acknowledge that clients, students, or participants in research have freedom of choice with regard to participation.

a. Psychologists are continually cognizant of their own needs and of their potentially influential position vis-à-vis persons such as clients, students, and subordinates. They avoid exploiting the trust and dependency of such persons. Psychologists make every effort to avoid dual relationships that could impair their professional judgment or increase the risk of exploitation. Examples of such dual relationships include, but are not limited to, research with and treatment of employees, students, supervisees, close friends, or relatives. Sexual intimacies with clients are unethical.

    b. When a psychologist agrees to provide services to a client at the request of a third party, the psychologist assumes the responsibility of clarifying the nature of the relationships to all parties concerned.

    c. Where the demands of an organization require psychologists to violate these Ethical Principles, psychologists clarify the nature of the conflict between the demands and these principles. They inform all parties of psychologists' ethical responsibilities and take appropriate action.

    d. Psychologists make advance financial arrangements that safeguard the best interests of and are clearly understood by their clients. They neither give nor receive any remuneration for referring clients for professional services. They contribute a portion of their services to work for which they receive little or no financial return.

    e. Psychologists terminate a clinical or consulting relationship when it is reasonably clear that the consumer is not benefiting from it. They offer to help the consumer locate alternative sources of assistance.

PRINCIPLE 7
PROFESSIONAL RELATIONSHIPS

Psychologists act with due regard for the needs, special competencies, and obligations of their colleagues in psychology and other professions. They respect the prerogatives and obligations of the institutions or organizations with which these other colleagues are associated.

    a. Psychologists understand the areas of competence of related professions. They make full use of all the professional, technical, and administrative resources that serve the best interests of consumers. The absence of formal relationships with other professional workers does not relieve psychologists of the responsibility of securing for their clients the best possible professional service, nor does it relieve them of the obligation to exercise foresight, diligence, and tact in obtaining the complementary or alternative assistance needed by clients.

    b. Psychologists know and take into account the traditions and practices of other professional groups with whom they work and cooperate fully with such groups. If a person is receiving similar services from another professional, psychologists do not offer their own services directly to such a person. If a psychologist is contacted by a person who is already receiving similar services from another professional, the psychologist carefully considers that professional relationship and proceeds with caution and sensitivity to the therapeutic issues as well as the client's welfare. The psychologist discusses these issues with the client so as to minimize the risk of confusion and conflict.

c. Psychologists who employ or supervise other professionals or professionals in training accept the obligation to facilitate the further professional development of these individuals. They provide appropriate working conditions, timely evaluations, constructive consultation, and experience opportunities.

d. Psychologists do not exploit their professional relationships with clients, supervisees, students, employees, or research participants sexually or otherwise. Psychologists do not condone or engage in sexual harassment. Sexual harassment is defined as deliberate or repeated comments, gestures, or physical contacts of a sexual nature that are unwanted by the recipient.

e. In conducting research in institutions or organizations, psychologists secure appropriate authorization to conduct such research. They are aware of their obligations to future research workers and ensure that host institutions receive adequate information about the research and proper acknowledgment of their contributions.

f. Publication credit is assigned to those who have contributed to a publication in proportion to their professional contributions. Major contributions of a professional character made by several persons to a common project are recognized by joint authorship, with the individual who made the principal contribution listed first. Minor contributions of a professional character and extensive clerical or similar nonprofessional assistance may be acknowledged in footnotes or in an introductory statement. Acknowledgment through specific citations is made for unpublished as well as published material that has directly influenced the research or writing. Psychologists who compile and edit material of others for publication publish the material in the name of the originating group, if appropriate, with their own name appearing as chairperson or editor. All contributors are to be acknowledged and named.

g. When psychologists know of an ethical violation by another psychologist, and it seems appropriate, they informally attempt to resolve the issue by bringing the behavior to the attention of the psychologist. If the misconduct is of a minor nature and/or appears to be due to lack of sensitivity, knowledge, or experience, such an informal solution is usually appropriate. Such informal corrective efforts are made with sensitivity to any rights to confidentiality involved. If the violation does not seem amenable to an informal solution, or is of a more serious nature, psychologists bring it to the attention of the appropriate local, state, and/or national committee on professional ethics and conduct.

PRINCIPLE 8
ASSESSMENT TECHNIQUES

In the development, publication, and utilization of psychological assessment techniques, psychologists make every effort to promote the welfare and best interests of the client. They guard against the misuse of assessment results. They respect the client's right to know the results, the interpretations made, and the bases for their conclusions and recommendations. Psychologists make every effort to maintain the security of tests and other assessment techniques within limits of legal mandates. They strive to ensure the appropriate use of assessment techniques by others.

a. In using assessment techniques, psychologists respect the right of clients to have full explanations of the nature and purpose of the techniques in language the clients can understand, unless an explicit exception to this right has been agreed upon in advance. When the explanations are to be provided by others, psychologists establish procedures for ensuring the adequacy of these explanations.

b. Psychologists responsible for the development and standardization of psychological tests and other assessment techniques utilize established scientific procedures and observe the relevant APA standards.

c. In reporting assessment results, psychologists indicate any reservations that exist regarding validity or reliability because of the circumstances of the assessment or the inappropriateness of the norms for the person tested. Psychologists strive to ensure that the results of assessments and their interpretations are not misused by others.

d. Psychologists recognize that assessment results may become obsolete. They make every effort to avoid and prevent the misuse of obsolete measures.

e. Psychologists offering scoring and interpretation services are able to produce appropriate evidence for the validity of the programs and procedures used in arriving at interpretations. The public offering of an automated interpretation service is considered a professional-to-professional consultation. Psychologists make every effort to avoid misuse of assessment reports.

f. Psychologists do not encourage or promote the use of psychological assessment techniques by inappropriately trained or otherwise unqualified persons through teaching, sponsorship, or supervision.

PRINCIPLE 9
RESEARCH WITH HUMAN PARTICIPANTS

The decision to undertake research rests upon a considered judgment by the individual psychologist about how best to contribute to psychological science and human welfare. Having made the decision to conduct research, the psychologist considers alternative directions in which research energies and resources might be invested. On the basis of this consideration, the psychologist carries out the investigation with respect and concern for the dignity and welfare of the people who participate and with cognizance of federal and state regulations and professional standards governing the conduct of research with human participants.

a. In planning a study, the investigator has the responsibility to make a careful evaluation of its ethical acceptability. To the extent that the weighing of scientific and human values suggests a compromise of any principle, the investigator incurs a correspondingly serious obligation to seek ethical advice and to observe stringent safeguards to protect the rights of human participants.

b. Considering whether a participant in a planned study will be a "subject at risk" or a "subject at minimal risk," according to recognized standards, is of primary ethical concern to the investigator.

c. The investigator always retains the responsibility for ensuring ethical practice in research. The investigator is also responsible for the ethical treatment of research participants by collaborators, assistants, students, and employees, all of whom, however, incur similar obligations.

d. Except in minimal-risk research, the investigator establishes a clear and fair agreement with research participants, prior to their participation, that clarifies the obligations and responsibilities of each. The investigator has the obligation to honor all promises and commitments included in that agreement. The investigator informs the participants of all aspects of the research that might reasonably be expected to influence willingness to participate and explains all other aspects of the research about which the participants inquire. Failure to make full disclosure prior to obtaining informed consent requires additional safeguards to protect the welfare and dignity of the research participants. Research with children or with participants who have impairments that would limit understanding and/or communication requires special safeguarding procedures.

e. Methodological requirements of a study may make the use of concealment or deception necessary. Before conducting such a study, the investigator has a special responsibility to (i) determine whether the use of such techniques is justified by the study's prospective scientific, educational, or applied value; (ii) determine whether alternative procedures are available that do not use concealment or deception; and (iii) ensure that the participants are provided with sufficient explanation as soon as possible.

f. The investigator respects the individual's freedom to decline to participate in or to withdraw from the research at any time. The obligation to protect this freedom requires careful thought and consideration when the investigator is in a position of authority or influence over the participant. Such positions of authority include, but are not limited to, situations in which research participation is required as part of employment or in which the participant is a student, client, or employee of the investigator.

g. The investigator protects the participant from physical and mental discomfort, harm, and danger that may arise from research procedures. If risks of such consequences exist, the investigator informs the participant of that fact. Research procedures likely to cause serious or lasting harm to a participant are not used unless the failure to use these procedures might expose the participant to risk of greater harm, or unless the research has great potential benefit and fully informed and voluntary consent is obtained from each participant. The participant should be informed of procedures for contacting the investigator within a reasonable time period following participation should stress, potential harm, or related questions or concerns arise.

h. After the data are collected, the investigator provides the participant with information about the nature of the study and attempts to remove any misconceptions that may have arisen. Where scientific or humane values justify delaying or withholding this information, the investigator incurs a special responsibility to monitor the research and to ensure that there are no damaging consequences for the participant.

i. Where research procedures result in undesirable consequences for the individual participant, the investigator has the responsibility to detect and remove or correct these consequences, including long-term effects.

j. Information obtained about a research participant during the course of an investigation is confidential unless otherwise agreed upon in advance. When the possibility exists that others may obtain access to such information, this possibility, together with the plans for protecting confidentiality, is explained to the participant as part of the procedure for obtaining informed consent.

PRINCIPLE 10
CARE AND USE OF ANIMALS

An investigator of animal behavior strives to advance understanding of basic behavioral principles and/or to contribute to the improvement of human health and welfare. In seeking these ends, the investigator ensures the welfare of animals and treats them humanely. Laws and regulations notwithstanding, an animal's immediate protection depends upon the scientist's own conscience.

a. The acquisition, care, use, and disposal of all animals are in compliance with current federal, state or provincial, and local laws and regulations.

b. A psychologist trained in research methods and experienced in the care of laboratory animals closely supervises all procedures involving animals and is responsible for ensuring appropriate consideration of their comfort, health, and humane treatment.

c. Psychologists ensure that all individuals using animals under their supervision have received explicit instruction in experimental methods and in the care, maintenance, and handling of the species being used. Responsibilities and activities of individuals participating in a research project are consistent with their respective competencies.

d. Psychologists make every effort to minimize discomfort, illness, and pain of animals. A procedure subjecting animals to pain, stress, or privation is used only when an alternative procedure is unavailable and the goal is justified by its prospective scientific, educational, or applied value. Surgical procedures are performed under appropriate anesthesia; techniques to avoid infection and minimize pain are followed during and after surgery.

e. When it is appropriate that the animal's life be terminated, it is done rapidly and painlessly.

APPENDIX IV
CODE OF ETHICS FOR MENTAL HEALTH COUNSELORS

PREAMBLE

Mental health counselors believe in the dignity and worth of the individual. They are committed to increasing knowledge of human behavior and understanding of themselves and others. While pursuing these endeavors, they make every reasonable effort to protect the welfare of those who seek their services or of any subject that may be the object of study. They use their skills only for purposes consistent with these values and do not knowingly permit their misuse by others. While demanding for themselves freedom of inquiry and community, mental health counselors accept the responsibility this freedom confers: competence, objectivity in the application of skills and concern for the best interests of clients, colleagues, and society in general. In the pursuit of these ideals, mental health counselors subscribe to the following principles.

PRINCIPLE 1. RESPONSIBILITY

In their commitment to the understanding of human behavior, mental health counselors value objectivity and integrity, and in providing services they maintain the highest standards. They accept responsibility for the consequences of their work and make every effort to insure that their services are used appropriately.

(a) Mental health counselors accept ultimate responsibility for selecting appropriate areas for investigation and the methods relevant to minimize the possibility that their finding will be misleading. They provide thorough discussion of the limitations of their data and alternative hypotheses, especially where their work touches on social policy or might be misconstrued to the detriment of specific age, sex, ethnic, socioeconomic, or other social categories. In publishing reports of their work, they never discard observations that may modify the interpretation of results. Mental health counselors take credit only for the work they have actually done. In pursuing research, mental health counselors ascertain that their efforts will not lead to changes in individuals or organizations unless such changes are part of the agreement at the time of obtaining informed consent. Mental health counselors clarify in advance the expectations for sharing and utilizing research data. They avoid dual relationships that may limit objectivity, whether theoretical, political, or monetary, so that interference with data, subjects, and milieu is kept to a minimum.

(b) As employees of an institution or agency, mental health counselors have the responsibility of remaining alert to institutional pressures which may distort reports of counseling findings or use them in ways counter to the promotion of human welfare.

(c) When serving as members of governmental or other organizational bodies, mental health counselors remain accountable as individuals to the Code of Ethics of the American Mental Health Counselors Association (AMHCA).

(d) As teachers, mental health counselors recognize their primary obligation to help others acquire knowledge and skill. They maintain high standards of scholarship and objectivity by presenting counseling information fully and accurately, and by giving appropriate recognition to alternative viewpoints.

(e) As practitioners, mental health counselors know that they bear a heavy social responsibility because their recommendations and professional actions may alter the lives of others. They, therefore, remain fully cognizant of their impact and alert to personal, social, organizational, financial, or political situations or pressures that might lead to misuse of their influence.

(f) Mental health counselors provide reasonable and timely feedback to employees, trainees, supervisors, students, clients, and others whose work they may evaluate.

PRINCIPLE 2. COMPETENCE

The maintenance of high standards of professional competence is a responsibility shared by all mental health counselors in the interest of the public and the profession as a whole. Mental health counselors recognize the boundaries of their competence and the limitations of their techniques and only provide services, use techniques, or offer opinions as professionals that meet recognized standards. Throughout their careers, mental health counselors maintain knowledge of professional information related to the services they render.

(a) Mental health counselors accurately represent their competence, education, training, and experience.

(b) As teachers, mental health counselors perform their duties based on careful preparation so that their instruction is accurate, up-to-date, and scholarly.

(c) Mental health counselors recognize the need for continuing training to prepare themselves to serve persons of all ages and cultural backgrounds. They are open to new procedures and sensitive to differences between groups of people and changes in expectations and values over time.

(d) Mental health counselors with the responsibility for decisions involving individuals or policies based on test results should know and understand literature relevant to the tests used and testing problems with which they deal.

(e) Mental health counselors/practitioners recognize that their effectiveness depends in part upon their ability to maintain sound interpersonal relations, that temporary or more enduring aberrations on their part may interfere with their abilities or distort their appraisals of others. Therefore, they refrain from undertaking any activity in which their personal problems are likely to lead to inadequate professional services or harm to a client, or, if they are already engaged in such activity when they become aware of their personal problems, they would seek competent professional assistance to determine whether they should suspend or terminate services to one or all of their clients.

(f) The mental health counselor has a responsibility both to the individual who is served and to the institution with which the service is performed to maintain high standards of professional conduct. The mental health counselor strives to maintain the highest levels of professional services offered to the individuals to be served. The mental health counselor also strives to assist the agency, organization, or institution in providing the highest caliber of professional services. The acceptance of employment in an institution implies that the mental health counselor is in substantial agreement with the general policies and principles of the institution. If, despite concerted efforts, the member cannot reach agreement with the employer as to acceptable standards of conduct that allow for changes in institutional policy conducive to the positive growth and development of counselees, then terminating the affiliation should be seriously considered.

(g)   Ethical behavior among professional associates, mental health counselors and non-mental health counselors, is expected at all times. When information is possessed that raises serious doubt as to the ethical behavior of professional colleagues, whether association members or not, the mental health counselor is obligated to take action to attempt to rectify such a-condition. Such action shall utilize the institution's channels first and then utilize procedures established by the state, division, or the association.

(h)   The mental health counselor is aware of the intimacy of the counseling relationship and maintains a healthy respect for the personhood of the client and avoids engaging in activities that seek to meet the mental health counselor's personal needs at the expense of the client. Through awareness of the negative impact of both racial and sexual stereotyping and discrimination, the member strives to ensure the individual rights and personal dignity of the client in the counseling relationship.

PRINCIPLE 3. MORAL AND LEGAL STANDARDS

Mental health counselors' moral, ethical, and legal standards of behavior are a personal matter to the same degree as they are for any other citizen, except as these may compromise the fulfillment of their professional responsibilities, or reduce the trust in counseling or counselors held by the general public. Regarding their own behavior, mental health counselors should be aware of the prevailing community standards and of the possible impact upon the quality of professional services provided by their conformance to or deviation from these standards. Mental health counselors should also be aware of the possible impact of their public behavior upon the ability of colleagues to perform their professional duties.

(a)   To protect public confidence in the profession of counseling, mental health counselors will avoid public behavior that is clearly in violation of accepted moral and legal standards.

(b)   To protect students, mental health counselors/teachers will be aware of the diverse backgrounds of students and, when dealing with topics that may give offense, will see that the material is treated objectively, that it is clearly relevant to the course, and that it is treated in a manner for which the student is prepared.

(c)   Providers of counseling services conform to the statutes relating to such services as established by their state and its regulating professional board(s).

(d)   As employees, mental health counselors refuse to participate in employer's practices that are inconsistent with the moral and legal standards established by federal or state legislation regarding the treatment of employees or of the public. In particular and for example, mental health counselors will not condone practices that result in illegal or otherwise unjustifiable discrimination on the basis of race, sex, religion, or national origin in hiring, promotion, or training.

(e)   In providing counseling services to clients, mental health counselors avoid any action that will violate or diminish the legal and civil rights of clients or of others who may be affected by the action.

(f)   Sexual conduct, not limited to sexual intercourse, between mental health counselors and clients is specifically in violation of this code of ethics. This does not, however, prohibit the use of explicit instructional aids including films and videotapes. Such use is within accepted practices of trained and competent sex therapists.

PRINCIPLE 4. PUBLIC STATEMENTS

Mental health counselors in their professional roles may be expected or required to make public statements providing counseling information, professional opinions, or supply information about the availability of counseling products and services. In making such statements, mental health counselors take full account of the limits and uncertainties of present counseling knowledge and techniques. They represent, as objectively as possible, their professional qualifications, affiliations, and functions, as well as those of the institutions or organizations with which the statements may be associated. All public statements, announcements of services, and promotional activities should serve the purpose of providing sufficient information to aid the consumer public in making informed judgments and choices on matters that concern it.

(a)   When announcing professional services, mental health counselors limit the information to: name, highest relevant degree conferred, certification or licensure, address, telephone number, office hours, cost of services, and a brief explanation of the types of services offered but evaluative as to their quality of uniqueness. They will not contain testimonials by implication. They will not claim uniqueness of skill or methods beyond those acceptable and public scientific evidence.

(b)   In announcing the availability of counseling services or products, mental health counselors will not display their affiliations with organizations or agencies in a manner that implies the sponsorship or certification of the organization or agency. They will not name their employer or professional associations unless the services are in fact to be provided by or under the responsible, direct supervision and continuing control of such organizations or agencies.

(c)   Mental health counselors associated with the development or promotion of counseling devices, books, or other products offered for commercial sale will make every effort to insure that announcements and advertisements are presented in a professional and factually informative manner without unsupported claims of superiority, and must be supported by scientifically acceptable evidence or by willingness to aid and encourage independent professional scrutiny or scientific test.

(d)   Mental health counselors engaged in radio, television, or other public media activities will not participate in commercial announcements recommending to the general public the purchase or use of any proprietary or single-source product or service.

(e)   Mental health counselors who describe counseling or the service of professional counselors to the general public accept the obligation to present the material fairly and accurately, avoiding misrepresentation through sensationalism, exaggeration, or superficiality. Mental health counselors will be guided by the primary obligation to aid the public in forming their own informed judgments, opinions, and choices.

(f) As teachers, mental health counselors ensure their statements in catalogs and course outlines are accurate, particularly in terms of subject matter to be covered, bases for grading, and nature of classroom experiences.

(g) Mental health counselors accept the obligation to correct others who may represent their professional qualifications or associations with products or services in a manner incompatible with these guidelines.

PRINCIPLE 5. CONFIDENTIALITY

Mental health counselors have a primary obligation to safeguard information about individuals obtained in the course of teaching, practice, or research. Personal information is communicated to others only with the person's written consent or in those circumstances where there is clear and imminent danger to the client, to others, or to society. Disclosures of counseling information are restricted to what is necessary, relevant, and verifiable.

(a) All materials in the official record shall be shared with the client, who shall have the right to decide what information may be shared with anyone beyond the immediate provider of service and to be informed of the implications of the materials to be shared.

(b) The anonymity of clients served in public and other agencies is preserved, if at all possible, by withholding names and personal identifying data. If external conditions require reporting such information, the client shall be so informed.

(c) Information received in confidence by one agency or person shall not be forwarded to another person or agency without the client's written permission.

(d) Service providers have a responsibility to insure the accuracy and to indicate the validity of data shared with their parties.

(e) Case reports presented in classes, professional meetings, or in publications shall be so disguised that no identification is possible unless the client or responsible authority has read the report and agreed in writing to its presentation or publication.

(f) Counseling reports and records are maintained under conditions of security and provisions are made for their destruction when they have outlived their usefulness. Mental health counselors insure that privacy and confidentiality are maintained by all persons in the employ or volunteers, and community aides.

(g) Mental health counselors who ask that an individual reveal personal information in the course of interviewing, testing, or evaluation, or who allow such information to be divulged, do so only after making certain that the person or authorized representative is fully aware of the purposes of the interview, testing, or evaluation and of the ways in which the information will be used.

(h) Sessions with clients are taped or otherwise recorded only with their written permission or the written permission of a responsible guardian. Even with guardian written consent, one should not record a session against the expressed wishes of a client.

(i) Where a child or adolescent is the primary client, the interests of the minor shall be paramount.

(j)   In work with families, the rights of each family member should be safeguarded. The provider of service also has the responsibility to discuss the contents of the record with the parent and/or child, as appropriate, and to keep separate those parts that should remain the property of each family member.

PRINCIPLE 6. WELFARE OF THE CONSUMER

Mental health counselors respect the integrity and protect the welfare of the people and groups with whom they work. When there is a conflict of interest between the client and the mental health counselors' employing institution, the mental health counselors clarify the nature and direction of their loyalties and responsibilities and keep all parties informed of their commitments. Mental health counselors fully inform consumers as to the purpose and nature of any evaluative, treatment, educational, or training procedure, and they freely acknowledge that clients, students, or subjects have freedom of choice with regard to participation.

(a)   Mental health counselors are continually cognizant both of their own needs and of their inherently powerful position "vis-à-vis" clients, in order to avoid exploiting the client's trust and dependency. Mental health counselors make every effort to avoid dual relationships that might impair their professional judgment or increase the risk of client exploitation. Examples of such dual relationships include treating an employee or supervisor, treating a close friend or family relative, and sexual relationships with clients.

(b)   Where mental health counselors' work with members of an organization goes beyond reasonable conditions of employment, mental health counselors recognize possible conflicts of interest that may arise. When such conflicts occur, mental health counselors clarify the nature of the conflict and inform all parties of the nature and directions of the loyalties and responsibilities involved.

(c)   When acting as supervisors, trainers, or employers, mental health counselors accord recipients informed choice, confidentiality, and protection from physical and mental harm.

(d)   Financial arrangements in professional practice are in accord with professional standards that safeguard the best interests of the client and that are clearly understood by the client in advance of billing. This may best be done by the use of a contract. Mental health counselors are responsible for assisting clients in finding needed services in those instances where payment of the usual fee would be a hardship. No commission or rebate or other form of remuneration may be given or received for referral of clients for professional services, whether by an individual or by an agency.

(e)   Mental health counselors are responsible for making their services readily accessible to clients in a manner that facilitates the client's ability to make an informed choice when selecting a service provider. This responsibility includes a clear description of what the client may expect in the way of tests, reports, billing, therapeutic regime and schedules, and the use of the mental health counselor's Statement of Professional Disclosure.

(f)   Mental health counselors who find that their services are not beneficial to the client have the responsibility to make this known to the responsible persons.

(g)   Mental health counselors are accountable to the parties who refer and support counseling services and to the general public and are cognizant of the indirect or long-range effects of their intervention.

(h)   The mental health counselor attempts to terminate a private service or consulting relationship when it is reasonably clear to the mental health counselor that the consumer is not benefiting from it. If a consumer is receiving services from another mental health professional, mental health counselors do not offer their services directly to the consumer without informing the professional persons already involved in order to avoid confusion and conflict for the consumer.

(i)   The mental health counselor has the responsibility to screen prospective group participants, especially when the emphasis is on self-understanding and growth through self-disclosure. The member should maintain an awareness of the group participants' compatibility throughout the life of the group.

(j)   The mental health counselor may choose to consult with any other professionally competent person about a client. In choosing a consultant, the mental health counselor should avoid placing the consultant in a conflict of interest situation that would preclude the consultant's being a proper party to the mental health counselor's efforts to help the clients.

(k)   If the mental health counselor is unable to be of professional assistance to the client, the mental health counselor should avoid initiating the counseling relationship or the mental health counselor terminates the relationship. In either event, the member is obligated to suggest appropriate alternatives. (It is incumbent upon the mental health counselor to be knowledgeable about referral resources so that a satisfactory referral can be initiated.) In the event the client declines the suggested referral, the mental health counselor is not obligated to continue the relationship.

(l)   When the mental health counselor has other relationships, particularly of an administrative, supervisory, and/or evaluative nature, with an individual seeking counseling services, the mental health counselor should not serve as the counselor but should refer the individual to another professional. Only in instances where such an alternative is unavailable and where the individual's situation definitely warrants counseling intervention should the mental health counselor enter into and/or maintain a counseling relationship. Dual relationships with clients that might impair the member's objectivity and professional judgment (such as with close friends or relatives, sexual intimacies with any client, etc.) must be avoided and/or the counseling relationship terminated through referral to another competent professional.

(m)   All experimental methods of treatment must be clearly indicated to prospective recipients, and safety precautions are to be adhered to by the mental health counselor instituting treatment.

(n)   When the member is engaged in short-term group treatment/training programs, for example, marathons and other encounter-type or growth groups, the member ensures that there is professional assistance available during and following the group experience.

PRINCIPLE 7. PROFESSIONAL RELATIONSHIP

Mental health counselors act with due regard to the needs and feelings of their colleagues in counseling and other professions. Mental health counselors respect the prerogatives and obligations of the institutions or organizations with which they are associated.

(a) Mental health counselors understand the areas of competence of related professions and make full use of other professional, technical, and administrative resources that best serve the interests of consumers. The absence of formal relationships with other professional workers does not relieve mental health counselors from the responsibilti of securing for their clients the best possible professional service; indeed, this circumstance presents a challenge to the professional competence of mental health counselors, requiring special sensitivity to problems outside their areas of training, and foresight, diligence, and tact in obtaining the professional assistance needed by clients.

(b) Mental health counselors know and take into account the traditions and practices of other professional groups with which they work, and cooperate fully with members of such groups when research, services, and other functions are shared or in working for the benefit of public welfare.

(c) Mental health counselors strive to provide positive conditions for those they employ and they spell out clearly the conditions of such employment. They encourage their employees to engage in activities that facilitate their further professional development.

(d) Mental health counselors respect the viability, reputation, and the proprietary right of organizations they serve. Mental health counselors show due regard for the interest of their present or prospective employers. In those instances where they are critical of policies, they attempt to effect change by constructive action within the organization.

(e) In the pursuit of research, mental health counselors give sponsoring agencies, host institutions, and publication channels the same respect and opportunity for giving informed consent that they accord to individual research participants. They are aware of their obligation to future research workers and insure that host institutions are given feedback information and proper acknowledgment.

(f) Credit is assigned to those who have contributed to a publication, in proportion to their contribution.

(g) When a mental health counselor violates ethical standards, mental health counselors who know firsthand of such activities should, if possible, attempt to rectify the situation. Failing an informal solution, mental health counselors should bring such unethical activities to the attention of the appropriate state, and/or national committee on ethics and professional conduct. Only after all professional alternatives have been utilized will a mental health counselor begin legal action for resolution.

PRINCIPLE 8. UTILIZATION OF ASSESSMENT TECHNIQUES

In the development, publication, and utilization of counseling assessment techniques, mental health counselors follow relevant standards. Individuals examined, or their legal guardians, have the right to know the results, the interpretations made, and where appropriate, the particulars on which final judgment was based. Test users should take precautions to protect test security but not at the expense of an individual's right to understand the basis for decisions that adversely affect that individual or that individual's dependents.

(a) The client has the right to have and the provider has the responsibility to give explanations of test results in language the client can understand.

(b)   When a test is published or otherwise made available for operational use, it should be accompanied by a manual (or other published or readily available information) that makes every reasonable effort to describe fully the development of the test, the rationale, specifications followed in writing items analysis or other research. The test, manual, record forms, and other accompanying material should help users make correct interpretations of the test results and should warn against common misuses. The test manual should state explicitly the purposes and application for which the test is recommended and identify any special qualifications required to administer the test and to interpret it properly. Evidence of validity and reliability, along with other relevant research data, should be presented in support of any claims made.

(c)   Norms presented in test manuals should refer to defined and clearly described populations. These populations should be the groups with whom users of the test will ordinarily wish to compare the persons tested. Test users should consider the possibility of bias in tests or in test items. When indicated, there should be an investigation of possible differences in validity for ethnic, sex, or other subsamples that can be identified when the test is given.

(d)   Mental health counselors who have the responsibility for decisions about individuals or policies that are based on test results should have a thorough understanding of counseling or educational measurement and of validation and other test research.

(e)   Mental health counselors should develop procedures for systematically eliminating from data files test score information that has, because of the lapse of time, become obsolete.

(f)   Any individual or organization offering test scoring and interpretation services must be able to demonstrate that their programs are based on appropriate research to establish the validity of the programs and procedures used in arriving at interpretations. The public offering of an automated test interpretation service will be considered as a professional-to-professional consultation. In this the formal responsibility of the consultant is to the consultee but his/her ultimate and overriding responsibility is to the client.

(g)   Counseling services for the purpose of diagnosis, treatment, or personalized advice are provided only in the context of a professional relationship, and are not given by means of public lectures or demonstrations, newspapers or magazine articles, radio or television programs, mail, or similar media. The preparation of personnel reports and recommendations based on test data secured solely by mail is unethical unless such appraisals are an integral part of a continuing client relationship with a company, as a result of which the consulting clinical mental health counselor has intimate knowledge of the client's personal situation and can be assured thereby that his or her written appraisals will be adequate to the purpose and will be properly interpreted by the client. These reports must not be embellished with such detailed analysis of the subject's personality traits as would be appropriate only for intensive interviews with the subjects.

PRINCIPLE 9. PURSUIT OF RESEARCH ACTIVITIES

The decision to undertake research should rest upon a considered judgment by the individual mental health counselor about how best to contribute to counseling and to human welfare. Mental health counselors carry out their investigations with respect for the people who participate and with concern for their dignity and welfare.

(a) In planning a study, the investigator has the personal responsibility to make a careful evaluation of its ethical acceptability, taking into account the following principles for research with human beings. To the extent that this appraisal, weighing scientific and humane values, suggests a deviation from any principle, the investigator incurs an increasingly serious obligation to seek ethical advice and to observe more stringent safeguards to protect the rights of the human research participants.

(b) Mental health counselors know and take into account the traditions and practices of other professional groups with members of such groups when research, services, and other functions are shared or in working for the benefit of public welfare.

(c) Ethical practice requires the investigator to inform the participant of all features of the research that reasonably might be expected to influence willingness to participate, and to explain all other aspects of the research about which the participant inquires. Failure to make full disclosure gives added emphasis to the investigator's abiding responsibility to protect the welfare and dignity of the research participants.

(d) Openness and honesty are essential characteristics of the relationship between investigator and research participant. When the methodological requirements of a study necessitate concealment or deception, the investigator is required to insure as soon as possible the participant's understanding of the reasons for this action and to restore the quality of the relationship with the investigator.

(e) In the pursuit of research, mental health counselors give sponsoring agencies, host institutions, and publication channels the same respect and opportunity for giving informed consent that they accord to individual research participants. They are aware of their obligation to future research workers and insure that host institutions are given feedback information and proper acknowledgment.

(f) Credit is assigned to those who have contributed to a publication, in proportion to their contribution.

(g) The ethical investigator protects participants from physical and mental discomfort, harm, and danger. If the risk of such consequences exists, the investigator is required to inform the participant of that fact, secure consent before proceeding, and take all possible measures to minimize distress. A research procedure may not be used if it is likely to cause serious and lasting harm to participants.

(h) After the data are collected, ethical practice requires the investigator to provide the participant with a full clarification of the nature of the study and to remove any misconceptions that may have arisen. Where scientific or humane values justify delaying or withholding information, the investigator acquires a special responsibility to assure that there are no damaging consequences for the participants.

(i) Where research procedures may result in undesirable consequences for the participant, the investigator has the responsibility to detect and remove or correct these consequences, including, where relevant, long-term aftereffects.

(j) Information obtained about the research participants during the course of an investigation is confidential. When the possibility exists that others may obtain access to such information, ethical research practice requires that the possibility, together with the plans for protecting confidentiality, be explained to the participants as a part of the procedure for obtaining informed consent.

PRINCIPLE 10. PRIVATE PRACTICE

(a)   A mental health counselor, where permitted by legislation or judicial decision, should assist the profession in fulfilling its duty to make counseling services available in private settings.

(b)   In advertising services as a private practitioner, the mental health counselor should advertise the services in such a manner so as to accurately inform the public as to services, expertise, profession, and techniques of counseling in a professional manner. A mental health counselor who assumes an executive leadership role in the organization shall not permit his/her name to be used in professional notices during periods when not actively engaged in the private practice of counseling. The mental health counselor may list the following: highest relevant degree, type and level of certification or license, type and/or description of services, and other relevant information. Such information should not contain false, inaccurate, misleading, partial, out-of-context, or deceptive material or statements.

(c)   The mental health counselor may join in partnership/corporation with other mental health counselors and/or other professionals provided that each mental health counselor of the partnership or corporation makes clear the separate specialties by name in compliance with the regulations of the locality.

(d)   A mental health counselor has an obligation to withdraw from a counseling relationship if it is believed that employment will result in the violation of the code of ethics, if their mental capacity or physical condition renders it difficult to carry out an effective professional relationship, or if the mental health counselor is discharged by the client because the counseling relationship is no longer productive for the client.

(e)   A mental health counselor should adhere to and support the regulations for private practice of the locality where the services are offered.

(f)   Mental health counselors are discouraged from deliberate attempts to utilize one's institutional affiliation to recruit clients for one's private practice. Mental health counselors are to refrain from offering their services in the private sector, when they are employed by an institution in which this is prohibited by stated policies reflecting conditions for employment.

(g)   In establishing fees for professional counseling services, mental health counselors should consider the financial status of clients and locality. In the event that the established fee structure is inappropriate for a client, assistance should be provided in finding services of acceptable cost.

PRINCIPLE 11. CONSULTING

(a)   The mental health counselor acting as consultant must have a high degree of self-awareness of his or her own values, knowledge, skills, and needs in entering a helping relationship that involves human and/or organizational change and that the focus of the relationship be on the issues to be resolved and not on the person(s) presenting the problem.

(b)   There should be understanding and agreement between the mental health counselor and client for the problem definition, change goals, and predicted consequences of interventions selected.

(c)   The mental health counselor must be reasonably certain that she or he or the organization represented has the necessary competencies and resources for giving the kind of help that is needed now or may develop later and that appropriate referral resources are available to the consultant, if needed later.

(d)   The mental health counselor relationship must be one in which client adaptability and growth toward self-direction are encouraged and cultivated. The mental health counselor must maintain this role consistently and not become a decision maker or substitute for the client.

(e)   When announcing consultant availability for services, the mental health counselor conscientiously adheres to professional standards.

(f)   The mental health counselor is expected to refuse a private fee or other remuneration for consultation with persons who are entitled to these services through the member's employing institution or agency. The policies of a particular agency may make explicit provisions for private practice with agency counselees by members of its staff. In such instances, the counselees must be apprised of other options open to them should they not seek private counseling services.

PRINCIPLE 12. CLIENT'S RIGHTS

The following apply to all consumers of mental health services, including both in- and outpatients in all state, county, local, and private care mental health facilities, as well as patients/clients of mental health practitioners in private practice.

The client has the right:

(a)   to be treated with consideration and respect;

(b)   to expect quality service provided by concerned, competent staff;

(c)   to a clear statement of the purposes, goals, techniques, rules of procedure, and limitations as well as potential dangers of the services to be performed and all other information related to or likely to affect the ongoing counseling relationship;

(d)   to obtain information about their case record and to have this information explained clearly and directly;

(e)   to full, knowledgeable, and responsible participation in the ongoing treatment plan, to the maximum feasible extent;

(f)   to expect complete confidentiality and that no information will be released without written consent;

(g)   to see and discuss their charges and payment records; and

(h)   to refuse any recommended services and be advised of the consequences of this action.

APPENDIX V
SPECIALTY GUIDELINES FOR THE DELIVERY OF SERVICES BY COUNSELING PSYCHOLOGISTS

These Specialty Guidelines were prepared by the APA Committee on Standards for Providers of Psychological Services (COSPOPS), chaired by Durand F. Jacobs, with the advice of the officers and committee chairpersons of the Division of Counseling Psychology (Division 17). Barbara A. Kirk and Milton Schwebel served successively as the counseling psychology representative of COSPOPS, and Arthur Centor and Richard Kilburg were the Central Office liaisons to the committee. Norman Kagan, Samuel H. Osipow, Carl E. Thoresen, and Allen E. Ivey served successively as Division 17 presidents.

The Specialty Guidelines that follow are based on the generic *Standards for Providers of Psychological Services* originally adopted by the American Psychological Association (APA) in September 1974 and revised in January 1977 (APA, 1974b, 1977b). Together with the generic *Standards,* these Specialty Guidelines state the official policy of the Association regarding delivery of services by counseling psychologists. Admission to the practice of psychology is regulated by state statute. It is the position of the Association that licensing be based on generic, and not on specialty, qualifications. Specialty guidelines serve the additional purpose of providing potential users and other interested groups with essential information about particular services available from the several specialties in professional psychology.

Professional psychology specialties have evolved from generic practice in psychology and are supported by university training programs. There are now at least four recognized professional specialties—clinical, counseling, school, and industrial/organizational psychology.

The knowledge base in each of these specialty areas has increased, refining the state of the art to the point that a set of uniform specialty guidelines is now possible and desirable. The present Guidelines are intended to educate the public, the profession, and other interested parties regarding specialty professional practices. They are also intended to facilitate the continued systematic development of the profession.

The content of each Specialty Guideline reflects a consensus of university faculty and public and private practitioners regarding the knowledge base, services provided, problems addressed, and clients served.

Traditionally, all learned disciplines have treated the designation of specialty practice as a reflection of preparation in greater depth in a particular subject matter, together with a voluntary limiting of focus to a more restricted area of practice by the professional. Lack of specialty designation does not preclude general providers of psychological services from using the methods or dealing with the populations of any specialty, except insofar as psychologists voluntarily refrain from providing services they are not trained to render. It is the intent of these guidelines, however, that after the grandparenting period, psychologists not put themselves forward as *specialists* in a given area of practice unless they meet the qualifications noted in the Guidelines (see Definitions). Therefore, these Guidelines are meant to apply only to those psychologists who voluntarily wish to be designated as *counseling psychologists.* They do not apply to other psychologists.

These Guidelines represent the profession's best judgment of the conditions, credentials, and experience that contribute to competent professional practice. The APA strongly encourages, and plans to participate in, efforts to identify professional practitioner behaviors and job functions and to validate the relation between these and desired client outcomes. Thus, future revisions of these Guidelines will increasingly reflect the results of such efforts.

These Guidelines follow the format and, wherever applicable, the wording of the generic *Standards*.[1] (Note: Footnotes appear at the end of the Specialty Guidelines. . . .) The intent of these Guidelines is to improve the quality, effectiveness, and accessibility of psychological services. They are meant to provide guidance to providers, users, and sanctioners regarding the best judgment of the profession on these matters. Although the Specialty Guidelines have been derived from and are consistent with the generic *Standards,* they may be used as separate documents. However, *Standards for Providers of Psychological Services* (APA, 1977b) shall remain the basic policy statement and shall take precedence where there are questions of interpretation.

Professional psychology in general and counseling psychology as a specialty have labored long and diligently to codify a uniform set of guidelines for the delivery of services by counseling psychologists that would serve the respective needs of users, providers, third-party purchasers, and sanctioners of psychological services.

The Committee on Professional Standards, established by the APA in January 1980, is charged with keeping the generic *Standards* and the Specialty Guidelines responsive to the needs of the public and the profession. It is also charged with continually reviewing, modifying, and extending them progressively as the profession and the science of psychology develop new knowledge, improved methods, and additional modes of psychological services.

The Specialty Guidelines for the Delivery of Services by Counseling Psychologists that follow have been established by the APA as a means of self-regulation to protect the public interest. They guide the specialty practice of counseling psychology by specifying important areas of quality assurance and performance that contribute to the goal of facilitating more effective human functioning.

PRINCIPLES AND IMPLICATIONS OF THE SPECIALTY GUIDELINES

These Specialty Guidelines emerged from and reaffirm the same basic principles that guided the development of the generic *Standards for Providers of Psychological Services* (APA, 1977b):

1. These Guidelines recognize that admission to the practice of psychology is regulated by state statute.
2. It is the intention of the APA that the generic *Standards* provide appropriate guidelines for statutory licensing of psychologists. In addition, although it is the position of the APA that licensing be generic and not in specialty areas, these Specialty Guidelines in counseling psychology provide an authoritative reference for use in credentialing specialty providers of counseling psychological services by such groups as divisions of the APA and state associations and by boards and agencies that find such criteria useful for quality assurance.

3. A uniform set of Specialty Guidelines governs the quality of services to all users of counseling psychological services in both the private and the public sectors. Those receiving counseling psychological services are protected by the same kinds of safeguards, irrespective of sector; these include constitutional guarantees, statutory regulation, peer review, consultation, record review, and supervision.

4. A uniform set of Specialty Guidelines governs counseling psychological service functions offered by counseling psychologists, regardless of setting or form of remuneration. All counseling psychologists in professional practice recognize and are responsive to a uniform set of Specialty Guidelines, just as they are guided by a common code of ethics.

5. Counseling psychology Guidelines establish clear, minimally acceptable levels of quality for covered counseling psychological service functions, regardless of the nature of the users, purchasers, or sanctioners of such covered services.

6. All persons providing counseling psychological services meet specified levels of training and experience that are consistent with, and appropriate to, the functions they perform. Counseling psychological services provided by persons who do not meet the APA qualifications for a professional counseling psychologist (see Definitions) are supervised by a professional counseling psychologist. Final responsibility and accountability for services provided rest with professional counseling psychologists.

7. When providing any of the covered counseling psychological service functions at any time and in any setting, whether public or private, profit or nonprofit, counseling psychologists observe these Guidelines in order to promote the best interests and welfare of the users of such services. The extent to which counseling psychologists observe these Guidelines is judged by peers.

8. These Guidelines, while assuring the user of the counseling psychologist's accountability for the nature and quality of services specified in this document, do not preclude the counseling psychologist from using new methods or developing innovative procedures in the delivery of counseling services.

These Specialty Guidelines have broad implications both for users of counseling psychological services and for providers of such services:

1. Guidelines for counseling psychological services provide a foundation for mutual understanding between provider and user and facilitate more effective evaluation of services provided and outcomes achieved.

2. Guidelines for counseling psychologists are essential for uniformity in specialty credentialing of counseling psychologists.

3. Guidelines give specific content to the profession's concept of ethical practice as it applies to the functions of counseling psychologists.

4. Guidelines for counseling psychological services may have significant impact on tomorrow's education and training models for both professional and support personnel in counseling psychology.

5. Guidelines for the provision of counseling psychological services in human service facilities influence the determination of acceptable structure, budgeting, and staffing patterns in these facilities.

6. Guidelines for counseling psychological services require continual review and revision.

The Specialty Guidelines here presented are intended to improve the quality and delivery of counseling psychological services by specifying criteria for key aspects of the practice setting. Some settings may require additional and/or more stringent criteria for specific areas of service delivery.

Systematically applied, these Guidelines serve to establish a more effective and consistent basis for evaluating the performance of individual service providers as well as to guide the organization of counseling psychological service units in human service settings.

DEFINITIONS

Providers of counseling psychological services refers to two categories of persons who provide counseling psychological services:

A. Professional counseling psychologists.[2] Professional counseling psychologists have a doctoral degree from a regionally accredited university or professional school providing an organized, sequential counseling psychology program in an appropriate academic department in a university or college, or in an appropriate department or unit of a professional school. Counseling psychology programs that are accredited by the American Psychological Association are recognized as meeting the definition of a counseling psychology program. Counseling psychology programs that are not accredited by the American Psychological Association meet the definition of a counseling psychology program if they satisfy the following criteria:

1. The program is primarily psychological in nature and stands as a recognizable coherent organizational entity within the institution.

2. The program provides an integrated, organized sequence of study.

3. The program has an identifiable body of students who are matriculated in that program for a degree.

4. There is a clear authority with primary responsibility for the core and specialty areas, whether or not the program cuts across administrative lines.

5. There is an identifiable psychology faculty, and a psychologist is responsible for the program.

The professional counseling psychologist's doctoral education and training experience[3] is defined by the institution offering the program. Only counseling psychologists, that is, those who meet the appropriate education and training requirements, have the minimum professional qualifications to provide unsupervised counseling psychological services. A professional counseling psychologist and others providing counseling psychological services under supervision (described below) form an integral part of a multilevel counseling psychological service delivery system.

B. All other persons who provide counseling psychological services under the supervision of a professional counseling psychologist. Although there may be variations in the titles of such persons, they are not referred to as counseling psychologists. Their functions may be indicated by use of the adjective *psychological* preceding the noun, for example, *psychological associate*, *psychological assistant*, *psychological technician*, or *psychological aide*.

Counseling psychological services refers to services provided by counseling psychologists that apply principles, methods, and procedures for facilitating effective functioning during the life-span developmental process.[4,5] In providing such services, counseling psychologists approach practice with a significant emphasis on positive aspects of growth and adjustment and with a developmental orientation. These services are intended to help persons acquire or alter personal-social skills, improve adaptability to changing life demands, enhance environmental coping skills, and develop a variety of problem-solving and decision-making capabilities. Counseling psychological services are used by individuals, couples, and families of all age groups to cope with problems connected with education, career choice, work, sex, marriage, family, other social relations, health, aging, and handicaps of a social or physical nature. The services are offered in such organizations as educational, rehabilitation, and health institutions and in a variety of other public and private agencies committed to service in one or more of the problem areas cited above. Counseling psychological services include the following:

A. Assessment, evaluation, and diagnosis. Procedures may include, but are not limited to, behavioral observation, interviewing, and administering and interpreting instruments for the assessment of educational achievement, academic skills, aptitudes, interests, cognitive abilities, attitudes, emotions, motivations, psychoneurological status, personality characteristics, or any other aspect of human experience and behavior that may contribute to understanding and helping the user.

B. Interventions with individuals and groups. Procedures include individual and group psychological counseling (e.g., education, career, couples, and family counseling) and may use a therapeutic, group process, or social-learning approach, or any other deemed to be appropriate. Interventions are used for purposes of prevention, remediation, and rehabilitation; they may incorporate a variety of psychological modalities, such as psychotherapy, behavior therapy, marital and family therapy, biofeedback techniques, and environmental design.

C. Professional consultation relating to A and B above, for example, in connection with developing in-service training for staff or assisting an educational institution or organization to design a plan to cope with persistent problems of its students.

D. Program development services in the areas of A, B, and C above, such as assisting a rehabilitation center to design a career-counseling program.

E. Supervision of all counseling psychological services, such as the review of assessment and intervention activities of staff.

F. Evaluation of all services noted in A through E above and research for the purpose of their improvement.

A *counseling psychological service unit* is the functional unit through which counseling psychological services are provided; such a unit may be part of a larger psychological service organization comprising psychologists of more than one specialty and headed by a professional psychologist:

A. A counseling psychological service unit provides predominantly counseling psychological services and is composed of one or more professional counseling psychologists and supporting staff.

B. A counseling psychological service unit may operate as a functional or geographic component of a larger multipsychological service unit or of a governmental, educational, correctional, health, training, industrial, or commercial organizational unit, or it may operate as an independent professional service.[6]

C. A counseling psychological service unit may take the form of one or more counseling psychologists providing professional services in a multidisciplinary setting.

D. A counseling psychological service unit may also take the form of a private practice, composed of one or more counseling psychologists serving individuals or groups, or the form of a psychological consulting firm serving organizations and institutions.

Users of counseling psychological services include:

A. Direct users or recipients of counseling psychological services.

B. Public and private institutions, facilities, or organizations receiving counseling psychological services.

C. Third-party purchasers—those who pay for the delivery of services but who are not the recipients of services.

D. Sanctioners—those who have a legitimate concern with the accessibility, timeliness, efficacy, and standards of quality attending the provision of counseling psychological services. Sanctioners may include members of the user's family, the court, the probation officer, the school adminstrator, the employer, the union representative, the facility director, and so on. Sanctioners may also include various governmental, peer review, and accreditation bodies concerned with the assurance of quality.

GUIDELINE 1
PROVIDERS

1.1 *Each counseling psychological service unit offering psychological services has available at least one professional counseling psychologist and as many more professional counseling psychologists as are necessary to assure the adequacy and quality of services offered.*

INTERPRETATION: The intent of this Guideline is that one or more providers of psychological services in any counseling psychological service unit meet the levels of training and experience of the professional counseling psychologist as specified in the preceding definitions.[7]

When a professional counseling psychologist is not available on a full-time basis, the facility retains the services of one or more professional counseling psychologists on a regular part-time basis. The counseling psychologist so retained directs the psychological services, including supervision of the support staff, has the authority and participates sufficiently to assess the need for services, reviews the content of services provided, and assumes professional responsibility and accountability for them.

The psychologist directing the service unit is responsible for determining and justifying appropriate ratios of psychologists to users and psychologists to support staff, in order to ensure proper scope, accessibility, and quality of services provided in that setting.

1.2 *Providers of counseling psychological services who do not meet the requirements for the professional counseling psychologist are supervised directly by a professional counseling psychologist who assumes professional responsibility and accountability for the services provided. The level and extent of supervision may vary from task to task so long as the supervising psychologist retains a sufficiently close supervisory relationship to meet this Guideline. Special proficiency training or supervision may be provided by a professional psychologist of another specialty or by a professional from another discipline whose competence in the given area has been demonstrated by previous training and experience.*

INTERPRETATION: In each counseling psychological service unit there may be varying levels of responsibility with respect to the nature and quality of services provided. Support personnel are considered to be responsible for their functions and behavior when assisting in the provision of counseling psychological services and are accountable to the professional counseling psychologist. Ultimate professional responsibility and accountability for the services provided require that the supervisor review reports and test protocols, and review and discuss intervention plans, strategies, and outcomes. Therefore, the supervision of all counseling psychological services is provided directly by a professional counseling psychologist in a face-to-face arrangement involving individual and/or group supervision. The extent of supervision is determined by the needs of the providers, but in no event is it less than 1 hour per week for each support staff member providing counseling psychological services.

To facilitate the effectiveness of the psychological service unit, the nature of the supervisory relationship is communicated to support personnel in writing. Such communications delineate the duties of the employees, describing the range and type of services to be provided. The limits of independent action and decision making are defined. The description of responsibility specifies the means by which the employee will contact the professional counseling psychologist in the event of emergency or crisis situations.

1.3 *Wherever a counseling psychological service unit exists, a professional counseling psychologist is responsible for planning, directing, and reviewing the provision of counseling psychological services. Whenever the counseling psychological service unit is part of a larger professional psychological service encompassing various psychological specialties, a professional psychologist shall be the administrative head of the service.*

INTERPRETATION: The counseling psychologist who directs or coordinates the unit is expected to maintain an ongoing or periodic review of the adequacy of services and to formulate plans in accordance with the results of such evaluation. He or she coordinates the activities of the counseling psychology unit with other professional, administrative, and technical groups, both within and outside the institution or agency. The counseling psychologist has related responsibilities including, but not limited to, directing the training and research activities of the service, maintaining a high level of professional and ethical practice, and ensuring that staff members function only within the areas of their competency.

To facilitate the effectiveness of counseling services by raising the level of staff sensitivity and professional skills, the counseling psychologist designated as director is responsible for participating in the selection of staff and support personnel whose qualifications and skills (e.g., language, cultural and experiential background, race, sex, and age) are relevant to the needs and characteristics of the users served.

1.4 *When functioning as part of an organizational setting, professional counseling psychologists bring their backgrounds and skills to bear on the goals of the organization, whenever appropriate, by participation in the planning and development of overall services.*[8]

INTERPRETATION: Professional counseling psychologists participate in the maintenance of high professional standards by representation on committees concerned with service delivery.

As appropriate to the setting, their activities may include active participation, as voting and as office-holding members, on the facility's professional staff and on other executive, planning, and evaluation boards and committees.

1.5 *Counseling psychologists maintain current knowledge of scientific and professional developments to preserve and enhance their professional competence.*

INTERPRETATION: Methods through which knowledge of scientific and professional developments may be gained include, but are not limited to, reading scientific and professional publications, attendance at professional workshops and meetings, participation in staff development programs, and other forms of continuing education.[9] The counseling psychologist has ready access to reference material related to the provision of psychological services. Counseling psychologists are prepared to show evidence periodically that they are staying abreast of current knowledge and practices in the field of counseling psychology through continuing education.

1.6 *Counseling psychologists limit their practice to their demonstrated areas of professional competence.*

INTERPRETATION: Counseling psychological services are offered in accordance with the providers' areas of competence as defined by verifiable training and experience. When extending services beyond the range of their usual practice, counseling psychologists obtain pertinent training or appropriate professional supervision. Such training or supervision is consistent with the extension of functions performed and services provided. An extension of services may involve a change in the theoretical orientation of the counseling psychologist, in the modality or techniques used, in the type of client, or in the kinds of problems or disorders for which services are to be provided.

1.7 *Professional psychologists who wish to qualify as counseling psychologists meet the same requirements with respect to subject matter and professional skills that apply to doctoral education and training in counseling psychology.*[10]

INTERPRETATION: Education of doctoral-level psychologists to qualify them for specialty practice in counseling psychology is under the auspices of a department in a regionally accredited university or of a professional school that offers the doctoral degree in counseling psychology. Such education is individualized, with due credit being given for relevant course work and other requirements that have previously been satisfied. In addition, doctoral-level training supervised by a counseling psychologist is required. Merely taking an internship in counseling psychology or acquiring experience in a practicum setting is not adequate preparation for becoming a counseling psychologist when prior education has not been in that area. Fulfillment of such an individualized educational program is attested to by the awarding of a certificate by the supervising department or professional school that indicates the successful completion of preparation in counseling psychology.

1.8 *Professional counseling psychologists are encouraged to develop innovative theories and procedures and to provide appropriate theoretical and/or empirical support for their innovations.*

INTERPRETATION: A specialty of a profession rooted in a science intends continually to explore and experiment with a view to developing and verifying new and improved ways of serving the public and documents the innovations.

GUIDELINE 2
PROGRAMS

2.1 *Composition and organization of a counseling psychological service unit:*

   2.1.1 *The composition and programs of a counseling psychological service unit are responsive to the needs of the persons or settings served.*

INTERPRETATION: A counseling psychological service unit is structured so as to facilitate effective and economical delivery of services. For example, a counseling psychological service unit serving predominantly a low-income, ethnic, or racial minority group has a staffing pattern and service programs that are adapted to the linguistic, experiential, and attitudinal characteristics of the users.

2.1.2 *A description of the organization of the counseling psychological service unit and its lines of responsibility and accountability for the delivery of psychological services is available in written form to staff of the unit and to users and sanctioners upon request.*

INTERPRETATION: The description includes lines of responsibility, supervisory relationships, and the level and extent of accountability for each person who provides psychological services.

2.1.3 *A counseling psychological service unit includes sufficient numbers of professional and support personnel to achieve its goals, objectives, and purposes.*

INTERPRETATION: The work load and diversity of psychological services required and the specific goals and objectives of the setting determine the numbers and qualifications of professional and support personnel in the counseling psychological service unit. Where shortages in personnel exist, so that psychological services cannot be rendered in a professional manner, the director of the counseling psychological service unit initiates action to remedy such shortages. When this fails, the director appropriately modifies the scope or work load of the unit to maintain the quality of the services rendered and, at the same time, makes continued efforts to devise alternative systems for delivery of services.

2.2 *Policies:*

2.2.1 *When the counseling psychological service unit is composed of more than one person or is a component of a larger organization, a written statement of its objectives and scope of services is developed, maintained, and reviewed.*

INTERPRETATION: The counseling psychological service unit reviews its objectives and scope of services annually and revises them as necessary to ensure that the psychological services offered are consistent with staff competencies and current psychological knowledge and practice. This statement is discussed with staff, reviewed with the appropriate administrator, and distributed to users and sanctioners upon request, whenever appropriate.

2.2.2 *All providers within a counseling psychological service unit support the legal and civil rights of the users.*[11]

INTERPRETATION: Providers of counseling psychological services safeguard the interests of the users with regard to personal, legal, and civil rights. They are continually sensitive to the issue of confidentiality of information, the short-term and long-term impacts of their decisions and recommendations, and other matters pertaining to individual, legal, and civil rights. Concerns regarding the safeguarding of individual rights of users include, but are not limited to, problems of access to professional records in educational institutions, self-incrimination in judicial proceedings, involuntary commitment to hospitals, protection of minors or legal incompetents, discriminatory practices in employment selection procedures, recommendation for special education provisions, information relative to adverse personnel actions in the armed services, and adjudication of domestic relations disputes in divorce and custodial proceedings. Providers of counseling psychological services take affirmative action by making themselves available to local committees, review boards, and similar advisory groups established to safeguard the human, civil, and legal rights of service users.

2.2.3 *All providers within a counseling psychological service unit are familiar with and adhere to the American Psychological Association's* Standards for Providers of Psychological Services, Ethical Principles of Psychologists, Standards for Educational and Psychological Tests, Ethical Principles in the Conduct of Research With Human Participants, *and other official policy statements relevant to standards for professional services issued by the Association.*

INTERPRETATION: Providers of counseling psychological services maintain current knowledge of relevant standards of the American Psychological Association.

2.2.4 *All providers within a counseling psychological service unit conform to relevant statutes established by federal, state, and local governments.*

INTERPRETATION: All providers of counseling psychological services are familiar with and conform to appropriate statutes regulating the practice of psychology. They also observe agency regulations that have the force of law and that relate to the delivery of psychological services (e.g., evaluation for disability retirement and special education placements). In addition, all providers are cognizant that federal agencies such as the Veterans Administration, the Department of Education, and the Department of Health and Human Services have policy statements regarding psychological services. Providers are familiar as well with other statutes and regulations, including those addressed to the civil and legal rights of users (e.g., those promulgated by the federal Equal Employment Opportunity Commission), that are pertinent to their scope of practice.

It is the responsibility of the American Psychological Association to maintain current files of those federal policies, statutes, and regulations relating to this section and to assist its members in obtaining them. The state psychological associations and the state licensing boards periodically publish and distribute appropriate state statutes and regulations, and these are on file in the counseling psychological service unit or the larger multipsychological service unit of which it is a part.

2.2.5 *All providers within a counseling psychological service unit inform themselves about and use the network of human services in their communities in order to link users with relevant services and resources.*

INTERPRETATION: Counseling psychologists and support staff are sensitive to the broader context of human needs. In recognizing the matrix of personal and social problems, providers make available to clients information regarding human services such as legal aid societies, social services, employment agencies, health resources, and educational and recreational facilities. Providers of counseling psychological services refer to such community resources and, when indicated, actively intervene on behalf of the users.

Community resources include the private as well as the public sectors. Consultation is sought or referral made within the public or private network of services whenever required in the best interest of the users. Counseling psychologists, in either the private or the public setting, utilize other resources in the community whenever indicated because of limitations within the psychological service unit providing the services. Professional counseling psychologists in private practice know the types of services offered through local community mental health clinics and centers, through family-service, career, and placement agencies, and through reading and other educational improvement centers and know the costs and the eligibility requirements for those services.

2.2.6 *In the delivery of counseling psychological services, the providers maintain a cooperative relationship with colleagues and co-workers in the best interest of the users.*[12]

INTERPRETATION: Counseling psychologists recognize the areas of special competence of other professional psychologists and of professionals in other fields for either consultation or referral purposes. Providers of counseling psychological services make appropriate use of other professional, research, technical, and administrative resources to serve the best interests of users and establish and maintain cooperative arrangements with such other resources as required to meet the needs of users.

2.3 *Procedures:*

2.3.1 *Each counseling psychological service unit is guided by a set of procedural guidelines for the delivery of psychological services.*

INTERPRETATION: Providers are prepared to provide a statement of procedural guidelines, in either oral or written form, in terms that can be understood by users, including sanctioners and local administrators. This statement describes the current methods, forms, procedures, and techniques being used to achieve the objectives and goals for psychological services.

2.3.2 *Providers of counseling psychological services develop plans appropriate to the providers' professional practices and to the problems presented by the users.*

INTERPRETATION: A counseling psychologist, after initial assessment, develops a plan describing the objectives of the psychological services and the manner in which they will be provided.[13] To illustrate, the agreement spells out the objective (e.g., a career decision), the method (e.g., short-term counseling), the roles (e.g., active participation by the user as well as the provider), and the cost. This plan is in written form. It serves as a basis for obtaining understanding and concurrence from the user and for establishing accountability and provides a mechanism for subsequent peer review. This plan is, of course, modified as changing needs dictate.

A counseling psychologist who provides services as one member of a collaborative effort participates in the development, modification (if needed), and implementation of the overall service plan and provides for its periodic review.

2.3.3 *Accurate, current, and pertinent documentation of essential counseling psychological services provided is maintained.*

INTERPRETATION: Records kept of counseling psychological services include, but are not limited to, identifying data, dates of services, types of services, significant actions taken, and outcome at termination. Providers of counseling psychological services ensure that essential information concerning services rendered is recorded within a reasonable time following their completion.

2.3.4 *Each counseling psychological service unit follows an established record retention and disposition policy.*

INTERPRETATION: The policy on record retention and disposition conforms to state statutes or federal regulations where such are applicable. In the absence of such regulations, the policy is (a) that the full record be maintained intact for at least 4 years after the completion of planned services or after the date of last contact with the user, whichever is later; (b) that if a full record is not retained, a summary of the record be maintained for an additional 3 years; and (c) that the record may be disposed of no sooner than 7 years after the completion of planned services or after the date of last contact, whichever is later.

In the event of the death or incapacity of a counseling psychologist in independent practice, special procedures are necessary to ensure the continuity of active service to users and the proper safeguarding of records in accordance with this Guideline. Following approval by the affected user, it is appropriate for another counseling psychologist, acting under the auspices of the professional standards review committee (PSRC) of the state, to review the record with the user and recommend a course of action for continuing professional service, if needed.

Depending on local circumstances, appropriate arrangements for record retention and disposition may also be recommended by the reviewing psychologist.

This Guideline has been designed to meet a variety of circumstances that may arise, often years after a set of psychological services has been completed. Increasingly, psychological records are being used in forensic matters, for peer review, and in response to requests from users, other professionals, and other legitimate parties requiring accurate information about the exact dates, nature, course, and outcome of a set of psychological services. The 4-year period for retention of the full record covers the period of either undergraduate or graudate study of most students in postsecondary educational institutions, and the 7-year period for retention of at least a summary of the record covers the period during which a previous user is most likely to return for counseling psychological services in an educational institution or other organization or agency.

2.3.5 *Providers of counseling psychological services maintain a system to protect confidentiality of their records.* [14]

INTERPRETATION: Counseling psychologists are responsible for maintaining the confidentiality of information about users of services, from whatever source derived. All persons supervised by counseling psychologists, including nonprofessional personnel and students, who have access to records of psychological services maintain this confidentiality as a condition of employment and/or supervision.

The counseling psychologist does not release confidential information, except with the written consent of the user directly involved or his or her legal representative. The only deviation from this rule is in the event of clear and imminent danger to, or involving, the user. Even after consent for release has been obtained, the counseling psychologist clearly identifies such information as confidential to the recipient of the information. [15] If directed otherwise by statute or regulations with the force of law or by court order, the psychologist seeks a resolution to the conflict that is both ethically and legally feasible and appropriate.

Users are informed in advance of any limits in the setting for maintenance of confidentiality of psychological information. For instance, counseling psychologists in agency, clinic, or hospital settings inform their clients that psychological information in a client's record may be available without the client's written consent to other members of the professional staff associated with service to the client. Similar limitations on confidentiality of psychological information may be present in certain educational, industrial, military, or other institutional settings, or in instances in which the user has waived confidentiality for purposes of third-party payment.

Users have the right to obtain information from their psychological records. However, the records are the property of the psychologist or the facility in which the psychologist works and are, therefore, the responsibility of the psychologist and subject to his or her control.

When the user's intention to waive confidentiality is judged by the professional counseling psychologist to be contrary to the user's best interests or to be in conflict with the user's civil and legal rights, it is the responsibility of the counseling psychologist to discuss the implications of releasing psychological information and to assist the user in limiting disclosure only to information required by the present circumstance.

Raw psychological data (e.g., questionnaire returns or test protocols) in which a user is identified are released only with the written consent of the user or his or her legal representative and released only to a person recognized by the counseling psychologist as qualified and competent to use the data.

Any use made of psychological reports, records, or data for research or training purposes is consistent with this Guideline. Additionally; providers of counseling psychological services comply with statutory confidentiality requirements and those embodied in the American Psychological Association's *Ethical Principles of Psychologists* (APA, 1981b).

Providers of counseling psychological services who use information about individuals that is stored in large computerized data banks are aware of the possible misuse of such data as well as the benefits and take necessary measures to ensure that such information is used in a socially responsible manner.

GUIDELINE 3
ACCOUNTABILITY

3.1 *The promotion of human welfare is the primary principle guiding the professional activity of the counseling psychologist and the counseling psychological service unit.*

INTERPRETATION: Counseling psychologists provide services to users in a manner that is considerate, effective, economical, and humane. Counseling psychologists are responsible for making their services readily accessible to users in a manner that facilitates the users' freedom of choice.

Counseling psychologists are mindful of their accountability to the sanctioners of counseling psychological services and to the general public, provided that appropriate steps are taken to protect the confidentiality of the service relationship. In the pursuit of their professional activities, they aid in the conservation of human, material, and financial resources.

The counseling psychological service unit does not withhold services to a potential client on the basis of that user's race, color, religion, gender, sexual orientation, age, or national origin; nor does it provide services in a discriminatory or exploitative fashion. Counseling psychologists who find that psychological services are being provided in a manner that is discriminatory or exploitative to users and/or contrary to these Guidelines or to state or federal statutes take appropriate corrective action, which may include the refusal to provide services. When conflicts of interest arise, the counseling psychologist is guided in the resolution of differences by the principles set forth in the American Psychological Association's *Ethical Principles of Psychologists* (APA, 1981b) and "Guidelines for Conditions of Employment of Psychologists" (APA, 1972).[16]

Recognition is given to the following considerations in regard to the withholding of services: (a) the professional right of counseling psychologists to limit their practice to a specific category of users with whom they have achieved demonstrated competence (e.g., adolescents or families); (b) the right and responsibility of counseling psychologists to withhold an assessment procedure when not validly applicable; (c) the right and responsibility of counseling psychologists to withhold services in specific instances in which their own limitations or client characteristics might impair the quality of the services; (d) the obligation of counseling psychologists to seek to ameliorate through peer review, consultation, or other personal therapeutic procedures those factors that inhibit the provision of services to particular individuals; and (e) the obligation of counseling psychologists who withhold services to assist clients in obtaining services from other sources.[17]

3.2 *Counseling psychologists pursue their activities as members of the independent, autonomous profession of psychology.*[18]

INTERPRETATION: Counseling psychologists, as members of an independent profession, are responsible both to the public and to their peers through established review mechanisms. Counseling psychologists are aware of the implications of their activities for the profession as a whole. They seek to eliminate discriminatory practices instituted for self-serving purposes that are not in the interest of the users (e.g., arbitrary requirements for referral and supervision by another profession). They are cognizant of their responsibilities for the development of the profession, participate where possible in the training and career development of students and other providers, participate as appropriate in the training of paraprofessionals or other professionals, and integrate and supervise the implementation of their contributions within the structure established for delivering psychological services. Counseling psychologists facilitate the development of, and participate in, professional standards review mechanisms.[19]

Counseling psychologists seek to work with other professionals in a cooperative manner for the good of the users and the benefit of the general public. Counseling psychologists associated with multidisciplinary settings support the principle that members of each participating profession have equal rights and opportunities to share all privileges and responsibilities of full membership in human service facilities and to administer service programs in their respective areas of competence.

3.3 There are periodic, systematic, and effective evaluations of counseling psychological services.[20]

INTERPRETATION: When the counseling psychological service unit is a component of a larger organization, regular evaluation of progress in achieving goals is provided for in the service delivery plan, including consideration of the effectiveness of counseling psychological services relative to costs in terms of use of time and money and the availability of professional and support personnel.

Evaluation of the counseling psychological service delivery system is conducted internally and, when possible, under independent auspices as well. This evaluation includes an assessment of effectiveness (to determine what the service unit accomplished), efficiency (to determine the total costs of providing the services), continuity (to ensure that the services are appropriately linked to other human services), availability (to determine appropriate levels and distribution of services and personnel), accessibility (to ensure that the services are barrier free to users), and adequacy (to determine whether the services meet the identified needs for such services).

There is a periodic reexamination of review mechanisms to ensure that these attempts at public safeguards are effective and cost efficient and do not place unnecessary encumbrances on the providers or impose unnecessary additional expenses on users or sanctioners for services rendered.

3.4 Counseling psychologists are accountable for all aspects of the services they provide and are responsive to those concerned with these services.[21]

INTERPRETATION: In recognizing their responsibilities to users, sanctioners, third-party purchasers, and other providers, and where appropriate and consistent with the users' legal rights and privileged communications, counseling psychologists make available information about, and provide opportunity to participate in, decisions concerning such issues as initiation, termination, continuation, modification, and evaluation of counseling psychological services.

Depending on the settings, accurate and full information is made available to prospective individual or organizational users regarding the qualifications of providers, the nature and extent of services offered, and where appropriate, financial and social costs.

Where appropriate, counseling psychologists inform users of their payment policies and their willingness to assist in obtaining reimbursement. To assist their users, those who accept reimbursement from a third party are acquainted with the appropriate statutes and regulations, the procedures for submitting claims, and the limits on confidentiality of claims information, in accordance with pertinent statutes.

GUIDELINE 4
ENVIRONMENT

4.1 *Providers of counseling psychological services promote the development in the service setting of a physical, organizational, and social environment that facilitates optimal human functioning.*

INTERPRETATION: Federal, state, and local requirements for safety, health, and sanitation are observed.

As providers of services, counseling psychologists are concerned with the environment of their service unit, especially as it affects the quality of service, but also as it impinges on human functioning in the larger context. Physical arrangements and organizational policies and procedures are conducive to the human dignity, self-respect, and optimal functioning of users and to the effective delivery of service. Attention is given to the comfort and the privacy of providers and users. The atmosphere in which counseling psychological services are rendered is appropriate to the service and to the users, whether in an office, clinic, school, college, university, hospital, industrial organization, or other institutional setting.

FOOTNOTES

[1]The footnotes appended to these Specialty Guidelines represent an attempt to provide a coherent context of other policy statements of the Association regarding professional practice. The Guidelines extend these previous policy statements where necessary to reflect current concerns of the public and the profession.

[2]The following two categories of professional psychologists who met the criteria indicated below on or before the adoption of these Specialty Guidelines on January 31, 1980, are also considered counseling psychologists: Category 1—persons who completed (a) a doctoral degree program primarily psychological in content at a regionally accredited university or professional school and (b) 3 postdoctoral years of appropriate education, training, and experience in providing counseling psychological services as defined herein, including a minimum of 1 year in a counseling setting; Category 2—persons who on or before September 4, 1974, (a) completed a master's degree from a program primarily psychological in content at a regionally accredited university or professional school and (b) held a license or certificate in the state in which they practiced, conferred by a state board of psychological examiners, or the endorsement of the state psychological association through voluntary certification, and who, in addition, prior to January 31, 1980, (c) obtained 5 post-master's years of appropriate education, training, and experience in providing counseling psychological services as defined herein, including a minimum of 2 years in a counseling setting.

After January 31, 1980, professional psychologists who wish to be recognized as professional counseling psychologists are referred to Guideline 1.7.

[3]The areas of knowledge and training that are a part of the educational program for all professional psychologists have been presented in two APA documents, *Education and Credentialing in Psychology II* (APA, 1977a) and *Criteria for Accreditation of Doctoral Training Programs and Internships in Professional Psychology* (APA, 1979). There is consistency in the presentation of core areas in the education

and training of all professional psychologists. The description of education and training in these Guidelines is based primarily on the document *Education and Credentialing in Psychology II*. It is intended to indicate broad areas of required curriculum, with the expectation that training programs will undoubtedly want to interpret the specific content of these areas in different ways depending on the nature, philosophy, and intent of the programs.

[4]Functions and activities of counseling psychologists relating to the teaching of psychology, the writing or editing of scholarly or scientific manuscripts, and the conduct of scientific research do not fall within the purview of these Guidelines.

[5]These definitions should be compared with the APA (1967) guidelines for state legislation (hereinafter referred to as state guidelines), which define *psychologist* (i.e., the generic professional psychologist, not the specialist counseling psychologist) and the *practice of psychology* as follows:

A person represents himself [or herself] to be a psychologist when he [or she] holds himself [or herself] out to the public by any title or description of services incorporating the words "psychology," "psychological," "psychologist," and/or offers to render or renders services as defined below to individuals, groups, organizations, or the public for a fee, monetary or otherwise.

The practice of psychology within the meaning of this act is defined as rendering to individuals, groups, organizations, or the public any psychological service involving the application of principles, methods, and procedures of understanding, predicting, and influencing behavior, such as the principles pertaining to learning, perception, motivation, thinking, emotions, and interpersonal relationships; the methods and procedures of interviewing, counseling, and psychotherapy; of constructing, administering, and interpreting tests of mental abilities, aptitudes, interests, attitudes, personality characteristics, emotion, and motivation; and of assessing public opinion.

The application of said principles and methods includes, but is not restricted to: diagnosis, prevention, and amelioration of adjustment problems and emotional and mental disorders of individuals and groups; hypnosis; educational and vocational counseling; personnel selection and management; the evaluation and planning for effective work and learning situations; advertising and market research; and the resolution of interpersonal and social conflicts.

Psychotherapy within the meaning of this act means the use of learning, conditioning methods, and emotional reactions, in a professional relationship, to assist a person or persons to modify feelings, attitudes, and behavior which are intellectually, socially, or emotionally maladjustive or ineffectual.

The practice of psychology shall be as defined above, any existing statute in the state of _____ to the contrary notwithstanding. (APA, 1967, pp. 1098–1099)

[6]The relation of a psychological service unit to a larger facility or institution is also addressed indirectly in the APA (1972) "Guidelines for Conditions of Employment of Psychologists" (hereinafter referred to as CEP Guidelines), which emphasize the roles, responsibilities, and prerogatives of the psychologist when he or she is employed by or provides services for another agency, institution, or business.

[7]This Guideline replaces earlier recommendations in the 1967 state guidelines concerning exemption of psychologists from licensure. Recommendations 8 and 9 of those guidelines read as follows:

Persons employed as psychologists by accredited academic institutions, governmental agencies, research laboratories, and business corporations should be exempted, provided such employees are performing those duties for which they are employed by such organizations, and within the confines of such organizations.

Persons employed as psychologists by accredited academic institutions, governmental agencies, research laboratories, and business corporations consulting or offering their research findings or providing scientific information *to like organizations* for a fee should be exempted. (APA, 1967, p. 1100)

On the other hand, the 1967 state guidelines specifically denied exemptions under certain conditions, as noted in Recommendations 10 and 11:

Persons employed as psychologists who offer or provide psychological services to the public for a fee, over and above the salary that they receive for the performance of their regular duties, should not be exempted.

Persons employed as psychologists by organizations that sell psychological services to the public should not be exempted. (APA, 1967, pp. 1100–1101)

The present APA policy, as reflected in this Guideline, establishes a single code of practice for psychologists providing covered services to users in any setting. The present position is that a psychologist providing any covered service meets local statutory requirements for licensure or certification. See the section entitled Principles and Implications of the Specialty Guidelines for further elaboration of this point.

[8]A closely related principle is found in the APA (1972) CEP Guidelines:

It is the policy of APA that psychology as an independent profession is entitled to parity with other health and human service professions in institutional practices and before the law. Psychologists in interdisciplinary settings such as colleges and universities, medical schools, clinics, private practice groups, and other agencies expect parity with other professions in such matters as academic rank, board status, salaries, fringe benefits, fees, participation in administrative decisions, and all other conditions of employment, private contractual arrangements, and status before the law and legal institutions. (APA, 1972, p. 333)

[9]See CEP Guidelines (section entitled Career Development) for a closely related statement:

Psychologists are expected to encourage institutions and agencies which employ them to sponsor or conduct career development programs. The purpose of these programs would be to enable psychologists to engage in study for professional advancement and to keep abreast of developments in their field. (APA, 1972, p. 332)

[10]This Guideline follows closely the statement regarding "Policy on Training for Psychologists Wishing to Change Their Specialty" adopted by the APA Council of Representatives in January 1976. Included therein was the implementing provision that "this policy statement shall be incorporated in the guidelines of the Committee on Accreditation so that appropriate sanctions can be brought to bear on university and internship training programs that violate [it]" (Conger, 1976, p. 424).

[11]See also APA's (1981b) *Ethical Principles of Psychologists,* especially Principles 5 (Confidentiality), 6 (Welfare of the Consumer), and 9 (Research With Human Participants); and see *Ethical Principles in the Conduct of Research With Human Participants* (APA, 1973a). Also, in 1978 Division 17 approved in principle a statement on "Principles for Counseling and Psychotherapy With Women," which was designed to protect the interests of female users of counseling psychological services.

[12]Support for this position is found in the section on relations with other professions in *Psychology as a Profession:*

Professional persons have an obligation to know and take into account the traditions and practices of other professional groups with whom they work and to cooperate fully with members of such groups with whom research, service, and other functions are shared. (APA, 1968, p. 5)

[13]One example of a specific application of this principle is found in APA's (1981a) revised *APA/CHAMPUS Outpatient Psychological Provider Manual.* Another example, quoted below, is found in Guideline 2 in APA's (1973b) "Guidelines for Psychologists Conducting Growth Groups":

The following information should be made available in *writing* [italics added] to all prospective participants:
(a)   An explicit statement of the purpose of the group;
(b)   Types of techniques that may be employed;
(c)   The education, training, and experience of the leader or leaders;
(d)   The fee and any additional expense that may be incurred;

(*e*)   A statement as to whether or not a follow-up service is included in the fee;

(*f*)   Goals of the group experience and techniques to be used;

(*g*)   Amounts and kinds of responsibility to be assumed by the leader and by the participants. For example, (*i*) the degree to which a participant is free not to follow suggestions and prescriptions of the group leader and other group members; (*ii*) any restrictions on a participant's freedom to leave the group at any time; and

(*h*)   Issues of confidentiality. (p. 933)

[14]See Principle 5 (Confidentiality) in *Ethical Principles of Psychologists* (APA, 1981b).

[15]Support for the principles of privileged communication is found in at least two policy statements of the Association:

In the interest of both the public and the client and in accordance with the requirements of good professional practice, the profession of psychology seeks recognition of the privileged nature of confidential communications with clients, preferably through statutory enactment or by administrative policy where more appropriate. (APA, 1968, p. 8)

Wherever possible, a clause protecting the privileged nature of the psychologist-client relationship be included.

When appropriate, psychologists assist in obtaining general "across the board" legislation for such privileged communications. (APA, 1967, p. 1103)

[16]The CEP Guidelines include the following;

It is recognized that under certain circumstances, the interests and goals of a particular community or segment of interest in the population may be in conflict with the general welfare. Under such circumstances, the psychologist's professional activity must be primarily guided by the principle of "promoting human welfare." (APA, 1972, p. 334)

[17]This paragraph is adapted in part from the CEP Guidelines (APA, 1972, p. 333).

[18]Support for the principle of the independence of psychology as a profession is found in the following:

As a member of an autonomous profession, a psychologist rejects limitations upon his [or her] freedom of thought and action other than those imposed by his [or her] moral, legal, and social responsibilities. The Association is always prepared to provide appropriate assistance to any responsible member who becomes subjected to unreasonable limitations upon his [or her] opportunity to function as a practitioner, teacher, researcher, administrator, or consultant. The Association is always prepared to cooperate with any responsible professional organization in opposing any unreasonable limitations on the professional functions of the members of that organization.

This insistence upon professional autonomy has been upheld over the years by the affirmative actions of the courts and other public and private bodies in support of the right of the psychologist— and other professionals—to pursue those functions for which he [or she] is trained and qualified to perform. (APA, 1968, p. 9)

Organized psychology has the responsibility to define and develop its own profession, consistent with the general canons of science and with the public welfare.

Psychologists recognize that other professions and other groups will, from time to time, seek to define the roles and responsibilities of psychologists. The APA opposes such developments on the same principle that it is opposed to the psychological profession taking positions which would define the work and scope of responsibility of other duly recognized professions. (APA, 1972, p. 333)

[19]APA support for peer review is detailed in the following excerpt from the APA (1971) statement entitled "Psychology and National Health Care":

All professions participating in a national health plan should be directed to establish review mechanisms (or performance evaluations) that include not only peer review but active participation by persons representing the consumer. In situations where there are fiscal agents, they should also have representation when appropriate. (p. 1026)

[20]This Guideline on program evaluation is based directly on the following excerpts from two APA position papers:

> The quality and availability of health services should be evaluated continuously by both consumers and health professionals. Research into the efficiency and effectiveness of the system should be conducted both internally and under independent auspices. (APA, 1971, p. 1025)
>
> The comprehensive community mental health center should devote an explicit portion of its budget to program evaluation. All centers should inculcate in their staff attention to and respect for research findings; the larger centers have an obligation to set a high priority on basic research and to give formal recognition to research as a legitimate part of the duties of staff members.
>
> . . . Only through explicit appraisal of program effects can worthy approaches be retained and refined, ineffective ones dropped. Evaluative monitoring of program achievements may vary, of course, from the relatively informal to the systematic and quantitative, depending on the importance of the issue, the availability of resources, and the willingness of those responsible to take risks of substituting informed judgment for evidence. (Smith & Hobbs, 1966, pp. 21–22)

[21]See also the CEP Guidelines for the following statement: "A psychologist recognizes that . . . he [or she] alone is accountable for the consequences and effects of his [or her] services, whether as teacher, researcher, or practitioner. This responsibility cannot be shared, delegated, or reduced" (APA, 1972, p. 334).

REFERENCES

AMERICAN PSYCHOLOGICAL ASSOCIATION, COMMITTEE ON LEGISLATION. A model for state legislation affecting the practice of psychology. *American Psychologist*, 1967, *22*, 1095–1103.

AMERICAN PSYCHOLOGICAL ASSOCIATION. *Psychology as a profession.* Washington, D.C.: Author, 1968.

AMERICAN PSYCHOLOGICAL ASSOCIATION. Psychology and national health care. *American Psychologist*, 1971, *26*, 1025–1026.

AMERICAN PSYCHOLOGICAL ASSOCIATION. Guidelines for conditions of employment of psychologists. *American Psychologist*, 1972, *27*, 331–334.

AMERICAN PSYCHOLOGICAL ASSOCIATION. *Ethical principles in the conduct of research with human participants.* Washington, D.C.: Author, 1973. (a)

AMERICAN PSYCHOLOGICAL ASSOCIATION. Guidelines for psychologists conducting growth groups. *American Psychologist*, 1973, *28*, 933. (b)

AMERICAN PSYCHOLOGICAL ASSOCIATION. *Standards for educational and psychological tests.* Washington, D.C.: Author, 1974. (a)

AMERICAN PSYCHOLOGICAL ASSOCIATION. *Standards for providers of psychological services.* Washington, D.C.: Author, 1974. (b)

AMERICAN PSYCHOLOGICAL ASSOCIATION. *Education and credentialing in psychology II.* Report of a meeting, June 4–5, 1977. Washington, D.C.: Author, 1977. (a)

AMERICAN PSYCHOLOGICAL ASSOCIATION. *Standards for providers of psychological services* (Rev. ed.). Washington, D.C.: Author, 1977. (b)

AMERICAN PSYCHOLOGICAL ASSOCIATION. *Criteria for accreditation of doctoral training programs and internships in professional psychology.* Washington, D.C.: Author, 1979 (amended 1980).

AMERICAN PSYCHOLOGICAL ASSOCIATION. *APA/CHAMPUS outpatient psychological provider manual* (Rev. ed.). Washington, D.C.: Author, 1981. (a)

AMERICAN PSYCHOLOGICAL ASSOCIATION. *Ethical principles of psychologists* (Rev. ed.). Washington, D.C.: Author, 1981. (b)

CONGER, J. J. Proceedings of the American Psychological Association, Incorporated, for the year 1975: Minutes of the annual meeting of the Council of Representatives. *American Psychologist*, 1976, *31*, 406–434.

SMITH, M. B. & HOBBS, N. *The community and the community mental health center.* Washington, D.C.: American Psychological Association, 1966.

APPENDIX VI
CODE OF ETHICS, NATIONAL ASSOCIATION OF SOCIAL WORKERS

I. The social worker's conduct and comportment as a social worker
   A. *Propriety.* The social worker should maintain high standards of personal conduct in the capacity or identity as social worker.
      1. The private conduct of the social worker is a personal matter to the same degree as is any other person's, except when such conduct compromises the fulfillment of professional responsibilities.
      2. The social worker should not participate in, condone, or be associated with dishonesty, fraud, deceit, or misrepresentation.
      3. The social worker should distinguish clearly between statements and actions made as a private individual and as a representative of the social work profession or an organization or group.
   B. *Competence and professional development.* The social worker should strive to become and remain proficient in professional practice and the performance of professional functions.
      1. The social worker should accept responsibility or employment only on the basis of existing competence or the intention to acquire the necessary competence.
      2. The social worker should not misrepresent professional qualifications, education, experience, or affiliations.
   C. *Service.* The social worker should regard as primary the service obligation of the social work profession.
      1. The social worker should retain ultimate responsibility for the quality and extent of the service that individual assumes, assigns, or performs.
      2. The social worker should act to prevent practices that are inhumane or discriminatory against any person or group of persons.
   D. *Integrity.* The social worker should act in accordance with the highest standards of professional integrity and impartiality.
      1. The social worker should be alert to and resist the influences and pressures that interfere with the exercise of professional discretion and impartial judgment required for the performance of professional functions.
      2. The social worker should not exploit professional relationships for personal gain.
   E. *Scholarship and research.* The social worker engaged in study and research should be guided by the conventions of scholarly inquiry.
      1. The social worker engaged in research should consider carefully its possible consequences for human beings.
      2. The social worker engaged in research should ascertain that the consent of participants in the research is voluntary and informed, without any implied deprivation or penalty for refusal

to participate, and with due regard for participants' privacy and dignity.

3. The social worker engaged in research should protect participants from unwarranted physical or mental discomfort, distress, harm, danger, or deprivation.

4. The social worker who engages in the evaluation of services or cases should discuss them only for the professional purposes and only with persons directly and professionally concerned with them.

5. Information obtained about participants in research should be treated as confidential.

6. The social worker should take credit only for work actually done in connection with scholarly and research endeavors and credit contributions made by others.

II. The social worker's ethical responsibility to clients

F.   *Primacy of clients' interests.* The social worker's primary responsibility is to clients.

1. The social worker should serve clients with devotion, loyalty, determination, and the maximum application of professional skill and competence.

2. The social worker should not exploit relationships with clients for personal advantage, or solicit the clients of one's agency for private practice.

3. The social worker should not practice, condone, facilitate, or collaborate with any form of discrimination on the basis of race, color, sex, sexual orientation, age, religion, national origin, marital status, political belief, mental or physical handicap, or any other preference or personal characteristic, condition, or status.

4. The social worker should avoid relationships or commitments that conflict with the interests of clients.

5. The social worker should under no circumstances engage in sexual activities with clients.

6. The social worker should provide clients with accurate and complete information regarding the extent and nature of the services available to them.

7. The social worker should apprise clients of their risks, rights, opportunities, and obligations associated with social service to them.

8. The social worker should seek advice and counsel of colleagues and supervisors whenever such consultation is in the best interest of clients.

9. The social worker should terminate service to clients, and pro-

fessional relationships with them, when such service and relationships are no longer required or no longer serve the clients' needs or interests.

10.   The social worker should withdraw services precipitously only under unusual circumstances, giving careful consideration to all factors in the situation and taking care to minimize possible adverse effects.

11.   The social worker who anticipates the termination or interruption of service to clients should notify clients promptly and seek the transfer, referral, or continuation of services in relation to the clients' needs and preferences.

G.   *Rights and prerogatives of clients.* The social worker should make every effort to foster maximum self-determination on the part of clients.

1.   When the social worker must act on behalf of a client who has been adjudged legally incompetent, the social worker should safeguard the interests and rights of that client.

2.   When another individual has been legally authorized to act in behalf of a client, the social worker should deal with that person always with the client's best interest in mind.

3.   The social worker should not engage in any action that violates or diminishes the civil or legal rights of clients.

H.   *Confidentiality and privacy.* The social worker should respect the privacy of clients and hold in confidence all information obtained in the course of professional service.

1.   The social worker should share with others confidences revealed by clients, without their consent, only for compelling professional reasons.

2.   The social worker should inform clients fully about the limits of confidentiality in a given situation, the purposes for which information is obtained, and how it may be used.

3.   The social worker should afford clients reasonable access to any official social work records concerning them.

4.   When providing clients with access to records, the social worker should take due care to protect the confidences of others contained in those records.

5.   The social worker should obtain informed consent of clients before taping, recording, or permitting third party observation of their activities.

I.   *Fees.* When setting fees, the social worker should ensure that they are fair, reasonable, considerate, and commensurate with the service performed and with due regard for the clients' ability to pay.

1.   The social worker should not divide a fee or accept or give anything of value for receiving or making a referral.

III. The social worker's ethical responsibility to colleagues

J. *Respect, fairness, and courtesy.* The social worker should treat colleagues with respect, courtesy, fairness, and good faith.

   1. The social worker should cooperate with colleagues to promote professional interests and concerns.

   2. The social worker should respect confidences shared by colleagues in the course of their professional relationships and transactions.

   3. The social worker should create and maintain conditions of practice that facilitate ethical and competent professional performance by colleagues.

   4. The social worker should treat with respect, and represent accurately and fairly, the qualifications, views, and findings of colleagues and use appropriate channels to express judgments on these matters.

   5. The social worker who replaces or is replaced by a colleague in professional practice should act with consideration for the interest, character, and reputation of that colleague.

   6. The social worker should not exploit a dispute between a colleague and employers to obtain a position or otherwise advance the social worker's interest.

   7. The social worker should seek arbitration or mediation resolution for compelling professional reasons.

   8. The social worker should extend to colleagues of other professions the same respect and cooperation that is extended to social work colleagues.

   9. The social worker who serves as an employer, supervisor, or mentor to colleagues should make orderly and explicit arrangements regarding the conditions of their continuing professional relationship.

   10. The social worker who has the responsibility for employing and evaluating the performance of other staff members should fulfill such responsibility in a fair, considerate, and equitable manner, on the basis of clearly enunciated criteria.

   11. The social worker who has the responsibility for evaluating the performance of employees, supervisees, or students should share evaluations with them.

K. *Dealing with colleagues' clients.* The social worker has the responsibility to relate to the clients of colleagues with full professional consideration.

   1. The social worker should not solicit the clients of colleagues.

   2. The social worker should not assume professional responsibility

for the clients of another agency or a colleague without appropriate communication with that agency or colleague.

3. The social worker who serves the clients of colleagues, during a temporary absence or emergency, should serve those clients with the same consideration as that afforded any client.

IV. The social worker's ethical responsibility to employers and employing organizations

  L. *Commitments to employing organization.* The social worker should adhere to commitments made to the employing organization.

    1. The social worker should work to improve the employing agency's policies and procedures, and the efficiency and effectiveness of its services.

    2. The social worker should not accept employment or arrange student field placements in an organization which is currently under public sanction by NASW for violating personnel standards, or imposing limitations on or penalties for professional actions on behalf of clients.

    3. The social worker should act to prevent and eliminate discrimination in the employing organization's work assignments and in its employment policies and practices.

    4. The social worker should use with scrupulous regard, and only for the purpose for which they are intended, the resources of the employing organization.

V. The social worker's ethical responsibility to the social work profession

  M. *Maintaining the integrity of the profession.* The social worker should uphold and advance the values, ethics, knowledge, and mission of the profession.

    1. The social worker should protect and enhance the dignity and integrity of the profession and should be responsible and vigorous in discussion and criticism of the profession.

    2. The social worker should take action through appropriate channels against unethical conduct by any other member of the profession.

    3. The social worker should act to prevent the unauthorized and unqualified practice of social work.

    4. The social worker should make no misrepresentation in advertising as to qualifications, competence, service, or results to be achieved.

  N. *Community service.* The social worker should assist the profession in making social services available to the general public.

    1. The social worker should contribute time and professional expertise to activities that promote respect for the utility, the integrity, and the competence of the social work profession.

2. The social worker should support the formulation, development, enactment, and implementation of social policies of concern to the profession.

O. *Development of knowledge.* The social worker should take responsibility for identifying, developing, and fully utilizing knowledge for professional practice.

    1. The social worker should base practice upon recognized knowledge relevant to social work.

    2. The social worker should critically examine and keep current with emerging knowledge relevant to social work.

    3. The social worker should contribute to the knowledge base of social work and share research knowledge and practice wisdom with colleagues.

VI. The social worker's ethical responsibility to society

P. *Promoting the general welfare.* The social worker should promote the general welfare of society.

    1. The social worker should act to prevent and eliminate discrimination against any person or group on the basis of race, color, sex, sexual orientation, age, religion, national origin, marital status, political belief, mental or physical handicap, or any other preference or personal characteristic, condition, or status.

    2. The social worker should act to ensure that all persons have access to the resources, services, and opportunities which they require.

    3. The social worker should act to expand choice and opportunity for all persons, with special regard for disadvantaged or oppressed groups and persons.

    4. The social worker should promote conditions that encourage respect for the diversity of cultures which constitute American society.

    5. The social worker should provide appropriate professional services in public emergencies.

    6. The social worker should advocate changes in policy and legislation to improve social conditions and to promote social justice.

    7. The social worker should encourage informed participation by the public in shaping social policies and institutions.

APPENDIX VII
ASGW PROFESSIONAL STANDARDS FOR GROUP COUNSELING

PREAMBLE

Whereas counselors may be able to function effectively with individual clients, they are also required to possess specialized knowledge and skills that render them effective in group counseling. The Association for Specialists in Group Work supports the preparation of group practitioners as part of and in addition to counselor education. The *Professional Standards for Group Counseling* represent the minimum core of group leader (cognitive and applied) competencies that have been identified by the Association for Specialists in Group Work.

DEFINITION OF GROUP COUNSELING

Consists of the interpersonal processes and activities focused on conscious thoughts and behavior performed by individuals who have the professional credentials to work with and counsel groups of individuals regarding career, educational, personal, social and developmentally related concerns, issues, tasks or problems.

DESIGNATED GROUP COUNSELING AREAS

In order to work as a professional in group counseling, an individual must meet and demonstrate minimum competencies in the generic core of group counseling standards. These are applicable to all training programs regardless of level of work or specialty area. In addition to the generic core competencies (and in order to practice in a specific area of expertise), the individual will be required to meet one or more specialty area standards (school counseling and guidance, student personnel services in high education, or community/mental health agency counseling).

GROUP COUNSELOR KNOWLEDGE COMPETENCIES

The qualified group leader has *demonstrated specialized knowledge* in the following aspects of group work:

1. Be able to state for at least three major theoretical approaches to group counseling the distinguishing characteristics of each and the commonalities shared by all.
2. Basic principles of group dynamics and the therapeutic ingredients of groups.
3. Personal characteristics of group leaders that have an impact on members; knowledge of personal strengths, weaknesses, biases, values and their impact on others.
4. Specific ethical problems and considerations unique to group counseling.
5. Body of research on group counseling in one's specialty area (school counseling, college students personnel, or community/mental health agency).

6. Major modes of group work, differentiation among the modes, and the appropriate instances in which each is used (such as group guidance, group counseling, group therapy, human relations training, etc.).

7. Process components involved in typical stages of a group's development (i.e., characteristics of group interaction and counselor roles).

8. Major facilitative and debilitative roles that group members may take.

9. Advantages and disadvantages of group counseling and the circumstances for which it is indicated or contraindicated.

GROUP COUNSELOR COMPETENCIES

The qualified group leader has shown the following abilities:

1. To screen and assess readiness levels of prospective clients.

2. To deliver a clear, concise, and complete definition of group counseling.

3. To recognize self-defeating behaviors of group members.

4. To describe and conduct a personally selected group counseling model appropriate to the age and clientele of group leader's specialty area(s).

5. To identify accurately nonverbal behavior among group members.

6. To exhibit appropriate pacing skills involved in stages of a group's development.

7. To identify and intervene effectively at critical incidents in the group process.

8. To work appropriately with disruptive group members.

9. To make use of the major strategies, techniques, and procedures of group counseling.

10. To provide and use procedures to assist transfer and support of changes by group members in the natural environment.

11. To use adjunct group structures such as psychological homework (i.e., self monitoring, contracting).

12. To use basic group leader interventions such as process comments, empathic responses, self-disclosures, confrontations, etc.

13. To facilitate therapeutic conditions and forces in group counseling.

14. To work cooperatively and effectively with a co-leader.

15. To open and close sessions, and terminate the group process.

16. To provide follow up procedures to assist maintenance and support of group members.

17. To utilize assessment procedures in evaluating effects and contributions of group counseling.

TABLE VIII-1   Training in Clinical Practice

TYPE OF SUPERVISED EXPERIENCE	MINIMUM NUMBER OF [CLOCK] HOURS REQUIRED: MASTER'S OR ENTRY LEVEL PROGRAM
1. Critique of group tapes (by self or others)	5
2. Observing group counseling (live or media presentation)	5
3. Participating as a member in a group	15
4. Leading a group with a partner and receiving critical feedback from a supervisor	15
5. Practicum: Leading a group alone, with critical self-analysis of performance; supervisor feedback on tape; and self-analysis	15
6. Fieldwork of Internship: Practice as a group leader with on-the-job supervision.	25

GLOSSARY

AACD: American Association for Counseling and Development.

AAMFT: American Association for Marriage and Family Therapy.

Acceptance: The ability to receive, to understand or believe in another person's outlook on life.

Accurate empathy: The ability to comprehend accurately how another person feels by putting oneself in that person's shoes and looking at a given situation as he or she would.

Action: Specific steps taken to bring about a change in a relationship or situation.

Action counseling: An integrative counseling approach that involves three major phases in the counseling process: (1) establishing a relationship; (2) gaining a commitment; and (3) implementing action.

Active listening: Tuning in carefully to the client's messages, decoding them, and responding accurately to the meaning behind the message.

Advanced empathy: An increased awareness of a client's verbal and nonverbal communication.

Advice-giving: Attempting to guide clients in the right direction by instructing them in the right course of action.

Affective domain: That aspect of the individual which involves the feelings the individual is experiencing.

Aggressiveness: Standing up for one's rights in a way that denies or discounts the rights of others.

Alcoholism: One form of chemical dependency in which the primary drug abused is alcohol.

Alienation: Repression or blocking of one's own feelings so they no longer seem to belong to oneself.

AMHCA: American Mental Health Counselors Association.

Anger: Strong displeasure or indignation stirred by a sense of injury or wrong.

Anorexia: A form of eating disorder in which the individual overly restricts his or her caloric input, leading to severe malnutrition and potential physiological harm.

Anxiety: A state of uneasiness and apprehension.

APA: American Psychological Association.

ASGW: Association for Specialists in Group Work.

Assertiveness: Standing up for one's own rights in a way that does not violate the rights of others.

Attending: Nonverbal behavior that communicate a focus on, or paying attention to, the other person.

Authenticity: An attitude of realness, or genuineness.

Behavioral counseling: An approach that focuses on the modification of the way an individual acts through the application of learning principles.

Behavioral domain: That aspect of an individual which involves the actual behavior of the individual.

Birth order: The position or order of birth in the family, e.g., first child, second child, middle child, youngest child.

Blocking: Sudden stop in a train of thought or in mid-sentence.

Brainstorming: Thoughts produced by a sudden inspiration or idea.

Career counseling: A focus on planning and making decisions about occupations and/or education.

Caring: To be concerned with or interested in another person.

Catharsis: The experience of having prior experiences that have been repressed or forgotten brought to the surface so that they can be dealt with fully.

Chemical dependency: A disease in which the individual continues to use mood-altering chemicals (alcohol, cocaine, heroin, etc.) in spite of the difficulties caused by that usage.

Clarification: An attempt by the counselor to have a client be more specific regarding his feelings/observations, so as to understand exactly what has been meant.

Client-centered therapy: An approach that emphasizes the importance of the quality of the relationship between client and therapist—allowing the client to move toward self-growth.

Cognitive domain: That aspect of the individual which involves the thinking process and its relationship to feelings and behavior.

Cognitive therapy: An approach that focuses on the idea of active restructuring of perceptions and concepts, so that inferences are made on the basis of adequate information and reasonable attitudes.

Commitment: A verbal decision to work toward a specified change in behavior and/or attitude.

Concreteness: Involves the specific, total expression of feelings and experiences regardless of content, as opposed to being general and abstract.

Conflict: A mental struggle occurring when conscious and unconscious forces want to go in two different directions.

Confrontation: Forcing someone to come face-to-face with some aspect of his or her life by helping that individual to become more integrated and consistent in behavior and relationships with others.

Congruence: The ability of counselors to be themselves, without needing to present a professional front or facade.

Contracting: An agreement between two parties aimed at changing the behavior of one of the persons involved.

Core conditions: Qualities and characteristics associated with establishing and maintaining effective counseling: being authentic and genuine; providing positive regard or nonpossessive warmth; and having a high degree of accurate empathic understanding of another.

Counseling: A formal relationship between a trained counselor and a client in which the counselor attempts to help the client explore and understand the client's problems in a way that will lead to a resolution of those problems.

Credentialing: Methods for determining whether or not an individual is properly trained.

Crisis: A state of mind, usually of a limited duration, marked by symptoms of stress and producing extreme discomfort, as well as feelings of being overwhelmed and/or helpless.

Crisis intervention: An approach to helping people in crisis with the primary goal being to avoid catastrophe.

Decision-making: A process by which the client learns to estimate the probable consequences of various deeds and then acts on them.

Defense mechanisms: The means (usually involuntary) by which the ego protects itself against impulses and affects of the id and superego operating to protect the individual or serve as a block to self-growth.

Defensiveness: An attempt to support or justify a particular occurrence, usually by arguing.

Denial: The refusal to acknowledge unpleasant realities by ignoring their existence.

Dependency: The state of being controlled by or sustained by someone or something.

Depression: An emotional state consisting of lowering of mood-tone, difficulty in thinking, and psychomotor retardation.

Desensitization: The act of alleviating a maladaptive response by subjecting it to the eliciting stimulus at times when the response has either a low probability of production or none, removing the association between the stimulus and the response.

Diagnosis: The identification of the root cause of a problem(s) from its signs and symptoms.

Disclosure: To reveal or divulge feelings and reactions to events and people as they occur.

Discounting: The act of disregarding something that has been seen, heard or felt as having little or no value.

Displaced aggression: A shift of aggression from the original target to a safer one.

Displacement: A shift of emotion from the original target to a safer one.

Dream analysis: Techniques sometimes used to uncover unconscious material.

Eating disorder: A disorder in which individuals have lost control over their eating behaviors to the extent that potential serious health problems exist. Includes anorexia, bulimia, and compulsive overeating.

Eclectic: Utilizing the most useful elements of various approaches in a systematic manner to accomplish a specific purpose.

Educational counseling: Counseling that focuses on clarifying educational goals and establishing steps toward reaching them.

Ego: That part of the psyche of which the prime function is the perception of reality and adaptation to it.

Emotionalizing: Using an exaggerated expression of emotion in an attempt to avoid dealing with problem areas by appearing (falsely) to be working through an emotional difficulty.

Empathy: The ability to adopt the client's internal frame of reference so that the client's private world and meaning are accurately understood and clearly communicated.

Encounter group: A personal growth group in which the focus is on expanding awareness through honest, genuine contact with other group members.

Ethical issue: Issue related to standards of conduct based on a consensus value set as applied to a topic of discussion or controversy.

Existential anxiety: Anxiety produced by the awareness and responsibility of the freedom to choose how one leads one's life or the awareness of being finite and facing the inevitable prospect of death.

Existential counseling: An approach that consists of numerous approaches that emphasize the philosophical concerns of what it means to become fully human, stressing the understanding of how the client has failed to realize his or her potential and then how to succeed in this existence.

Experiencing: Allowing one's emotions to surface and becoming fully aware of them in one's consciousness.

External locus of control: Aspect of motivation in which the individual does not control the outcome of a given situation but allows outside forces to dictate what occurs.

Facilitating: Helping persons become aware of the causes and forces at work in their lives and, in doing so, learn to exert some control over those forces.

Family counseling: An approach in which individuals are viewed in relationship to the rest of the family, not by themselves and all members are involved in working through the problem.

Fear: To regard with dread or apprehension.

Feedback: Providing information to another individual regarding that person's behavior and its effects on others.

Focusing: A technique used to place attention on a point of concentration for reviewing one's feelings about oneself, other people, and other events that take place in one's life.

Follow-up: Keeping in touch with a client after counseling is terminated to see how things are progressing.

Free association: A technique in which a patient is encouraged to share (spontaneously) whatever thoughts, words, expressions or feelings come to mind, without censorship.

Game-playing: A variety of techniques used by individuals to manipulate others to meet their needs and thus allow the individuals to avoid responsibility.

Genuineness: The most fundamental element in the development of the therapeutic climate; the ability to be oneself, without putting on a front or hiding behind a mask.

Gestalt: In counseling, the concept of a meaningful whole when a healthy personality exists between those experiences that are in immediate focus and those set in the background.

Gestalt counseling: An approach that is concerned primarily with perceptions/cognitions with the purpose being to increase the client's self-awareness.

Goals: Targets for desired change.

Grief: Deep sorrow.

Group counseling: The use of group interaction to facilitate self-understanding as well as individual behavior change.

Group leader: Person or persons ultimately responsible for the climate of group counseling.

Group process: Refers to the stages of group development and the interactions that characterize each stage.

Group therapy: The use of group interaction to help individuals alter their thinking, feeling, or behavior in order to alleviate severe emotional distress.

Guidance: Prevention-oriented activities to prevent problems of a social, personal, vocational, or educational nature.

Guilt: A feeling of remorse when one believes he or she has done something wrong.

Health counseling: An approach that emphasizes the total well-being of the person, including prevention measures.

Helping: The establishment of a therapeutic climate in which personal growth can occur.

Here-and-now: Awareness of what is going on in a person's life at the moment.

Honesty: To be frank and open in dealings and relationships with others.

Humanistic approach: An approach to counseling that emphasizes the inherent ability of the individual to move toward positive growth when anxiety and stress are minimal.

Humor: The ability to see something or express it as funny.

Id: That part of the psyche of which the prime function is to satisfy the needs of the organism by decreasing pain and increasing pleasure, with no concern for reality or morality.

Identification: A defense used to enhance self-worth by closely associating oneself with another one admires or respects.

Immediacy: The ability to be tuned into the interactions with, and the reactions to another as they occur in the here-and-now.

Incongruence: Inability of a person to be genuine; putting on a front or professional facade.

Inherent nature: Those characteristics which are present at birth in all individuals (unless there is some type of brain damage and/or mental retardation).

Insight: An awareness of one's values, beliefs, thought processes, or behavior patterns.

Intellectualization: To avoid dealing with feelings by an exaggerated cognitive expression that analyzes or describes the feeling without experiencing it.

Internal locus of control: That aspect of motivation in which the individual takes control from within and is responsible for those actions.

Interpreting: Relates to the counselor's explanation of the meanings associated with the uncovered conscious material of the client.

Intervention: A planned confrontation designed to force the individual to seek a change in attitude, feelings, thinking, or behavior.

Introjection: Involves taking on the attitudes and values of others in an attempt to control one's own behavior and to act in an acceptable manner so as to protect oneself.

Leadership: The ability to guide, conduct, or facilitate others.

Learned helplessness: Once a person has been labeled a failure, he or she tends to take on that role in all levels of life, viewing self as incompetent and lacking in self-efficacy.

Learning group: The use of group interaction to acquire specific information and knowledge.

Life script: The way we play out our lives based on ''tapes'' our subconscious mind plays.

Life style: Particular behaviors and cognitions an individual uses to cope with stress and satisfy needs.

Listening: The process of tuning in carefully to another's message and responding accurately to the meaning behind the message.

Marital counseling: An approach in which couples examine the quality of their relationship, decide what problems are preventing genuine intimacy, and make decisions toward correcting those conflicts.

Meaninglessness: A sense of a person or situation lacking in importance.

Modeling: An approach based on the idea that a person will imitate the behavior of others.

Mourning: The expression of grief or sorrow.

Neurosis: Irrational solutions to problems accompanied by anxiety.

Nonassertive: Failing to stand up for one's rights and allowing others to take advantage.

Nonpossessive warmth: Positive regard or respect for another.

Nonstructured activities: Group activities that are allowed to occur spontaneously without prior planning or direction.

Norm: The expected behavior in a given situation.

Orientation: Providing the new group member with information about the purpose, norms, expectations, and rules of a group.

Paradox: A technique in which the client is asked to behave in a manner opposite that which he or she expected.

Personal growth group: A group in which the focus is on the enhancement of personal living skills, especially those skills involved in relating to others.

Phenomenological approach: An approach to understanding human behavior which emphasizes the importance of the individual's perception of self and the situation.

Phobia: A morbid fear, or experiencing excessive anxiety in a specific situation.

Positive regard: Nonpossessive warmth or respect for another.

Problem-solving: A systematic approach to decision-making.

Projection: Involves transferring blame for one's own shortcomings onto others as well as attributing to others one's unacceptable desires or impulses.

Psychoanalysis: A method of therapy that investigates the unconscious and then deals with the ego-defense mechanisms found.

Psychosis: An emotional disorder of severe intensity and disruptive to a person's life.

Rational-emotive therapy: A counseling method that stresses logical reasoning and cognitive processes.

Rationalization: Coming up with logical, ethical, or socially approved (but not the real) reasons for one's behavior.

Reaction formation: A defensive reaction in which a dangerous impulse is replaced by a feeling or behavior pattern that is just the opposite.

Reflection: Responding to a client in such a way that the client understands how his or her behavior is perceived by others.

Regression: The reaction to stress that involves reverting back to a less mature level of adjustment in order to feel safe.

Reinforcement: Strengthening a behavior by the addition of a reward.

Relationship: The social interaction, association, or involvement that occurs between people.

Repression: The removal of painful or dangerous thoughts and experiences from consciousness.

Resistance: Reluctance to accept what is happening or proposed to.

Respect: An attitude of positive regard, consideration, or prizing of another person.

Role: The part or character one plays, other than one's true self.

Screening: Systematic examination based on background, skills, etc., in order to put together a compatible group.

Self-actualization: Emphasis on the inherent tendency of people to move in the direction of growth, health, adjustment, socialization, self-realization, and autonomy.

Self-as-instrument: The personal characteristics of the counselor are seen as the major factor in facilitating the personal growth of clients.

Self-exploration: The act of looking inside oneself to determine feelings, thoughts, and goals.

Self-understanding: Being aware or having knowledge of oneself through experience.

Sensitivity group: The use of group interaction to increase members' sensitivity to their own feelings as well as to their impact on others.

Socialization: The process that transmits values and purposes of a group to an individual.

Social learning theory: The viewpoint that one learns through contact or observation of others.

Sorrow: The expression of mental pain or anguish caused by a loss or disappointment.

Structured activities: Group activities that are planned and/or controlled by the leader in a deliberate effort to achieve a specific outcome.

Structuring: Deliberate efforts to provide direction to counseling activities.

Sublimation: Channeling aggressive or sexual impulses into socially acceptable activities.

Summarization: A brief account stating the main point and feelings of a verbal interaction.

Superego: The part of the psyche that represents the moral and traditional values society feels are important.

Supportive: Able to encourage or help another.

T-groups: Laboratory training groups that emphasize the development of human relations skills through group experimentation.

Termination: The process by which a counseling relationship is concluded.

Therapeutic elements: Aspects or factors related to the effectiveness of a therapeutic intervention.

Therapy group: A group established to help individuals with severe emotional distress by helping them alter their thinking, feeling, or behavior.

Timing: Saying or doing something at the right moment to enhance its effectiveness.

Training group: See T-group.

Transactional analysis: A counseling approach that stresses the interaction between the individuals as both a symptom and a cause of psychological difficulties.

Transference: A dynamic in which the patient projects onto the counselor feelings the patient has toward significant others in his or her life.

Trust: An attitude of confidence or faith in another.

Unconditional positive regard: Genuine acceptance of all aspects of the client's self-experience.

Unfinished business: Situations from the past about which clients have unexpressed feelings such as anger, pain, anxiety, grief, guilt, etc.

Values: A set of beliefs that determines the decisions one makes.

Valuing: Communicating a genuine attitude of prizing an individual as a person of worth and dignity.

Withdrawal: Avoiding emotional or psychological issues by pulling back from emotional involvement with the counselor.

Special thanks to Melinda Sanderson for her help in compiling this section.

BIBLIOGRAPHY

ALLEN, E. E. (1982). Multiple attending in therapy groups. *Personel and Guidance Journal, 60*(5), 318–320.

ALLPORT, G. (1961). *Pattern and growth in personality.* New York: Holt, Rinehart & Winston.

AMERICAN ASSOCIATION FOR COUNSELING AND DEVELOPMENT. (1981). *Ethical standards.* Washington, D.C.: Author.

AMERICAN PSYCHOLOGICAL ASSOCIATION. (1981). *Ethical standards of psychologists.* Washington, DC.: Author.

ASSOCIATION FOR COUNSELOR EDUCATION AND SUPERVISION. (1964). The counselor: Professional preparation and role. *Personnel and Guidance Journal, 42,* 536–54.

ASSOCIATION FOR SPECIALISTS IN GROUP WORK. (1980). *Ethical guidelines for group leaders.* Falls Church, VA: Author.

AXLINE, V. (1969). *Play therapy* (rev. ed.). New York: Ballantine Books.

AZRIN, N. H., & BESALEL, V. A. (1980). *Job club counselor's manual.* Baltimore: University Park Press.

BAKEMAN, M. (1971). *Job seeking skills: Reference manual.* Minneapolis: Multi-Resource Center.

BANDURA, A., ROSS, D., & ROSS, S. (1963). Vicarious reinforcement and imitative learning. *Journal of Abnormal and Social Psychology, 67,* 601–607.

BARLOW, S., HANSEN, W. D., FUKRIMAN, A. J., & FINLEY, R. (1982). Leader communication style: Effects on members of small groups. *Small Group Behavior, 13,* 518–531.

BARRERA, M., JR. (1979). An evaluation of a brief group therapy for depression. *Journal of Consulting and Clinical Psychology, 47,* 413–415.

BECK, A. T., RUSH, A. J., SHAW, B. F., & EMORY, G. (1978). *Cognitive therapy of depression: A treatment manual.* New York: Guilford Press.

BEDNAR, R. L., & KAUL, T. J. (1978). Experiential group research: Current perspectives. In S. L. Garfield & A. E. Bergin (Eds.), *Handbook of psychotherapy and behavior change* (2nd ed.). New York: John Wiley.

BELKIN, G. S. (1981). *Practical counseling in the schools* (2nd ed.). Dubuque, IA: Wm. C. Brown.

BELKIN, G. S. (1984). *Introduction to counseling* (2nd ed.). Dubuque, IA: Wm. C. Brown.

BERMAN, E. (1982). Authority and authoritarianism in group psychotherapy. *International Journal of Group Psychotherapy, 32,* 189–200.

BERZON, B., PIOVS, C., & FARSON, R. (1963). The therapeutic event in group psychotherapy: A study of subjective reports by group members. *Journal of Individual Psychology, 19,* 204–212.

BLOCH, S. (1986). Therapeutic factors in group psychotherapy. In A. J. Frances & R. E. Hales (Eds.), *Annual Review, Vol. 5* (pp. 678–698). Washington, DC: American Psychiatric Press.

BLOCH, S., CROUCH, E., & REIBSTEIN, J. (1981). Therapeutic factors in group psychotherapy: A review. *Archives of General Psychiatry, 38,* 519–526.

BLOCH, S., REIBSTEIN, J., & CROUCH, E. (1979). A method for the study of therapeutic factors in group psychotherapy. *British Journal of Psychiatry, 134,* 257–263.

BLOCHER, D. H. (1966). *Development counseling.* New York: Ronald Press.

BLUME, S. B. (1984). Psychotherapy in the treatment of alcoholism. In L. Grinspoon (Ed.), *Psychiatry Update: Vol. III* (pp. 338–346). Washington, DC: American Psychiatric Press.

BREWER, J. M. (1942). *History of vocational guidance.* New York: Harper.

BRUCH, H. (1978). *The golden cage.* Cambridge, MA: Harvard University Press.

BUSSE, E. W., & PFEIFFER, E. (Eds.). (1973). *Mental illness in later life.* Washington, DC: American Psychiatric Association.

BUTLER, T., & FUKRIMAN, A. (1980). Patient perspective on the curative process: A comparison of day treatment and outpatient psychotherapy groups. *Small Group Behavior, 11,* 371–388.

CARKHUFF, R. R. (1969). *Helping and human relations.* New York: Holt, Rinehart & Winston.

CARKHUFF, R. R. (1971). Training as a preferred mode of treatment. *Journal of Counseling Psychology, 18,* 123–131.

CARKHUFF, R. R. & BERENSON, B. G. (1967). *Beyond counseling and therapy.* New York: Holt, Rinehart & Winston.

COCHE, E., & DIES, R. R. (1981). Integrating research findings into the practice of group psychotherapy. *Psychotherapy Theory Research and Practice, 18,* 410–416.

COHEN, R. G., & LIPKIN, G. B. (1979). *Therapeutic group work for health professionals.* New York: Springer.

COLANGELO, N., DUSTIN, D., & FOXLEY, C. H. (1982). *The human relations experience: Exercises in multicultural nonsexist education.* Belmont, CA: Wadsworth.

COMBS, A. (1962). A perceptual view of the adequate personality. In A. Combs (Ed.), *Perceiving, behaving, becoming* (pp. 50–64). Washington, DC: Yearbook Association for Supervision and Curriculum Development.

COMBS, A., & SOPER, D. (1963). The perceptual organization of effective counselors. *Journal of Counseling Psychology, 10,* 222–226.

COMBS, A., SOPER, D., GOODING, C., BENTON, J., DICKMAN, J., & USHER, R. (1969). *Florida studies in the helping professions.* Gainesville: University of Florida Press.

COREY, G. (1981). *Theory and practice of group counseling.* Monterey, CA: Brooks/Cole.

COREY, G. (1982). *The skilled helper.* Monterey, CA: Brooks/Cole.

COREY, G. (1985). *Theory and practice of group counseling* (2nd ed.). Monterey, CA: Brooks/ Cole.

COREY, G., & COREY, M. S. (1982). *Groups: Process and practice* (2nd ed.). Monterey, CA: Brooks/Cole.

COREY, G., & COREY, M. S. (1987). *Group counseling: Theory and practice* (3rd. ed.). Monterey, CA: Brooks/Cole.

COREY, G., COREY, M. S., & CALLAHAN, P. (1984). *Issues and ethics in the helping professions* (2nd ed.). Monterey, CA: Brooks/Cole.

COREY, G., COREY, M. S., CALLAHAN, P. J., & RUSSELL, J. M. (1982). *Group technique.* Monterey, CA: Brooks/Cole.

CORSINI, R., & ROSENBERG, B. (1955). Mechanisms of group psychotherapy: Processes and dynamics. *Journal of Abnormal and Social Psychology, 51,* 406–411.

COVI, L., ROTH, D., & LIPMAN, R. S. (1982). Cognitive group psychotherapy of depression: The close-ended group. *American Journal of Psychotherapy, 34,* 459–469.

CRITES, J. O. (1981). *Career counseling: Models, methods, and materials.* New York: McGraw-Hill.

CULPON, F. M. (1979). Studying action sociometry: An element in the personal growth of the therapist. *Journal of Group Psychotherapy, 32,* 122–127.

DAANE, C. (1972). *Vocational exploration group: Theory and research.* Washington, DC: U.S. Department of Labor.

DAY, M. (1981). Process in classical psychodynamic groups. *International Journal of Group Psychotherapy, 31,* 153–174.

DICKOFF, H., & LAKIN, M. (1963). Patients' views of group psychotherapy: Retrospections and interpretations. *International Journal of Group Psychotherapy, 13,* 61–73.

DINKMEYER, D. C., & MURO, J. J. (1979). *Group counseling: Theory and practice* (2nd ed.). Itasca, IL: Peacock.

DINKMEYER, D. C., PEW, W. L., & DINKMEYER, D. C., JR. (1979). *Adlerian counseling and psychotherapy.* Monterey, CA: Brooks/Cole.

DUNCAN, J. A., & GUMAER, J. (Eds.). (1980). *Developmental groups for children.* Springfield, IL: Charles C Thomas.

DUPONT, H. (1979). Affective development: Stage and sequence. In R. L. Mosher (Ed.), *Adolescents' development and education* (pp. 163–183). Berkeley: McCutchan.

DUSKA, R., & WHELAN, M. (1975). *Moral development: A guide to Piaget and Kohlberg.* New York: Paulist Press.

DUSTIN, R., & GEORGE, R. L. (1977). *Action counseling for behavior change* (2nd ed.). Cranston, RI: Carroll Press.

EGAN, G. (1975). *The skilled helper.* Monterey, CA: Brooks/Cole.

ELLIS, A. (1982). *Rational-emotive therapy and cognitive behavior therapy.* New York: Springer.

ERIKSON, E. H. (1963). *Childhood and society* (2nd ed.). New York: W. W. Norton.

ERNST, N. S., & GLAZER-WALDMAN, H. R. (Eds.). (1983). *The aged patient.* Chicago: Yearbook Medical Publishers.

FALLOON, I. R. H. (1981). Interpersonal variables in behavioral group therapy. *British Journal of Medical Psychology, 54,* 133–141.

FIGLER, H. E. (1979). *PATH: A career workbook for liberal arts students.* Cranston, RI: Carroll Press.

FLAVELL, J. H. (1963). *The developmental psychology of Jean Piaget.* New York: D. Van Nostrand.

FLORA-TOSTADO, J. (1981). Patient and therapist agreement on curative factors in group psychotherapy. *Dissertation Abstracts International, 42,* 371–B.

FORREST, G. G. (1984). *Intensive psychotherapy of alcoholism.* Springfield, IL: Charles C Thomas.

FRANK, J. D. (1957). Some determinants, manifestations and effects of cohesiveness in therapy groups. *International Journal of Group Psychotherapy, 7,* 53–63.

FRANK, J. D. (1971). Therapeutic factors in psychotherapy. *American Journal of Psychotherapy, 25,* 350–361.

FRANK, J. D., HOEHN-SARIC, R., & IMBER, S. D. (1978). *Effective ingredients of successful psychotherapy.* New York: Brunner/Mazel.

FRANKL, V. (1969). *The will to meaning.* Cleveland: World Publishing Press.

FRANKS, C. M., & WILSON, G. T. (1973). *Behavior therapy: Theory and practice.* New York: Brunner/Mazel.

FREEDMAN, S., & HURLEY, J. (1979). Maslow's needs: Individuals' perceptions of helpful factors in growth groups. *Small Group Behavior, 10,* 355–367.

GARNER, D. M., & GARFINKEL, P. E. (Eds.). (1985). *Handbook of psychotherapy for anorexia nervosa and bulimia.* New York: Guilford Press.

GAZDA, G. M. (1984). *Group counseling* (3rd. ed.). Boston: Allyn & Bacon.

GAZDA, G. M. (1978). *Group counseling: A developmental approach* (2nd ed.). Boston: Allyn & Bacon.

GAZDA, G. M., ASBURY, F. S., BALZER, F. J., CHILDERS, W. C., & WALTERS, R. P. (1984). *Human relations development: A manual for educators* (3rd ed.). Newton, MA: Allyn & Bacon.

GEORGE, R. L., & CRISTIANI, T. C. (1986). *Counseling: Theory and practice* (2nd ed.). Englewood Cliffs, NJ: Prentice-Hall.

GEORGE, R. L., & CRISTIANI, T. (1983). Improving communication with older adults. In N. S. Ernst & H. R. Glazer-Waldman (Eds.), *The aged patient* (pp. 31–40). Chicago: Yearbook Medical Publishers.

GESELL, A., ILG, F. L., AMES, L. B., & BULLIS, G. E. (1946). *The child from five to ten.* New York: Harper.

GINOTT, H. G. (1961). *Group psychotherapy with children: The theory and practice of play therapy.* New York: McGraw-Hill.

GINOTT, H. G. (1968). Group therapy with children. In G. M. Gazda (Ed.), *Basic approaches to group psychotherapy and group counseling* (pp. 176–194). Springfield, IL: Charles C Thomas.

GLANZ, E. C. (1962). *Groups in guidance.* Boston: Allyn & Bacon.

HALL, A. (1985). Group psychotherapy for anorexia nervosa. In D. M. Garner & P. E. Garfinkel (Eds.), *Handbook of psychotherapy for anorexia nervosa and bulimia* (pp. 213–239). New York: Guilford Press.

HANSEN, J. C., STEVIC, R. R., & WARNER, R. W., JR. (1982). *Counseling theory and process* (3rd ed.). Boston: Allyn & Bacon.

HANSEN, J. C., WARNER, R. W., & SMITH, E. J. (1980). *Group counseling* (2nd ed.). Chicago: Rand McNally.

HARRISON, K., & COOPER, C. L. (1976). The use of groups in education: Identifying the issues. *Small Group Behavior, 7,* 259–270.

HAVIGHURST, R. J. (1972). *Human development and education* (3rd ed.). New York: Longman.

HILL, W. F. (1957). Analysis of interviews of group therapists' papers. *Provo Papers, 1,* 1.

IVEY, A. E. (1971). *Microcounseling: Innovations in interviewing training.* Springfield, IL: Charles C Thomas.

IVEY, A. E., & GLUCKSTERN, N. B. (1976). *Basic influencing skills: Participant manual.* North Amherst, MA: Author.

JESKE, J. O. (1973). Identification and therapeutic effectiveness in group therapy. *Journal of Counseling Psychology, 20,* 528–530.

JOHNSON, D. W. (1981). *Reaching out* (2nd ed.). Englewood Cliffs, NJ: Prentice-Hall.

JOHNSON, D. W., & JOHNSON, F. P. (1982). *Joining together* (2nd ed.). Englewood Cliffs, NJ: Prentice-Hall.

JONES, J. (1977). *Group psychotherapy as experiencing interpersonal perceiving and developing of values.* Stockholm: Almquist & Wiksell.

KAPP, F. T., GLASER, G., & BRISSENDEN, A. (1964). Group participation and self-perceived personality change. *Journal of Nervous and Mental Disorders, 139,* 255–265.

KAUL, T. J., & BEDNAR, R. L. (1986). Experiential group research. In S. L. Garfield & A. E. Besquin (Eds.), *Handbook of psychotherapy and behavior change* (3rd ed., pp. 671–714). New York: John Wiley & Sons.

KELMAN, H. C. (1963). The role of the group in the induction of therapeutic change. *International Journal of Group Psychotherapy, 13,* 399–432.

KENDALL, P. C. (1982). Individual versus group cognitive-behavioral self-control training: One-year follow-up. *Behavior Therapy, 13,* 241–247.

KINNEY, J., & LEATON, G. (1983). *Loosening the grip* (2nd ed.). St. Louis: C. V. Mosby.

KOTTLER, J. (1983). *Pragmatic group leadership.* Monterey, CA: Brooks/Cole.

LANDRETH, G. L. (1984). Encountering Carl Rogers: His views on facilitating groups. *Personnel and Guidance Journal, 62,* 323–325.

LATNER, J. (1973). *The Gestalt therapy book.* New York: The Julian Press.

LAWSON, G. W., ELLIS, D. C., & RIVERS, P. C. (1984). *Essentials of chemical dependency counseling.* Rockville, MD: Aspen.

LESZCZ, M., YALOM, I., & NORDEN, M. (1985). The value of inpatient group psychotherapy: Patients' perceptions. *International Journal of Group Psychotherapy, 35,* 46–59.

LIEBERMAN, M. A. (1980). Group methods. In F. H. Kanfer & A. P. Goldstein (Eds.), *Helping people change.* New York: Pergamon.

LIEBERMAN, M. A., YALOM, I. D., & MILES, M. B. (1973). *Encounter groups: First facts.* New York: Basic Books.

LOEVINGER, J. (1976). *Ego development: Conceptions and theories.* San Francisco: Jossey-Bass.

LONG, L. & COPE, C. (1980). Curative factors in a male felony offender. *Small Group Behavior, 11,* 389–398.

LONG, T. L., & SCHULTZ, E. W. (1973). Empathy: A quality of effective groups leaders. *Psychological Reports, 32,* 699–705.

MACKENZIE, K. R. (1981). Measurement of group climate. *International Journal of Group Psychotherapy, 31,* 287–295.

MASSON, R. L., & JACOBS, E. (1980). Group leadership: Practical points for beginners. *Personnel and Guidance Journal, 59,* 52–55.

MAY, O. P., & THOMPSON, C. L. (1973). Perceived levels of self-disclosure, mental health, and helpfulness of group leaders. *Journal of Counseling Psychology, 20,* 349–352.

MCCANDLESS, B. R. (1970). *Adolescents: Behavior and development.* Hinsdale, IL: Dryden.

MELNICK, J. (1980). Gestalt group process therapy. *The Gestalt Journal, 3*(2), 86–96.

MORRAN, D. K., ROBISON, F. F., & STOCKTON, R. (1985). Feedback exchange in counseling groups: An analysis of message content and receiver acceptance as a function of leader versus member delivery, session, and valence. *Journal of Counseling Psychology, 32,* 57–67.

MURO, J. J., & FREEMAN, S. L. (1968). *Reading in group counseling.* Scranton, PA: Intext.

NAPIER, R. W., & GERSHENFELD, M. K. (1983). *Making groups work.* Boston: Houghton Mifflin.

NEUMANN, P. A., & HALVERSON, P. A. (1983). *Anorexia nervosa and bulimia: A handbook for counselors and therapists.* New York: Van Nostrand Reinhold.

OAKLANDER, V. (1978). *Windows to our children.* Moab, UT: Real People Press.

OHLSEN, M. M. (1977). *Group counseling* (2nd ed.). New York: Holt, Rinehart & Winston.

OHLSEN, M. (1979). *Marriage counseling in groups.* Champaign, IL: Research Press.

OLSON, R. P., GANLEY, R., DEVINE, V. T., & DORSEY, G. C. JR. (1981). Long-term effects of behavioral versus insight-oriented therapy with inpatient alcoholics. *Journal of Consulting and Clinical Psychology, 49,* 866–877.

PATTERSON, C. H. (1958). The place of values in counseling and psychotherapy. *Journal of Counseling Psychology, 5,* 216–223.

REMER, R. (1981). The counselor and research: Introduction. *Personnel and Guidance Journal, 59,* 567–571.

ROBINSON, D. (1980). Self-help health groups. In P. B. Smith (Ed.), *Small groups and personal change.* London: Methuen.

ROGERS, C. R. (1951). *Client-centered therapy.* Boston: Houghton Mifflin.

ROGERS, C. (1961). *On becoming a person.* Boston: Houghton Mifflin.

ROGERS, C. (1962). Toward becoming a fully functioning person. In A. Combs (Ed.), *Perceiving, behaving, becoming* (pp. 21–33). Washington, DC: Yearbook Association for Supervision and Curriculum Development.

Rogers, C. (1975). Empathic: An unappreciated way of being. *Counseling Psychologist, 5,* 2–10.

ROHRBAUGH, M., & BARTELS, B. (1975). Participants' perceptions of 'curative factors' in therapy and growth groups. *Small Group Behavior, 6,* 430–456.

ROSE, S. D. (1977). *Group therapy: A behavioral approach.* Englewood Cliffs, NJ: Prentice-Hall.

ROSSEL, R. D. (1981). Chaos and control: Attempts to regulate the use of humor in self-analytic and therapy groups. *Small Group Behavior, 12,* 195–219.

RUTAN, J. S., & RICE, C. A. (1981). The charismatic leader: Asset or liability? *Psychotherapy: Theory, Research and Practice, 18,* 487–492.

SALISBURY, H. (1975). Counseling the elderly: A neglected area in counselor education. *Counselor Education and Supervision, 14,* 237–238.

SCHEIDLINGER, S. (1980). The psychology of leadership revisited: An overview. *Group, 4,* 5–17.

SCHWARTZ, R. C., BARRETT, M. J., & SABA, G. (1985). Family therapy for bulimia. In D. M. Garner & P. E. Garfinkel (Eds.), *Handbook of psychotherapy for anorexia nervosa and bulimia* (pp. 280–307). New York: Guilford Press.

SEEMANN, D. C. (1982). Leader style and anxiety level: Their relation to autonomic response. *Small Group Behavior, 13,* 192–203.

SELVINI-PALAZZOLI, M. (1974). *Anorexia nervosa.* London: Chaucer.

SHADISH, W. R. JR. (1980). Non-verbal interventions in clinical groups. *Journal of Consulting and Clinical Psychology, 48,* 164–168.

SHAFFER, C. S., SANK, L. I., SHAPIRO, J., & DONOVAN, D. C. (1982). Cognitive behavior therapy follow-up: Maintenance of treatment effects at six-months. *Journal of Group Psychotherapy, Psychodrama and Sociometry, 35,* 57–63.

SHAPIRO, J., SANK, L. I., SHAFFER, C. S., & DONOVAN, D. C. (1982). Cost effectiveness of individual versus group cognitive behavior therapy for problems of depression and anxiety in an HMO population. *Journal of Clinical Psychology, 38,* 674–677.

SHOSTROM, E. L. (1974). *The Personal Orientation Inventory.* San Diego: EDITS Publishers.

SMITH. E. L. (1976). *The growing edge of Gestalt therapy.* New York: Brunner/Mazel, Inc.

STEPHENSON, F. D. (1975). *Gestalt therapy primer.* Springfield, IL: Charles C Thomas.

SULZBACHER, S., WONG, B., McKEEN, J., GLOCK, J., & MacDONALD, B. (1981). Long-term therapeutic effects of a three-month intensive growth group. *Journal of Clinical Psychiatry, 42,* 148–153.

SUPER, D. E. (1957). *Vocational development: A framework for research.* New York: Teachers College Press.

TRUAX, C. B. (1968). Therapist interpersonal reinforcement of client self-exploration and therapeutic outcome in group psychotherapy. *Journal of Counseling Psychology, 15,* 225–231.

TRUAX, C. B., & CARKHUFF, R. R. (1965). Client and therapist transparency in the psychotherapeutic encounter. *Journal of Counseling Psychology, 12,* 3–9.

TRUAX, C. B., & CARKHUFF, R. R. (1967). *Toward effective counseling and psychotherapy.* Chicago: Aldine.

TYRON, C., & LILIENTHAL, J. W. (1950). Developmental tasks: I. The concept and its importance. In ASCD, *Fostering mental health in our schools: 1950 Yearbook* (pp. 46–63). Washington, DC: Author.

VANDER KOLK, C. J. (1985). *Introduction to group counseling and psychotherapy.* Columbus, OH: Charles E. Merrill.

WADSWORTH, B. J. (1971). *Piaget's theory of cognitive development.* New York: Longman.

WAREHIME, R. G. (1981). Interactional Gestalt theory. *Small Group Behavior, 12,* 37–54.

WEINER, M. (1974). Genetic versus interpersonal insight. *International Journal of Group Psychotherapy, 24,* 230–237.

WEINER, M. F. (1984). *Techniques of group psychotherapy.* Washington, DC: American Psychiatric Press.

WEINRICH, S. G. (Ed.). (1979). *Career counseling: Theoretical and practical perspectives.* New York: McGraw-Hill.

WHITE, R., & LIPPITT, R. (1961). Leader behavior and member reaction in three 'social climates.' In D. Cartwright & A. Zander (Eds.), *Group dynamics: Research and theory.* New York: Row, Peterson, 527–553.

WILLIAMS, A. F. (1973). Personality and other characteristics associated with cigarette smoking among young teenagers. *Journal of Health and Social Behavior, 14,* 374–380.

WILLIAMSON, E. (1958). Value orientation in counseling. *Personnel and Guidance Journal, 36,* 520–528.

YALOM, I. D. (1985). *The theory and practice of group psychotherapy* (3rd ed.). New York: Basic Books.

YALOM, I. D., HOUTS, P. S., & ZIMERBERG, S. M. (1967). Prediction of improvement in group therapy. *Archives of General Psychiatry, 17,* 159–168.

ZAMARRIPA, P. O., & KRUEGER, D. L. (1983). Implicit contracts regulating small group leadership: The influence of culture. *Small Group Behavior, 14,* 187–210.

ZIFF, J. D. (1980). Establishing guidelines for differential processing of structured experiences based on self-knowledge theory. *Group and Organization Studies, 5,* 234–246.

AUTHOR INDEX

SUBJECT INDEX